Violin

Chris Haigh

Exploring Jazz Violin

*An Introduction to Jazz Harmony,
Technique and Improvisation*

www.schott-music.com

SCHOTT

Mainz · London · Madrid · Berlin · New York · Paris · Prague · Tokyo · Toronto
© 2010 SCHOTT MUSIC Ltd, London · Printed in Germany

About the author

Chris Haigh has been a professional fiddle player for 25 years, with experience covering many different genres. He has played on over 75 albums, working with artists including Alison Moyet, All About Eve, Michael Ball, David Soul, Oumou Sangari, The Quireboys, Riverdance, Morcheeba, Rolf Harris, James Galway and Steps.

He has played swing jazz with The Kimbara Brothers, Diz Disley, Le Jazz, The Hot Club of London, and the Quecumbar Allstars. He leads a 7-piece Soviet swing band –The Kremlinaires.

Chris gives lessons and workshops on jazz violin technique and has taught jazz violin at Middlesex, Brunel and Newcastle universities and Truro College. Writing credits include three other fiddle books, including *The Fiddle Handbook*.

His website, www.fiddlingaround.co.uk, is probably the most comprehensive and widely visited source of fiddle information on the web.

ED 13351

British Library Cataloguing-in-Publication Data.
A catalogue record for this book is available from the British Library.
ISMN M-2201-3207-0
ISBN 978-1-84761-242-7

© 2010 Schott Music Ltd, London

All rights reserved. No part of this publication may be reproduced, stored in a retrieval system, or transmitted, in any form or by any means, electronic, mechanical, photocopying, recording or otherwise, without the prior written permission of Schott Music Ltd, 48 Great Marlborough Street, London W1F 7BB

Project management, layout and copy-editing by Scott Barnard for MusicPreparation (www.musicpreparation.co.uk)
Cover design by www.adamhaystudio.com
Main cover photo by George Doyle, Stockbyte Collection.
© 2010 Getty Images. All Rights Reserved

Printed in Germany S&Co.8695

Picture credits

p. 5   Jean-Luc Ponty
(Courtesy of Imma Casanelles)

Back cover image courtesy of Ilana Gorban

All other photographs courtesy of David Sinclair (www.jazzphotographs.com)
p. 29   Roby Lakatos
p. 43   Tcha Limberger
p. 59   Mark Fieldman
p. 96   Didier Lockwood
p. 156 Stephane Grappelli
p. 190 Chris Garrick
p. 202 Regina Carter
p. 207 Billy Bang

Acknowledgments

I am deeply grateful for the help and encouragement I've had from numerous jazz violinists to whom I've spoken whilst researching this book. They include: Jean-Luc Ponty, Chris Garrick, Billy Thompson, Mike Piggott, Alex Yellowlees, Graham Clark, Tcha Limberger, Tim Kliphuis, Sam Bardfeld and Ric Sanders.

I would like to dedicate this book to the memory of my former teacher, Johnny Van Derrick.

Discography

Paris Hot Club Style with Neil Stacey, Chris Haigh, Jez Cook, and Bernard O'Neill, Cooking Vinyl / IODA 2000

Off The Wall Chris Haigh, TZCD02, 2009
www.fiddlingaround.co.uk

The Ghost of Uncle Joe, The Kremlinaires, TZCD03, 2010
www.fiddlingaround.co.uk

Contents

Introduction

Starting Out	7
Jazz Violin Techniques	7
Different Approaches	7
Using the Backing Tracks	8
Using This Book	8
Practice Makes Perfect	8

1: It Don't Mean a Thing

Swing	9
Swingin' the Scale (head)	11
Swingin' the Scale (slurred pairs)	12
Playing a 'Head'	13
The Form of the Tune	14
Head First (head)	14
Slides	17
Head First (with slides)	18
Vibrato	19
Improvisation on the Melody	20
Head First (rephrased)	24
Adding to the Melody	25

2: Starting to Improvise

Come Home (head)	30
Riffs	31
How to Construct Your Own Licks	33
Come Home (scale fragments)	36
Starting from a Different Place	37
Bebop Scales	38
Playing by Ear	41
Snakes and Ladders (head)	42
Snakes and Ladders (solo version)	44

3: Pentatonic Scales

Major Pentatonics	47
Pentatonic Riffs	48
Tonal Centres	48
Mind the Gap (head)	49
Pentatonic Patterns	50
Minor Pentatonics	52
Higher Positions	53

Mind the Gap (solo version)	56
The Glass Slippers (head)	57
The Glass Slippers (solo version)	60
Other Pentatonic Scales	62

4: The Blues

The Blues Sequence	63
Finding the Blues	66
Head First (Blues Pentatonic version)	70
More Blue Notes	71
The Blues Scale	73
Pentatonic Blues or Blues Scale?	73
The Minor Blues	75
Repetition	76
Other Blues Sequences	77

5: Chords Part I

What is a Chord?	79
Where do Chords Come From?	80
Understanding Chord Symbols	81
Chords Based on Degrees of the Major Scale	81
Dealing with Chords	85
Major / Major 7th	85
Minor 7th	87
7th Chord	88
II-V-I Sequences	90
The Minor II-V-I	93
Temporary Dominants	93
Mind the Gap (Temporary Dominants)	94

6: Chords Part II

Cycle of Fifths	97
Cycle Ride (head)	100
Cycle Ride (solo version)	103
Diminished Chords	106
Augmented Chords	108
m7♭5 / 7♭9	110
Sus Chords	112
Slash Chords	112
Playing Outside	113

Whole-tone Scales	118

7: Masters of Swing

Joe Venuti	119
The Yodel	122
Double Stops (Joe Venuti)	124
Parallel 5ths	125
Harmonics	125
Jumpin' with Joe	126
Stuff Smith	128
Double Stops (Stuff Smith)	129
Substitutions	133
Rhythm Changes	135
Other Swing Players	136

8: Stéphane Grappelli

Grappelli's Childhood	137
Grappelli Discovers Jazz	138
Formation of the Hot Club	138
Grappelli's Playing Style (1934-9)	139
A New Vocabulary (1939-71)	144
Death of Django	144
Revival (1971 onwards)	145
Who's on Piano?	145
Grappelli's Playing Style (Post Hot Club – 1939 onwards)	146
Swing Parisienne (head)	153
Swing Parisienne (solo version)	154

9: Running Wild

Jean-Luc Ponty	157
Ponty meets Zappa	158
Cosmic Messenger	159
Cosmic Voyager	168
Didier Lockwood	169
Didier's Style	170
Whispers	171
Michal Urbaniak	172
L. Shankar	172

10: Other Styles, Other Players

Gypsy Jazz	173
Gypsy-jazz players	175
Bebop	176
Bebop players	179
Modal Jazz	180
Dorian Grey (head)	183
Dorian Grey (solo version)	184
Free Jazz	185
Free-jazz players	186
Latin	186
Cuban effect on Latin music	186
The Clave	187
Brazilian effect on Latin music	188

11: The Big Night

Can I Use Sheet Music?	191
The Key	191
Versions and Phrasing	192
Playing the Head	192
The Big Night (head)	193
Is there an Arrangement?	193
Learning the Chords	194
Analyzing the Chord Sequence	195
The Big Solo – when do I start?	195
Your Opening Gambit	196
Phrasing	196
The Punch Line	199
The Big Night (solo version)	200

12: Final Thoughts

Gear	203
Suggested Listening	204
Bibliography / Suggested Reading	206
Track Listing	208

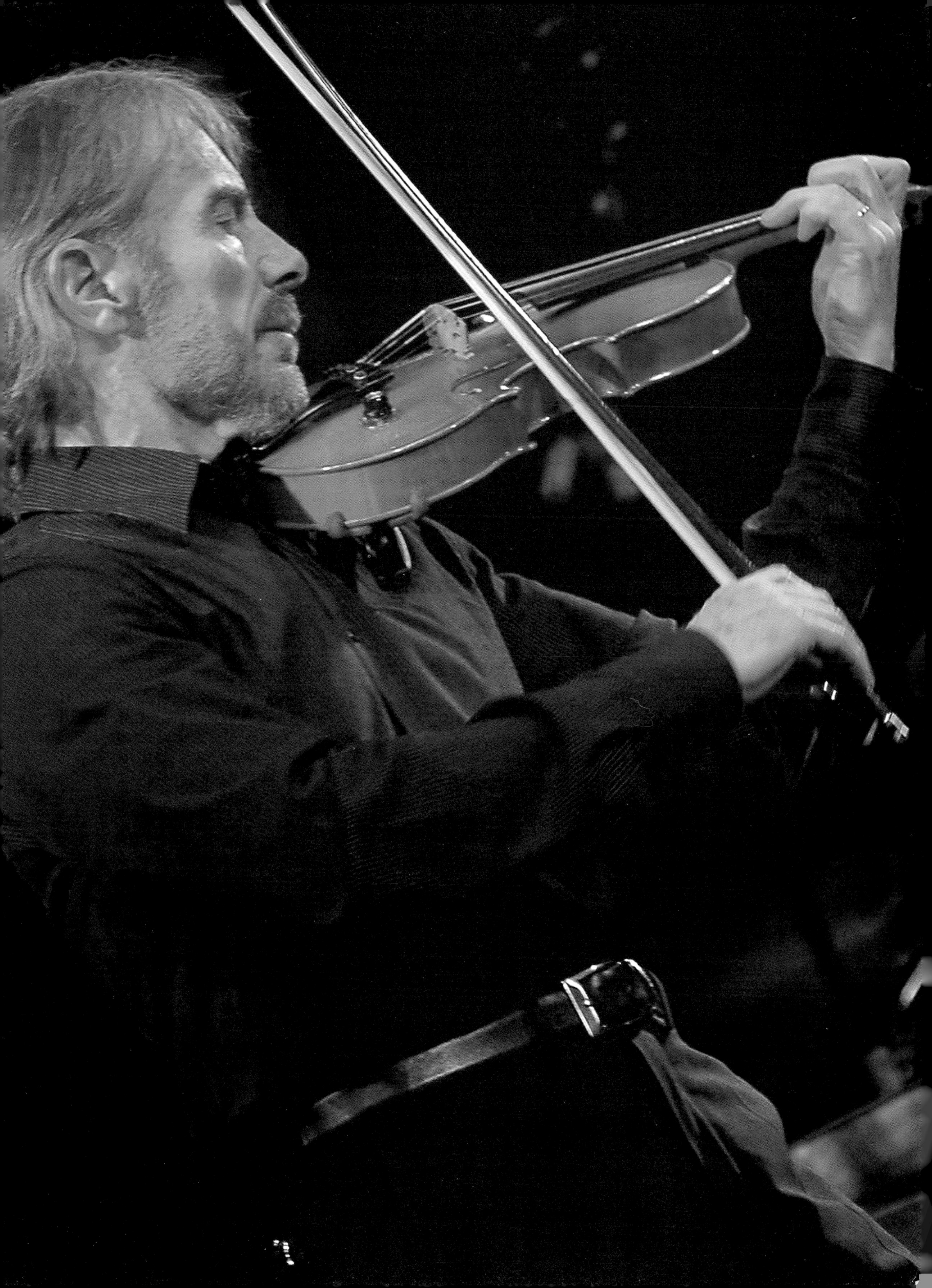

Introduction

Starting Out

Jazz violin is easy – just play what you feel. That's perhaps the worst piece of advice you'll ever hear. Starting to play jazz is like learning a foreign language. You can listen to it all day long but it won't make a word of sense until you slow it down, break it up and analyse it. You then need to learn the vocabulary, grammar and accent. You can't just expect to immediately start playing jazz by 'feeling' it, any more than you can speak a foreign language by instinct.

To some people, jazz improvisation is akin to something between rocket science and black magic… in fact the majority of it is simply nuts and bolts, and that's the approach we'll be taking in this book. Jazz theory can be very heavy going, so I've tried to take the simplest approach to explaining what you need to know. If you've never improvised before, it's not very helpful to be told at the outset that every chord has its own scale or mode that has to be understood and followed; you're liable to be paralysed with fear halfway through the first line when you meet an unfriendly $Fm^{7(\flat5)}$. Instead we'll start out looking for some very easy ways to improvise, which I've perfected over years of teaching and workshops to classical or folk players who break out into a sweat at the mere thought of improvisation.

As you work through this book we'll develop an understanding of chords and how you can relate to them and get your ears trained so that you can hear the possibilities as well as seeing them on the page or the fiddle strings. The first stage of dealing with chords will be simplistic, explaining how to use a single tonal centre through most, or all of a tune. We'll then go into more detail with how to stay 'safe' with individual chords or groups of chords, before moving on to extending the chords to create interest and surprise. Finally we'll be looking at the options of playing 'outside' the chords altogether.

Jazz Violin Techniques

One aspect of getting the right jazz feel is bowing. We'll also look at how to swing, different types of scale and finger pattern, the analysis of chords and sequences, how to use vibrato and harmonics, and how to construct phrases and structure a solo.

We'll study different types of tunes and sub-genres of jazz violin and examine the work and playing styles of the great players from the past and present.

Throughout, you'll be given 'licks' or 'riffs' which you can learn and use in your own solos, adapting them to suit whatever tunes you're playing. As a result of wading through many frustrating hours of other jazz fiddle books, I've avoided presenting you with long sequences of sight-reading; where I refer to other players' solos, I concentrate on short 'bite-sized' licks, with some explanation of how and where to use them.

Different Approaches

There's something of an ideological divide in the jazz violin world. At the traditional end there are players like **Joe Venuti** and **Stéphane Grappelli**. They mostly play swing, stylistically from the 1940s and earlier, and tend to play 'violinistically'; that is to say they use patterns,

Exploring Jazz Violin

shapes and sounds that are idiomatic to the instrument. They are *violinists playing jazz*. At the modern end are those players, including **Jean-Luc Ponty** and **Michal Urbaniak**, who are more interested in bebop, modal jazz and fusion. They tend to emulate wind players like **Charlie Parker**, **John Coltrane** or **Miles Davis**, and in outlook they are *jazz players who happen to play the violin*.

This book looks in detail at both approaches. The chances are that you'll already have a clear idea of which side of the fence looks most attractive to you, but don't let that limit you. There's a great deal you can learn from any jazz violinist. In writing this book, I've spoken to many contemporary players and will refer occasionally to their various approaches and opinions.

Using the Backing Tracks

Each chapter has one or more jazz tunes to learn and practise. Usually, the tune is presented in different versions: one with the head (melody) and one with a sample solo. On the CD you will find audio demonstrations of these, including the violin part with a live band. Also on the CD are backing track versions. For the most part, these are designed to work with both the head and solo versions.

Some of the backing tracks have a gypsy-jazz style backing with two rhythm guitars and a double bass, while most of the later tunes have a more modern feel, with piano, electric bass and drums.

Listen to the tracks with violin included and try playing along, then try with just the backing track version. Finally, use the backing to try out your own improvisational ideas.

Using This Book

It is assumed that you already have at least a basic knowledge of violin playing and music theory, but I'm also assuming that you know little or nothing of jazz. We start with some basics – the first four chapters looking at how to swing, develop a melody and improvise using pentatonic and blues scales. The next two chapters look at chords and how to deal with them – from a jazz theory point of view, these are the most difficult sections.

We then have a further three chapters introducing the work of some of the great players past and present; **Joe Venuti**, **Stuff Smith**, **Stéphane Grappelli**, **Jean-Luc Ponty** and **Didier Lockwood**. Chapter 10 looks at some of the sub-genres of jazz violin playing and the final chapter brings it all together, showing how to learn a new number and create a memorable solo under the most difficult of circumstances. You'll see what I mean!

Practice Makes Perfect

Each chapter can be worked through in around an hour, but don't be fooled into thinking that 11 hours of work will make you into a jazz violinist. Each concept, scale or lick may be something you can understand and play without too much trouble, but none of it is really useful until you can get it into the subconscious part of your brain, where you no longer have to think of how to play a bebop scale, or how to process a sharpened 9th. That needs practice, and lots of it! This book will give you the bricks, the tools and the blueprints that you need to be on your way as an up-and-coming jazz violinist.

1: It Don't Mean a Thing

In this chapter we'll look at the differences between the melody you read, and the melody you actually play. We'll look at an example of a jazz tune, examine its form, and see bar by bar, phrase by phrase, how it can be modified, customized and personalized. You may have thought that you had escaped from scales, but they're as important to jazz as they are to classical music – through slurs, accents, subtle bow pressure, and 'ghosting', you will see how to bring a scale to life and how to make it swing! We'll also look at syncopation, slides, vibrato, ornamentation and passing notes, all of which will allow you to bring sparkle and style to a tune, allowing for a different rendition each time.

Swing

Swing is the very essence of most jazz music, and the subtleties of bow length and pressure make the violin as capable as any instrument of swinging successfully. It's next to impossible to write swing music accurately in conventional music notation, but in this section we will endeavour to unlock the secrets of how to interpret a jazz melody.

Let's take a simple G major scale. Here it is written as conventional 'straight' quavers (eighth notes).

Fig 1.1 G major scale – straight quavers

You will have been taught to play a scale like this smoothly and evenly, with every note exactly the same length. Forget that. To play swing you will need to lengthen the 'on' beats and shorten the 'off' beats. Here are two written examples of how you could approximate this:

Fig 1.2 G major scale – dotted quavers

Fig 1.3 G major scale – triplet quavers

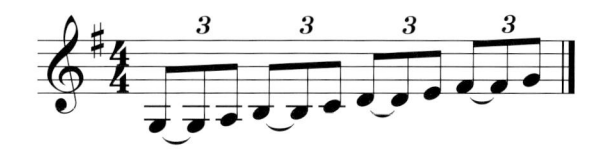

Neither is precisely what you're actually aiming for – the dotted version would sound too jagged if you played them literally as written, and the triplets could be very confusing. The rhythm of the words "hot po-ta-to, hot po-ta-to" gives a clearer indication of what we're after. The most important element of getting the feel right for swing is to use short bows.

The 'on' beats need be no more than an inch or two, whilst the 'off' beats hardly need any bow at all. Think of the off beats as 'ghost notes'; if you played the scale fairly fast, the off beats would virtually disappear (demonstrated on CD track 1). Practise this, slowly at first, watching your bows carefully to make sure they're not too long. Use the middle of the bow.

Exploring Jazz Violin

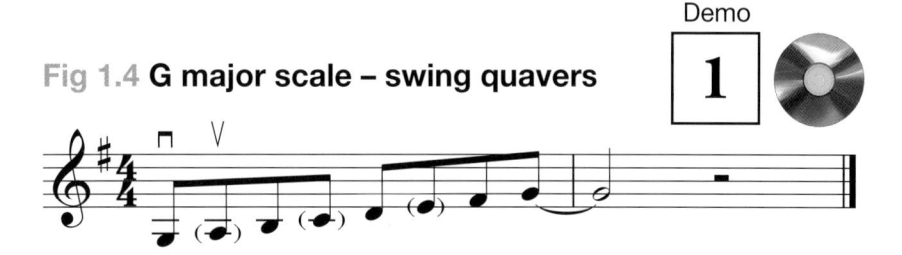

Fig 1.4 G major scale – swing quavers Demo 1

On the ghost notes, take the pressure off the bow (the pressure that comes mostly from the index finger of your right hand); allow your wrist to spring back to the same position you started from. It will make a slight whistling sound as you do the up bow; the fact that this is not a 'clean' note is not a problem at all.

Once you have mastered this bowing action (don't expect to get it straight away!) it should be possible to play an endless stream of swung notes without ever running out of bow. Practise the bar below several times until it feels comfortable to you.

Fig 1.5 Endless bowing

Aim for very precise articulation of the notes. Give each new down bow a little 'dig' of pressure with the index finger of your bow hand.

Fig 1.6 Down bows with accents

It works just as well with accents on the up bows. Try the phrase below, letting the bow spring back after each up bow, so that the bow returns to the same place:

Fig 1.7 Up bows with accents

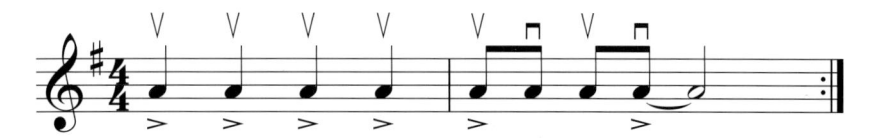

Here's a tune, which will make use (and hopefully make sense) of what we've just been looking at. **Joe Venuti**, one of the first great jazz fiddlers, had several similar tunes. Listen to CD track 2 to immerse yourself in the swing style, then have a go yourself.

Jazz musicians often embellish the written chord symbols. For example, in this next tune, you will hear a G^6 chord replacing the 'straight' G chord. It makes for a more jazzy sound.

1: It Don't Mean a Thing

Swingin' the Scale (head)

Demo Backing
2 3

Chris Haigh

Medium Swing ♩ = 160

© 2010 Schott Music Ltd, London

This tune uses mostly separate bows, with slurs either for the syncopated notes (about which more shortly), or to make it easier to return to the middle of the bow. You should be able to play most of this piece by using about six inches of the bow – from the middle towards the tip.

Now here's a different bowing pattern, which you might find a bit easier:

Fig 1.8 Slurred pairs

Listen to this next version of 'Swingin' the Scale', which includes the pattern above. Once you have the feel for it, try to play it using backing (track 3).

Exploring Jazz Violin

Swingin' the Scale (slurred pairs)

Demo 4 | Backing 3

Chris Haigh

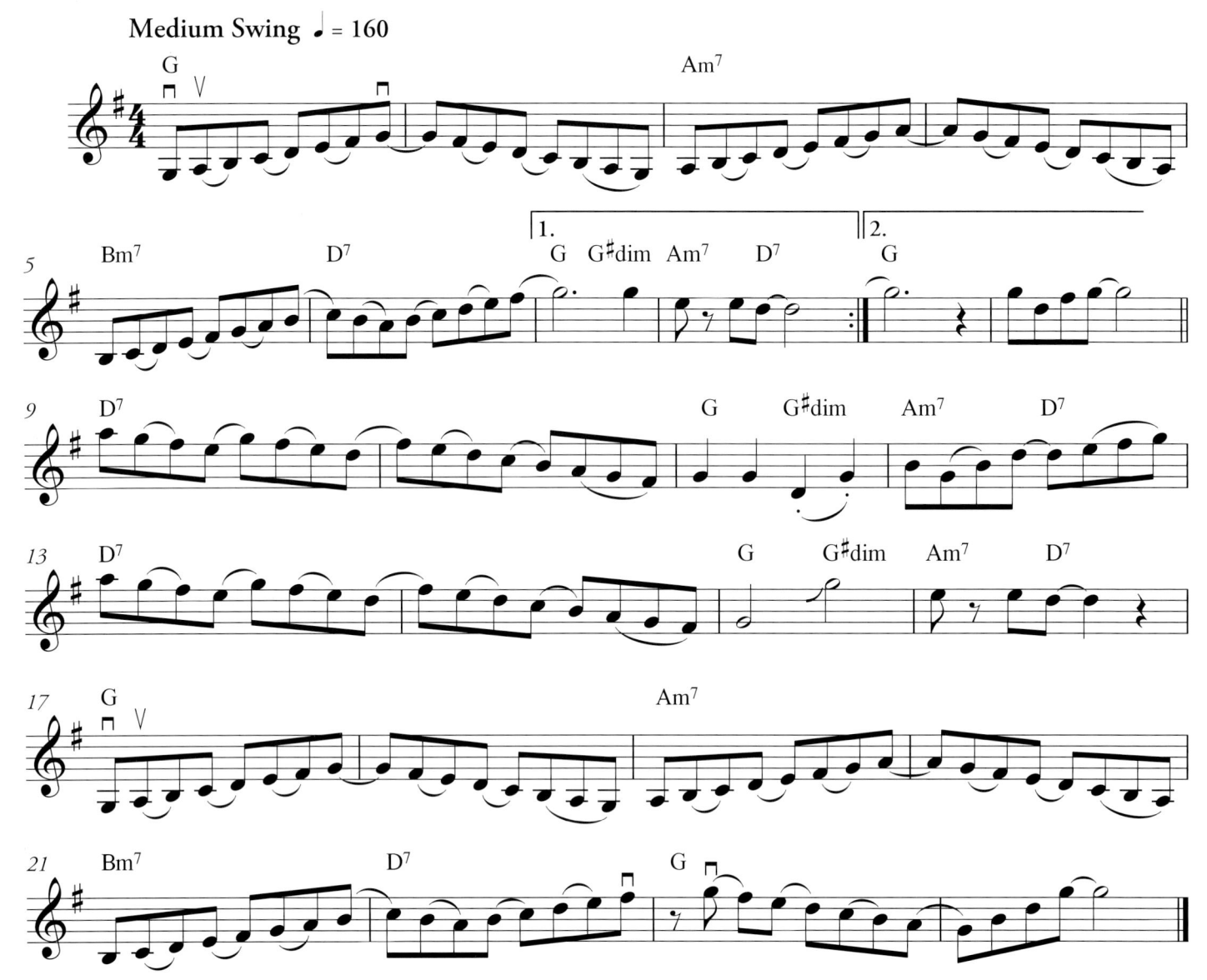

Medium Swing ♩ = 160

[musical notation]

© 2010 Schott Music Ltd, London

In this version, it's easier to play more smoothly than it was with separate bows, but it can still seem 'lumpy' when there are too many two-note slurs in a row. Here are a couple more patterns to try on 'Swingin' the Scale' which give a different emphasis:

Fig 1.9 Three-note slurs

[musical notation]

Fig 1.10 **Alternate separate bows / three-note slurs**

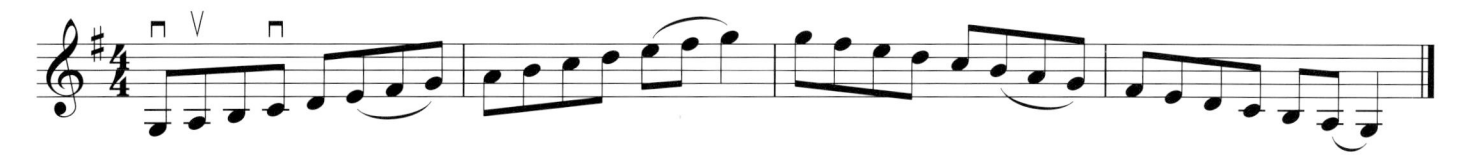

[musical notation]

So which is the right pattern to use? If you've played in an orchestra you'll know how important it is to get the correct up and down bows, not least because of the embarrassment that everyone from your fellow violinists, to the conductor, to the old guy at the back of the cheap seats can see straight away when you have made a mistake. Thankfully, you've said goodbye to all that!

The decision is now entirely yours, and as with so many things in jazz, there is no single right answer. Your short-term goal should be to get familiar with each bowing pattern, whilst aiming long term to let your right hand take care of itself, automatically selecting a suitable bowing for each phrase. Strive for smoothness, economy of effort, and a degree of unpredictability in your playing.

Checkpoint

You probably thought that if you started playing jazz you would escape from endless scales and arpeggios – you were wrong! But now they can be more enjoyable and musical when you make them swing. Use a few scales to practise the bowing patterns above as part of your regular practice routine, be sure to stretch yourself beyond the easier keys. Always look at your bow to make sure the bows are short, the notes smooth, the accents clearly articulated, and your bowing wrist relaxed. Once you are familiar with all the bowing patterns you'll always have a choice of different approaches to any phrase or run.

Listen to lots of swing jazz violin recordings. Anything by **Stéphane Grappelli** would be a good place to start, though, as we'll see in later chapters, there are many other fine players to investigate. Although you may not be able to tell exactly what bowing is being used, you'll eventually get used to the sound and feel of swing bowing.

Playing a 'Head'

In most music, the written melody is all there is. With jazz, however, the tune (melody) is usually just step one – the first clue in the treasure hunt. The tune is played at the beginning and end of the number, and it defines the chord sequence, the rhythm and the feel (or style) of the improvisation (which makes up the bulk of the performance). In jazz, the tune is often called the 'Head', meaning what comes at the top. If you see a bandleader pointing a finger at his own head during a number, it means that it's time to stop the interminable soloing and get back to playing the tune. Even with the melody, what you read is not exactly what you play, and interpreting the melody is an art in itself, as we will discover.

Exploring Jazz Violin

Your first challenge is to make a melody swing, and that's something that, as we've seen, is next to impossible to write down accurately. In a jazz 'lead sheet' – the written version of the Head – the quavers (eighth notes) are always written with equal lengths, it's up to you to apply the swing feel.

Here's a simple tune that we can use to cover the first steps of jazz playing. Listen to early recordings by the **Quintette du Hot Club de France** for a style reference. Before we get into playing it let's take a moment to look at its structure.

The Form of the Tune

You'll notice that 'Head First' is 32 bars long, in a form usually described as 'AABA' (each section being 8 bars in length). This is very typical of jazz tunes. The repeated 'A' section is almost the same each time, usually with just a slight variation for the first- and second-time ending. The 'B' section will be different to the 'A' section, and will certainly have a different chordal movement; this is often called the 'Bridge'. Once the tune has been played through and you're into the improvising section, you will need to be aware at all times where you are within the 32-bar sequence. Jazz numbers often originated from popular show tunes that had a separate verse and chorus. This is very rare in jazz; usually the verse has been discarded, and only the chorus is played.

Notice that there are chords written above the melody line. You don't need to pay them any attention at this stage, but they provide information, which will be vital as soon as you start to improvise.

Demo Backing
  5   6

Head First (head)

Chris Haigh

[Musical notation: Medium Swing ♩ = 165, in G major, 4/4 time]

Section A (bars 1–8): G | | Am7 | D7 | G A♭dim | Am7 D7 |

Section A (bars 9–16): G | | Am7 | D7 | G | B7 |

© 2010 Schott Music Ltd, London

1: It Don't Mean a Thing

B
17 Em   Em/E♭   Em/D   C♯dim

21 Em   A⁷   Am⁷   D⁷

A
25 G

29 Am⁷   D⁷   G

Play the tune through as if playing an orchestral piece. You'll find it sounds a bit 'stiff' and 'wooden'– we need to make it swing. Take bar 2 for example; we've already seen how jazz is 'written' with even quavers (eighth notes) but 'played' with a swing feel.

So you will need to lengthen the first and third notes of each pair of quavers (eighth notes) and shorten the second and fourth – I would bow it as shown below, putting an accent on the first and third notes and 'ghosting' the second and fourth:

Fig 1.11 **Bar 2 with a swing feel**

Bar 4 has three of these pairs:

Fig 1.12 **Bar 4**

Again, we ghost the second of each pair of quavers (eighth notes), and put more emphasis on the first. Play through this tune again using the above bowing patterns, you should notice an immediate change to the feel. The exception to this rule comes when the second note of a pair is tied to another note, as at the end of bar 19. When this occurs, the accent will normally lie on the second note of the pair, (the first note of the pair will still be longer). This is an example of 'Syncopation'.

Exploring Jazz Violin

Fig 1.13 **Bar 19 – syncopation**

Syncopation is an important part of swing playing; it involves placing the accent of a phrase 'off' the beat instead of 'on' the beat, creating surprise and a sense of urgency. This may already be written into the melody; we've seen another example of this in bar 18, where the last note of the phrase is brought forward or anticipated.

Fig 1.14 **Bar 18 – syncopation**

It's common to add syncopation to a melody even if it isn't written. Bar 4, which is very similar to bar 2, could be played:

Fig 1.15 **Bar 4 original version**

Fig 1.16 **Bar 4 with syncopation**

And you could give bar 21 a real kick, syncopating every note:

Fig 1.17 **Bar 21 original version**

Fig 1.18 **Bar 21 with syncopation**

Repeated syncopation like this can be hard to get the hang of. It may help you to tap your foot 'on' the beat whilst playing, otherwise there's a danger of losing track of where you are. You've seen now how a phrase can be modified by syncopation, look through 'Head First' and try to find some more places where you can add your own syncopation. Later on we'll try another version of the tune where some of these changes have been made.

1: It Don't Mean a Thing

Checkpoint

Many jazz standards are former pop or show tunes; therefore the original melody can sometimes seem a little staid when in a jazz idiom. So don't be afraid to impose your will on a tune, on the other hand don't go overboard with the syncopation; it will always be more effective if some of the original rhythms are left in for contrast.

When you finally get to the stage where you're improvising freely, don't neglect the head and think of it as merely 'the bit you have to get through before you start the exciting part'. You must always give the head as much personality, flair and colour as you put into your solo.

Assignment

Next time you listen to some jazz, make a conscious effort to define the head. Can you recognize the 'AABA' format, or does it have a different structure? Any swing recording will probably have at least a few titles you recognize, and for which it is easy to get hold of the sheet music. Look for collections of tunes, either by author (for example **Cole Porter** or **George Gershwin**), or by artist (for example **Django Reinhardt** and **Stéphane Grappelli**). There are also large anthologies of jazz tunes, often called "Real Books" or "Fake Books". Compare what you see with what you hear, and see how much the lead player (the musician playing the tune) has modified the head.

Slides

When playing jazz, one of the simplest and most prevalent techniques that you can use to 'loosen up' the notes, is to slide up to them.

Start about a semitone below your target note, and slide your finger upwards until you hit the right pitch. Make it quick and subtle; if you give the slide too much emphasis it could sound comical.

Fig 1.19 Slide

On the next page you'll see the tune 'Head First' again, but this time with some suggestions of where you might use a slide; have a listen, then try it out.

Exploring Jazz Violin

Head First (with slides)

Demo 7 | Backing 6

Chris Haigh

© 2010 Schott Music Ltd, London

In bars such as 1, 5 and 7 you can start the phrase with an upward slide as discussed above. In bars 3 and 8 you can make an effective slide by changing up to 3rd position; slide your second finger up from F to A or B to D (then come straight back down to 1st position for the next bar).

This kind of slide covers more distance on the finger board than the first kind, so be careful not to make a meal of it. Getting into 3rd position allows you to use a strong vibrato on these notes, which would otherwise have been open strings or on weak fourth fingers.

Downward slides are much less common but there is a place for them in bars 25 and 29. With these slides, we're producing a kind of a confidence trick. In bar 25, for example, we're going from a distinct D note (third finger) to a distinct B (first finger). Slide as far as you can before you place the next note, and it will sound as if the slide is continuous (even though there's a break as you move out of position and back to 1st position).

At bars 15 and 31 a slide is used to finish the phrase. It's important to understand that, whereas the slides discussed so far have all had a distinct target note, this 'end of phrase' slide drifts down from a distinct starting note to something indeterminate.

You can help this effect by:
1. Reducing your bow pressure towards the end of the note, so that it ends in a sort of 'whisper'; or
2. Make an increasingly wide vibrato towards the end of the note, just before you slide – to the extent that the note at the end is no longer clear.

These effects can be combined; they are used to particular effect by players like **Didier Lockwood**; he might apply the sliding-down effect repeatedly; for example this is how he might play bars 17–18 demonstrated on CD track 8:

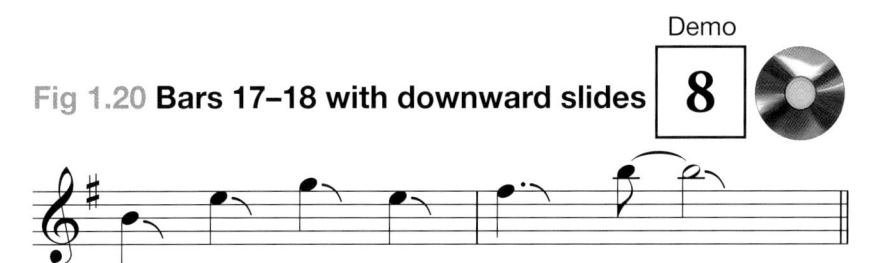

Fig 1.20 **Bars 17–18 with downward slides** Demo 8

Try to emulate the slides you have heard on the recording until they sound secure. How much you use slides is a matter of personal taste and style; it's definitely a good idea to keep them sparse and subtle, at least until you're completely confident about how you want to use them.

Vibrato

Before we go any further, a quick thought about vibrato. If you've had classical training, then I can absolutely guarantee that when you play 'Head First', or indeed any other jazz tune, you'll be using too much vibrato to start with. Classical training teaches you to use a smooth and consistent vibrato all the way through every note. Stop it! Use vibrato as an *effect* on certain notes; for example, on longer notes start without any at all, bringing the vibrato in towards the end of the note – giving it some shape. Vibrato, like the use of slides, is a matter of taste and style. **Stéphane Grappelli** is noted for his subtle use of a very smooth, fast vibrato whilst **Joe Venuti** used a very wide, crazy vibrato, whereas the jazz / rock and bebop players like **Jean-Luc Ponty** use virtually none at all. I asked Ponty about his transition from classical to jazz in terms of vibrato and bowing, he told me: "*I started listening very intensely to records of bebop and post-bop horn players and later on transferred that horn phrasing to the violin. It was obvious to me that classical vibrato had to be discarded and that I had to rethink my bow technique from scratch in order to adapt the violin to modern jazz*".

Exploring Jazz Violin

Assignment

You've probably not paid much attention to vibrato since that painful time when a demented wobbling of the left hand gradually turned into a smooth and elegant action, which I have no doubt it is today.

It's time to get re-acquainted. Try playing with no vibrato, and then with lots. Try altering the speed, width and intensity. Listen to the different jazz fiddlers mentioned above to compare their styles, and aim for the sound you prefer.

Improvisation on the Melody

When you approach a new jazz tune, the first thing you need to do is to memorize it, and get familiar with the fingering. However, once you've done that you should aim to never play it exactly the same again. The tune should always be recognizable, but you might only play 50% of the original notes and phrases – and that's before you begin your solo. Think of it in terms of the trip from your house to your local shop. You know the way very well, but decisions as to which side of the road to walk on, who to stop and talk to, where to cross the road and so on make every trip slightly different. Your aim is for fluency, swing and an element of surprise. Let's see how we can begin to change the melody a little to make it more individual.

Adding quavers

We've seen how the quavers (eighth notes) are the notes that provide the swing. What if there aren't any quavers in the original phrase that you want to swing? Bar 14, for example, has four crotchets (quarter notes).

Here's the original:

Fig 1.21 Bar 14

Try splitting them all like this:

Fig 1.22 Bar 14 – crotchets split into quavers

Remember we're looking for variety and surprise, not a succession of identical phrases. Here are some more interesting possibilities for bar 14:

Fig 1.23 Bar 14 – version 1

Fig 1.24 Bar 14 – version 2

We've tried breaking up some crotchets. Now let's do something similar to the semibreve in bar 15. A whole bar with a single sustained note is just begging to be given some swing, especially as it's followed by a one-bar rest:

Fig 1.25 Bar 15 – adding swing

Here's a longer version. (Try applying these same rhythms to bar 23.)

Fig 1.26 Bar 15 – even more swing

Adding syncopation

You could also add some syncopation to a phrase:

Fig 1.27 Bar 14 – original version

Fig 1.28 Bar 14 – added syncopation

Don't be tempted to swing and syncopate every note. Without some 'on the beat' crotchets for contrast, the swing and syncopation will be less effective.

Delay / extend / repeat

Another interesting way to spice up a melody is to delay, extend, anticipate or repeat a phrase. In bar 3 for example, you might decide that you so enjoy the long slide up to the A that you want to draw it out:

Fig 1.29 Bar 3 – original version

Fig 1.30 Bar 3 – delayed 2nd note

Exploring Jazz Violin

You could stretch a note even further, cutting out a chunk of the melody entirely to make room.

So the first line of the 'B' section (bars 17–20) could be changed by extending the F♯ in the second bar:

Fig 1.31 Bars 17–20 – original version

Fig 1.32 Bars 17–20 – extending a note length

You'll quickly realize that any change that you make to the rhythm of the melody may have consequences for the following phrase – the lengthening of one phrase may require the shortening of the next. This requires quick thinking, but eventually this will become second nature.

If you take a shine to a particular phrase, you could play it a few times before moving on. So the two notes in bar 9:

Fig 1.33 Bar 9 – original version

Could go forth and multiply...

Fig 1.34 Bar 9 – repeated pitches

Or could be cut off in their prime...

Fig 1.35 Bar 9 – reduced note lengths

Checkpoint

With all these changes in place, the tune has now become much more personal and, hopefully, spontaneous. The first few times that you try a new tune you might want to plan specific phrases in advance, or even learn the exact phrasing which another jazz violinist has recorded. This is a useful exercise and will always sound better than the original written version of the tune, however, if that's as far as you go, you've missed the point. Eventually you should be able to play a different set of variations on the melody every time you perform it. That way the tune will always seem fresh for both you and your audience.

Time for some initiative on your part. Here's a simple tune, completely devoid of swing. First let's play it as written.

Fig 1.36 **'Camptown Races'**

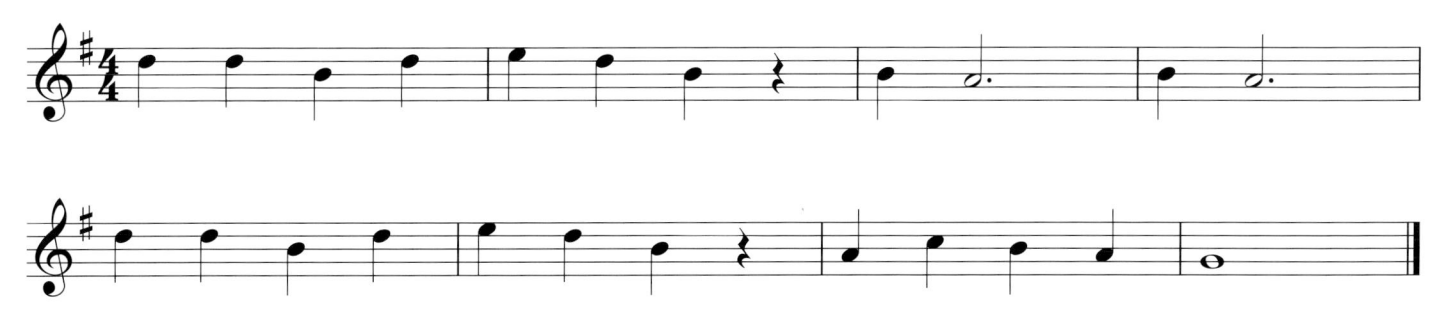

Now play it again, making each of these changes in turn, so that you can add your own touches:

1. Split all the crotchets into quavers (eighth notes), and make them **swing**

2. Find as many places as you can where you can add **syncopation**

3. Add some **slides**

4. Try applying different types of **vibrato**

5. Find a phrase in the melody where you can **repeat** it into the next bar, and make the appropriate changes to the next note or phrase to **accommodate** it

6. Choose a single note to **extend**, again shortening whatever comes next to make room for it

Exploring Jazz Violin

Here's an example of the tune 'Head First' using some of the techniques discussed so far, it uses split notes, syncopation and rephrasing. Listen and then play.

Demo Backing
9 6

Head First (rephrased)

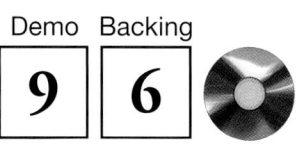

Chris Haigh

1: It Don't Mean a Thing

Adding to the Melody

Until now we've had fun poking and prodding at notes and phrases, altering their duration and position within the bar. Now it's time to take a step further, and start adding notes of different pitches, which didn't appear in the original melody.

Passing notes

Let's make things easy to start with by confining ourselves to the notes of the G major scale:

Fig 1.37 G major scale

The idea that this scale will work all the way through the chord sequence is something we'll come back to shortly. Let's find two notes from 'Head First' with an interval of at least a third between them, and fill in the gap with a relevant note from the scale of G major – bar 1 will work well for this.

Fig 1.38 Bar 1 – original version

Fig 1.39 Bar 1 – adding a passing note

And we could give a similar treatment to bar 17:

Fig 1.40 Bar 17 – original version

Fig 1.41 Bar 17 – adding a passing note

Since the notes we're adding are largely 'passing notes', which link or lead to more important melody notes, we could also safely use chromatic notes. A 'safe' note is basically one that sounds as if you meant it. To use a note that is outside the scale is potentially 'unsafe', but if it's clearly passing between, or leading towards, a strong melody note it will sound convincing. We can 'fill up the gap' between the two notes of bar 9 with a chromatic descending scale:

Fig 1.42 Bar 9 – original version

Fig 1.43 Bar 9 – inserting a chromatic scale

25

Exploring Jazz Violin

Here's a similar approach to bar 17:

Fig 1.44 Bar 17 – inserting a chromatic scale

Using chromatic notes to 'fill in the gaps' sounds more jazzy than just using the notes from a major scale. It doesn't matter if some of the notes don't belong to the chord you're playing over; so long as you start and end on the 'right' notes, the 'wrong' ones will sound fine. Have another look at 'Camptown Races' and try adding some chromatic scales.

Rolls or turns

Rolls (or turns) are a slightly more complex way of adding notes to a melody. If you've played any Celtic music you'll be familiar with the idea; start on the target note, play the note above in the scale, play the target note again, then a semitone below, and finally the target note again. You'd usually add this at the start of a bar or phrase. The example below demonstrates a turn at the beginning of bar 5.

Fig 1.45 Bar 5 – original version

Fig 1.46 Bar 5 – with a roll (turn)

If you're worried about how to play something so complicated as a quintuplet – don't be! The notes don't have to be equal. Your classical violin teacher isn't in the room!

More ornaments

As if the mantelpiece wasn't already full up, here are some more ornaments. Previously we looked at adding notes within the melody – i.e. filling gaps between two adjacent melody notes. We can also add notes from 'outside' the melody, usually above or below the notes at the beginning of a phrase.

A common way to embellish a melody is to approach a strong melody note from a semitone below; classical musicians would call this a lower appoggiatura.

Here's the original bar 18 from 'Head First', and then with lower appoggiaturas on each note:

Fig 1.47 Bar 18 – original version

Fig 1.48 Bar 18 – lower appoggiaturas

Go back to 'Camptown Races' again and try adding some lower appoggiaturas.

In bar 5 you could ornament the first note (C) by slipping in a D above it, this is an upper appoggiatura, as shown below:

Fig 1.49 Bar 5 – original version

Fig 1.50 Bar 5 – upper appoggiatura

A favourite **Grappelli** ornament would be to split a note like the A in bar 5, adding the next note up in the scale, before playing the original note again – a mordent:

Fig 1.51 Bar 5 – mordent

With mordents the added note will often be the next adjacent note from the scale, as above, but it may also be a third above or below, as in this variation of bar 7, where I've added a D a third above the B:

Fig 1.52 Bar 7 – original version

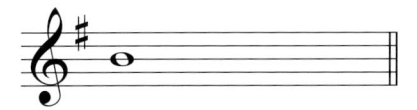

Fig 1.53 Bar 7 – mordent spanning a third

Again there are endless variations on this kind of ornament. Listen to **Stéphane Grappelli** playing the opening bars of any simple melody and you'll hear many examples; 'Dinah' on the *I Got Rhythm* album is a good place to start. Try some mordents on 'Camptown Races'.

Exploring Jazz Violin

Chapter Summary

Chapter one out of the way; let's see what we've covered so far? We've looked at how to play a version of the written melody, which, whilst still being clearly recognizable, also has many personal touches, more than enough to make every performance unique. Here are some of the techniques that we have used so far:

1. All pairs of quavers (eighth notes) in a written melody can be modified to become 'swung pairs'

2. By shortening, lengthening and tying notes together you can create syncopation, which builds a sense of urgency and surprise

3. Sliding up to, and occasionally down from, some notes will create a relaxed and jazzy feel

4. Get your vibrato under control! What is excellent for a classical player may be a disaster for a jazz violinist

5. Longer notes can be subdivided in all sorts of ways, adding to the swing and syncopation of a tune

6. Use small sections of a scale (major, minor or chromatic) to link two adjacent melody notes

7. Use notes that are 'outside' of the melody by playing notes above or below the melody notes

8. You can apply a roll to longer notes, particularly at the start of phrases

Assignment

It would be a good idea to start building a library of jazz violin recordings to listen to, and sheet music of tunes that you can play. **Stéphane Grappelli** is probably the best artist to start with, since most of what he recorded was 'standards' (well-known tunes which are played by the majority of jazz musicians).

A few suggestions for tunes to look for would include 'Autumn Leaves', 'Lady be Good', 'Honeysuckle Rose', 'Dinah', 'I Can't Give You Anything But Love', 'Crazy Rhythm', 'I Got Rhythm', 'Sweet Georgia Brown', 'Ain't Misbehavin'', 'It Don't Mean a Thing', 'Avalon', 'Sweet Sue', 'In a Sentimental Mood', 'Night and Day', 'How High the Moon' and 'Tea for Two'.

Try applying all the different decorative techniques discussed in this chapter to some of these tunes.

Try each technique in isolation; don't attempt to do everything at once. Eventually these ideas will become second nature and you'll begin to use them as an integral part of your playing.

2: Starting to Improvise

By this stage you may already be thinking that a jazz melody is a pretty flexible thing, and that you can take all sorts of liberties with it. We're going to develop that thought further, introducing the idea that any section of the tune can be removed or replaced, that you can learn 'licks' that can fill any gap in any tune, and that by using notes from the correct scale, you can improvise freely and easily over a simple chord sequence.

One of the problems that a lot of people face when starting out in jazz, is keeping track of where they are in the chord sequence. With many other musical styles, which don't include an element of improvisation, this problem doesn't occur – you'll always know where you are because you're always playing the melody. With jazz it's different – you're going to be meandering anywhere and everywhere, so it's crucial to be aware of how the chords are changing and where you are within the sequence. Listen to the demonstration version of the tune on the next page – 'Come Home'.

Exploring Jazz Violin

Come Home (head)

Chris Haigh

Demo 10 / Backing 11

Lively Swing ♩ = 185

Assignment

First, play the tune along with the backing track a few times to get familiar with it. Then, using the backing track but without playing, read through the tune, playing it in your head. Now try mixing the two approaches; play a few phrases then stop, but keep the tune going in your head; drop back in for a phrase or two, then drop out again. The point of this exercise is to start getting used to the idea that the chord sequence is going to continue whether you're playing or not, and that you need the freedom to be able to drop in and out at will.

© 2010 Schott Music Ltd, London

2: Starting to Improvise

Now play this two-bar phrase.

Fig 2.1 Phrase 1

With the chord sequence playing in the background, play this phrase 16 times, i.e. all the way through the sequence, listening carefully to how the notes relate differently to different chords. If it feels a bit uncomfortable when you hit the F chord, don't panic, the fact that you heard it is a good sign.

Now try alternating between listening for two bars and playing this phrase for two bars, again all the way through the sequence. Next, alternate between playing two bars of the original melody and playing this phrase for two bars. This kind of mental gymnastics is what jazz fiddle playing is all about.

Try the same thing with these next phrases:

Fig 2.2 Phrase 2

Fig 2.3 Phrase 3

Finally try playing all three phrases one after the other (two bars of the melody, then phrase 1, two bars of the melody then phrase 2 and so on).

Dropping phrases in and out in this way is the essence of jazz soloing.

Riffs

In jazz these kind of phrases are known as 'riffs' or 'licks'; think of them as the basic 'building blocks' of improvisation. They can either be spontaneously created, or else learnt and stored away as stock phrases for future use.

Some players' solos can be recognized by their use of particular riffs which may recur several times during a sequence. Depending on your point of view, this can serve as a distinctive 'trademark' of someone's playing; purists would say that this is not true improvisation, and that using riffs can sound repetitive or unimaginative. Personally, I am quite shameless about using riffs – whether original, borrowed or adapted.

When you learn a new riff it will have a particular rhythmic and harmonic context. That is to say, it will occur at a certain point within a bar and over a specific rhythm; it will also be played over a certain chord or set of chords.

Exploring Jazz Violin

It's important to listen to what's going on behind a riff when you first learn it, but then also to work out how to use the same riff in a different context. For example, here's a phrase that would work over a progression from the chords G[7] to C (as in bars 30–31 of 'Come Home')

Now, try this two-bar phrase:

Fig 2.4 G⁷ to C riff

It's a nice little lick – using a chromatic run up to the tonic of the dominant chord, G[7] (tonic and dominant are terms I'll explain in later chapters), and then a kind of arpeggio leading back up to the C chord. But it's not a very efficient use of your time to learn a riff that you can only use in one key. So, here it is in the key of G:

Fig 2.5 Riff transposed (D⁷ to G)

It's usually easy to transpose a riff up or down a 5th – this involves, as in this case, simply shifting to the adjacent strings.

It's a bit harder to transpose it to, let's say the key of B♭, but that shouldn't stop you:

Fig 2.6 Riff transposed (F⁷ to B♭)

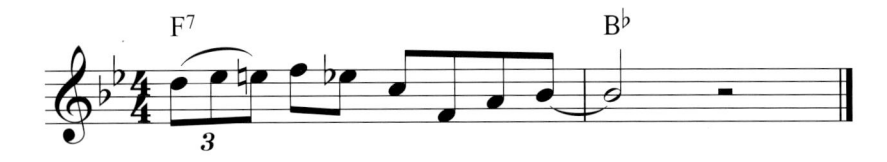

Some riffs, for example those that require an open string, may only work in a few keys. Most are universal, though they may require trickier fingering than the original. To really get the most out of a new riff, you need to practise it in every key. The best way to do this is to take it through the 'cycle of fifths' (about which we'll hear more later). So every time you repeat the phrase, transpose it a 5th lower (or a 4th higher); this will eventually take you through every key until you get back to where you started from. The next example shows the beginning of this.

Fig 2.7 **Riff in four keys**

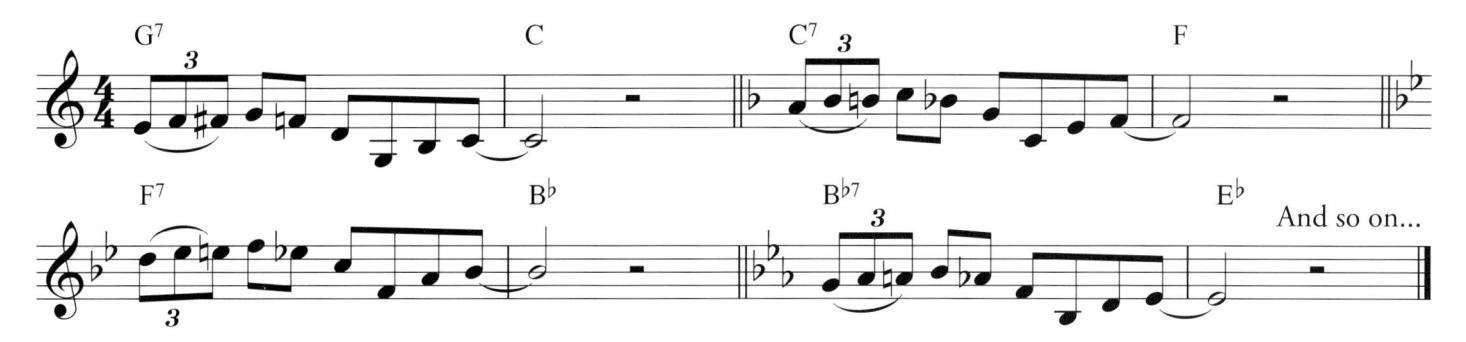

[musical notation: riff in G7-C, C7-F, F7-Bb, Bb7-Eb progressions, "And so on..."]

You may also want to tinker with the rhythm of a riff. The one we're looking at starts on the first beat of the bar, but what would it sound like on the second beat of the bar?

Fig 2.8 **Riff with altered phrasing**

[musical notation: G7 to C]

Sounds just as good, if not better.

Checkpoint

Licks or riffs are the building blocks of a solo, and are usually phrases of one or two bars in length. Whenever you hear a good riff in someone else's solo, try it out, write it down and memorize it. Eventually you will have a huge stock of licks that you can draw upon when constructing a solo. To make the most of a lick you should be able to transfer it to different parts of a tune, different keys and different songs.

How to Construct Your Own Licks

OK, so we've learnt how to work on a riff – once you've got hold of one (by fair means or foul!). But what about creating your own? The first problem you have to deal with is to decide what notes are available to you to choose from. The simplistic answer is 'hey, this is jazz, you can play whatever notes you like'. In common with politics, religion and philosophy, most statements about jazz can be both true and false at the same time, and this is no exception. However, at this stage in the game we're going to play it safe and say it's not true. For this tune, and many like it, the notes of a single major scale will make a good start. Let's play the C major scale.

Fig 2.9 **C major scale**

[musical notation: C major scale]

Exploring Jazz Violin

Play this scale repeatedly with the backing track for 'Come Home', and you'll find that it fits anywhere, to some extent; that is to say that on a scale of 1 to 10 (1 being 'comfortable' and 10 being 'excruciating'), it ranges from about 1 to 4. If you're into extreme sports, use the same chord sequence but try a B major scale – I think you'll spot the difference!

So we've established that you can play a C major scale anywhere in this tune, therefore a lick or series of licks can be constructed using any of these notes. The scale itself can be a good starting point, if we can find ways to make it more interesting and jazzy – for example, a little bit of syncopation will go a long way:

Fig 2.10 C major scale with a little syncopation

Or maybe a lot of syncopation:

Fig 2.11 C major scale, all notes syncopated

You could split the crotchets (quarter notes) into swung pairs:

Fig 2.12 C major scale – swung pairs

Or you could create step-like patterns:

Fig 2.13 C major scale with step patterns

2: Starting to Improvise

Or a kind of arpeggio / scale:

Fig 2.14 **C major arpeggio / scale**

Maybe give it a twist and include some rests:

Fig 2.15 **C major scale fragments with rests**

Try to find as many variations as you can, and be sure to keep the bar lengths in mind as you're practising; give yourself a starting note and finishing note, and a fixed length, and try filling in the gap. For example here's the space for a two-bar phrase:

Fig 2.16 **Two bars with a gap**

You could fill this gap with the phrase below:

Fig 2.17 **Two bars with filled gap**

It's not necessary to work out the ending to a phrase before you start, because as you approach your target note (the end of the scale or run) it should become clear at which point you need to 'tidy up' the end of the run. In the example above, you're following a pattern that repeats until bar two, beat two, at which point you 'home in' on the target note. Here's another one, this time it's four bars long:

Fig 2.18 **Four-bar run**

Exploring Jazz Violin

Using nothing but the notes of the major scale, you should be able to improvise endlessly, moving up and down with different patterns and rhythms and changing direction in different places.

Here's an example of how you might play the melody of 'Come Home' with the addition of fragments from the C major scale, or patterns created from it.

Come Home (scale fragments)

Demo 12 Backing 11

Chris Haigh

Lively Swing ♩ = 185

© 2010 Schott Music Ltd, London

2: Starting to Improvise

Assignment

Spend some time practising this new version, then try variations of your own, first based around the melody but with fragments of scale, then eventually without any of the melody.

Starting from a Different Place

Your first stab at improvisation, then, is based on the idea of using a single major scale all the way through the tune. It's a good start, but it has two immediate drawbacks.

1. This will only work with a very simple chord sequence, and whilst a lot of standards, particularly the older numbers, do have such sequences, many do not. Try the same technique with 'The Girl from Ipanema' and you'll have your first experience of over-confident-jazz-fiddler-shot-down-in-flames!

2. You'll already have noticed that even within the simple sequence we've been working on, the random use of the major scale isn't always very effective as the chords change. The C major scale over a chord of C works fine:

Fig 2.19 **C major scale over a chord of C**

But the same thing over a Dm^7 chord doesn't sound quite as good (try it for example, over bar 29 of 'Come Home').

Fig 2.20 **C major scale over a chord of Dm^7**

The problem is with the phrasing of these notes. Rhythmically, the notes being emphasized are the first of each swung pair: C, E, G and B; these notes make the arpeggio of a $Cmaj^7$ chord, not a Dm^7 chord. (If I've lost you at this point, because you're not sure about chord symbols, don't worry; we'll get to those in a later chapter, then you can worry!) It's a problem, however, that's very easily solved: simply start your C major scale on a D rather than a C. Lo and behold, the emphasized notes are now D, F, A and C, making a Dm^7 arpeggio.

Fig 2.21 **C major scale starting on a D**

Exploring Jazz Violin

So when you come to a new chord, it will help you to start your scale, or phrase, on the root note of the chord. To make it more interesting, but still safe, you could also start on the 3rd or 5th degree of the chord. Here's a Dm^7 chord with a C major scale, starting on an F (the 3rd of a Dm^7 chord):

Fig 2.22 C major scale starting on an F

At first you may need to look at the music to see what your starting notes should be, but after some practice your ears will get used to the idea, and you'll be able to make the right choices automatically, making your scale-based improvisation sound far more comfortable.

Assignment

Go back to 'Come Home' and try playing C major scale phrases up and down once more; but this time use your eyes and ears to make the scales fit better, by starting your phrase on the note most appropriate to the chord.

Bebop Scales

First of all let's look at an ordinary G major scale, two octaves. You could use this over a G major chord, or over any chord which is diatonic in the key of G. Diatonic means 'within the key'; all the diatonic chords are constructed using only notes from the scale of G major. You should practise this scale swing style – i.e. with a bowing of 'long-short' or 'doo-be, doo-be, doo-be'.

Fig 2.23 G major scale, two octaves

However, there are some practical problems with this scale from a jazz point of view.

The first bar (the first octave) has the accents (the long, stressed notes) on G, B, D and F♯ – the root, 3rd, 5th and 7th of the chord of Gmaj^7; this is ideal, as these are harmonically the 'strong' notes of the chord. However, the second bar (the second octave), is the other way round – all the harmonically 'weak' notes are now being stressed; the A (the 2nd), C (the 4th) and E (the 6th). Although all these notes fit in the scale of G major, they're far from ideal; they fit a chord of Am, not a chord of G.

Also, a scale, as well as having a starting point, should have a 'target note' – a strong note which marks the top of the scale. We really want it to be a G, not an A.

Because of these various problems, jazz musicians in the '40s started using what is known as the 'bebop' scale. Don't be put off by the name – bebop scales are applicable throughout jazz, not just in bebop.

The idea involves slipping in an extra note which makes the scale repeat properly at the beginning of each bar, instead of turning itself inside out every octave. A seven-note scale then becomes an eight-note scale. The most useful is the one below, sometimes called the 'bebop dominant scale'. The extra note is the 'flattened' 7th, so that the scale has both a flattened and a major 7th:

Fig 2.24 G bebop dominant scale

I've added some bowings to the scale above – spend some time practising this, as you'll need to become as familiar, if not more so, with this as you are with a conventional major scale.

The other main type of bebop scale involves adding a sharpened 5th (instead of the flattened 7th), this is sometimes called the 'bebop major scale'.

Fig 2.25 G bebop major scale

Let's try both of them again, but using the 'chain bowing' pattern (slurred pairs starting on the second quaver).

Fig 2.26 G bebop dominant scale, chain bowing

Fig 2.27 G bebop major scale, chain bowing

Exploring Jazz Violin

In real-life soloing of course, you won't be playing complete scales, but nevertheless the concept of bebop scales transfers readily to jazz licks. Here's a lick derived from the dominant bebop scale.

Fig 2.28 Bebop scale lick 1

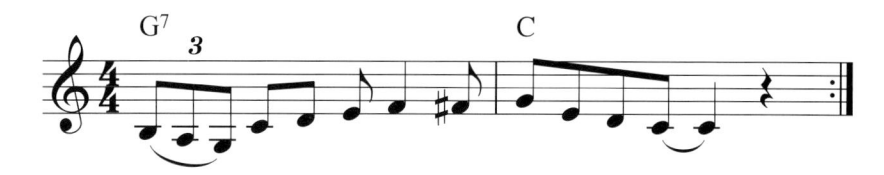

The next one is a descending (dominant bebop) scale with a slight diversion before it reaches the end.

Fig 2.29 Bebop scale lick 2

Here's one using the sharpened 5th from the major bebop scale:

Fig 2.30 Bebop scale lick 3

Checkpoint

Bebop scales are designed to phrase well with a swing rhythm, placing the harmonically strong notes on the strong accents, even when you get into the second octave of a scale pattern. The extra chromatic note, far from sounding wrong, adds melodic interest. These should become your default scales for jazz playing.

Now spend some time playing these scales over the chord sequence of 'Come Home'. You should find that it will work well over most, if not all of the sequence.

Playing by Ear

We now have a basis for improvisation, where instead of playing the written melody, we can play notes from the major scale instead. They can either be complete or partial scales, with or without added chromatic notes to reach a target note neatly, or phrases made up from these notes.

In the absence of much theoretical understanding of chords, we'll be largely playing by ear, constantly making decisions about which notes sound best or most comfortable as the chords change. Even within simple tunes you're likely to come across some chords which are not diatonic. When this happens your ear should 'warn' you that something has changed, even if you're not quite sure what it is.

For example you might be playing over a C major chord, which then becomes C^7. Listen carefully to the next example:

Fig 2.31 Chord change (C to C^7) — Demo 13

If you play the C major scale over the C^7 chord, you should be able to hear that one note sounds 'wrong'. It's the B, which is now demanding to change to a B♭. The B has become, temporarily at least, a note which you need to avoid, preferably replacing it with whatever the new chord requires. Here's another example, where a Dm^7 chord becomes D^7. Again listen carefully to the track:

Fig 2.32 Chord changes (C to Dm^7 to D^7) — Demo 14

Can you hear which note is out of place? It's the F♮ against the chord of D^7. This has become an 'avoid' note, to be replaced by an F♯. Here's another:

Fig 2.33 Chord changes (C to E^7 to Am^7) — Demo 15

When the C changes to E^7 your ear should 'tell' you that the C♮ needs to become a C♯. If the E^7 lasted any longer, and we continued our scale further, you'd also find out that the notes G and F would also needed changing, but by that time we're back on safe territory with the Am^7 chord. What we're doing in these examples is continuing to play as if we're in the key of C major, and basing our phrases on the notes from that key, but avoiding or modifying notes when the need arises in the expectation that we'll soon be back on 'safe ground' again. If the non-diatonic chords are short enough in duration

Exploring Jazz Violin

(for example half a bar in length), you can usually ignore them altogether, and treat them as 'passing chords'; the dissonance created, like that created by the chromatic notes of a bebop scale, is so temporary that the ear will 'forgive and forget'. For non-diatonic chords that last for a bar, you will need to 'duck and dive' for one or two notes. For anything longer, or if it's a slow tune where a bar of the 'wrong' chord can seem like half a lifetime, you'll need a different approach and will have to temporarily think in a new key.

This approach is very helpful when you're first learning jazz improvising. It helps to train your ear to be alert for changes in the chord sequence, and allows you to put off, at least for a while, the tiresome job of learning about the intricacies of chords.

Here's a tune we can use to demonstrate the various ideas about scale-based soloing. Listen to the demonstration track then play along with the backing.

Snakes and Ladders (head)

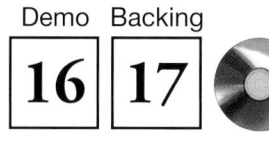

Demo 16 · Backing 17

Chris Haigh

© 2010 Schott Music Ltd, London

2: Starting to Improvise

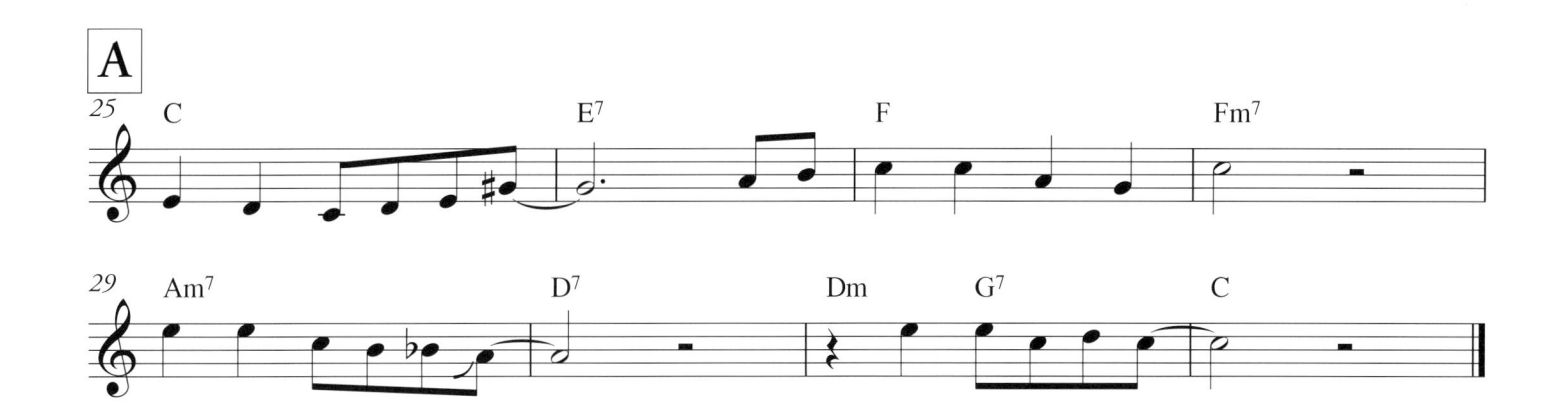

Exploring Jazz Violin

Now here's a solo based on this tune. It demonstrates two points in particular. Firstly, the advantages and pitfalls of trying to keep to the same tonal centre (C major) throughout a set of changes (abbreviation for chord changes); and secondly the use of bebop scales to give some semblance of order to your snakes-and-ladders ramblings.

Snakes and Ladders (solo version)

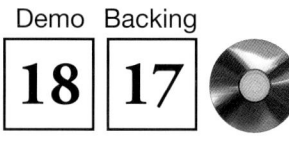

Chris Haigh

© 2010 Schott Music Ltd, London

The following describes the thought processes about how the note choices and phrases were decided upon for this solo.

Bars 1–4
The solo kicks off with a quote from the original melody, transposed up an octave. As an opening gambit this is always a safe bet, so long as you quickly develop it into something new. We hit the E^7 chord with G♮. You didn't see it coming, but your ear should tell you that this is not a 'safe' note for this chord. An E^7 demands a G♯, so we can quickly raise it by a semitone and pretend we intended that all along. The next phrase, over the F chord, centres on the note A, and leads up to another A for bar 4. On this occasion we spot in time that the A in bar 4 will be another 'avoid' or 'modify' note, so we flatten it to A♭ for the Fm^7 chord.

Bars 5–8
Bars 5 and 6 have a descending sequence that runs safely through Am^7 and D^7, whilst bars 7 and 8 have a slightly interrupted G dominant bebop scale. The fact that it starts over an Em^7 chord is no problem – Em is the relative minor of G major, and so can share the same scale.

Bars 9–12
We introduce a new lick in bar 9, which includes a G♮. Trying to repeat this lick in bar 10 (over E^7) means that we fall into the same trap as in bar 2, but again we make a quick recovery and raise it to a G♯. The same lick fits fairly comfortably over the next chord, F, but on the Fm^7 we have to flatten the A to A♭. Again, we didn't quite see it coming.

Bars 13–16
In bars 13 and 14 we have another descending pattern over Am^7 and D^7. We decide at the last minute to try to reach a low D in bar 15 with an undignified scramble to get there in time, then there's an ascending bebop scale landing on the target note of C in bar 16.

Bars 17–20
The bridge (bar 17) starts with a chromatic descending scale – the top part of a C dominant bebop scale, then bar 18 has a stab at the riff we worked on early in the chapter, so the time wasn't wasted after all!

Bars 21–24
Bar 21 has a common or garden C major scale. We decide at the last moment to approach the D in bar 22 from a semitone below, only to realize that C♮ is a better choice for a chord of D^7, so we then drop the C♯ by a semitone. Bar 23 has a descending G dominant bebop scale, followed in bar 24 by a C major scale starting on a D. This fits our chords well and means that we will end up safely on our target note of C by bar 25. By starting the C major scale on a D rather than a C, we avoid needing an extra chromatic note (from a bebop scale).

Bars 25–28
The simple phrase in bar 25 has G as its highest note. When repeating it in bar 26 we have to quickly raise it to a G♯, getting there by a short chromatic run. We have a new phrase for bar 27 which won't quite work in bar 28 – we have to lower the A to an A♭.

Bars 29–32
Bar 29 is part of the C major scale, with an extra chromatic G♯ to reach the A at the start of bar 30. Running down the scale we hit an F♮ and have to change it to an F♯ to fit the D^7 chord better. In bar 31 we find that the F♯ no longer fits, so we lower it again, before rounding off with a descending bebop scale to a G – a safe note in the C chord.

Exploring Jazz Violin

Checkpoint

The above solo was an exercise in crisis management; the result of playing by ear and not knowing what chords are coming next. This will work fine on completely diatonic chord sequences, and you can ramble freely up and down major or bebop scales without any danger of hitting 'avoid' notes. All you need to sound fluent is to start your scales and patterns on the right note for the chord, and use the extra chromatic notes to reach your target notes cleanly.

However, as you may be starting to realize, not all chord sequences are diatonic, and there may be lots of nasty surprises waiting for you. Be warned, it's not long before we're going to have to learn some proper theory about chords!

Chapter Summary

In this chapter we took a gentle step away from the melody and began looking more seriously at the business of improvisation using these steps:

1. We discovered how to insert short licks in place of parts of the melody.

2. We looked at how to make the best use of a lick by trying it in different keys and also rhythmic contexts.

3. We saw how the major scale could be used as a lick in itself, especially when we tinkered with it to make step-like patterns.

4. We examined the phrasing of a scale, and learnt how the problem of starting the second octave of a scale on the 'wrong' beat of the bar could be solved by adopting the bebop scale.

In the next chapter we'll look at a different kind of scale altogether.

3: Pentatonic Scales

Conventional major and minor scales are, as we've seen, a useful starting point for improvisation, but once you've learnt to use the pentatonic scale it's like turning water into wine! Simply by omitting the 4th and 7th degrees of the major scale, you can create a five-note (hence the name) scale, which will give you a tool that is instantly melodic.

Major Pentatonics

Here's the G major pentatonic scale:

Fig 3.1 G major pentatonic scale

As with any scale, the pentatonic scale is defined by the intervals it uses – G to A is one tone, A to B is one tone, B to D is one and a half tones, and D to E is one tone. So the intervals for any major pentatonic scale are: **tone**, **tone**, **one and a half tones**, **tone**. Looking at it another way, pentatonic scales use the 1st, 2nd, 3rd, 5th and 6th degrees of the major scale.

If you're confused by the fact that I call it a five-note scale but then show you six notes in the example above, this is because the upper G completes the scale – showing you that the scale could continue higher, using the same pattern of intervals.

So by the same rule, a C major pentatonic would be:

Fig 3.2 C major pentatonic scale

Assignment

Work out some more major pentatonic scales for yourself. At first you will probably have to think it out interval by interval, but soon you'll be able to play it by ear. Try extending the scales over two octaves.

So what's so clever about this scale? If you play these notes on a piano, you'll find that you can use any combination, or play all five notes simultaneously, and they'll sound harmonious. In fact, if you place your arm across all the black keys (which are arranged in a pentatonic scale), it will sound rather good. Try the same with the white keys (arranged in a major scale), and it will sound rather bad. Why is this? The painful dissonance comes from the semitone intervals present in the major scale, whereas the pentatonic scale doesn't contain any semitones.

Pentatonic Riffs

So we've seen that any group of adjacent notes from the pentatonic scale will sound melodic, and you'll find that it's very easy to construct riffs which are light and airy and appear 'thought out'. Jazz violinist **Chris Garrick**, who described pentatonic riffs to me as essential building blocks for jazz improvisations, considers them "*very violinistic*", in that they are comfortable under the fingers. Here are a few examples:

Fig 3.3 **Pentatonic riff 1**

Fig 3.4 **Pentatonic riff 2**

Fig 3.5 **Pentatonic riff 3**

A clear indication that there's something special about this scale is the fact that it appears in traditional folk music throughout the world, and that many popular, well-known tunes are based on it ('Marie's Wedding', 'Swing Low, Sweet Chariot', 'Ole Man River', 'Amazing Grace', the first section of 'I Got Rhythm' and 'Dinah', to name but a few).

Tonal Centres

The concept of a tonal centre is a useful one when improvising with pentatonic scales. The tonal centre is the 'home' note around which the tune revolves – the root note of the key the tune is based on. If the tune has a single tonal centre, you should be able to play the root note of the key all the way through, with the feeling that the melody will want to resolve to this note at some point. With the pentatonic scale you can think of the four upper degrees as 'planets' revolving around the tonal centre of the root note. Unless the tonal centre changes (i.e. a temporary key change) the five notes of the pentatonic will always work.

Here's a melody built entirely on the G major pentatonic scale – 'Mind the Gap'.

Mind the Gap (head)

Chris Haigh

Notice how, although the chords keep changing, only the same five notes are used throughout the melody. This is a good indication that when we start to improvise we can use a similar approach.

You should also notice that the tonal centre, G, remains constant throughout. (To digress slightly, you may also realize that this tune does not follow the 'AABA' format, but has a more linear structure.)

Exploring Jazz Violin

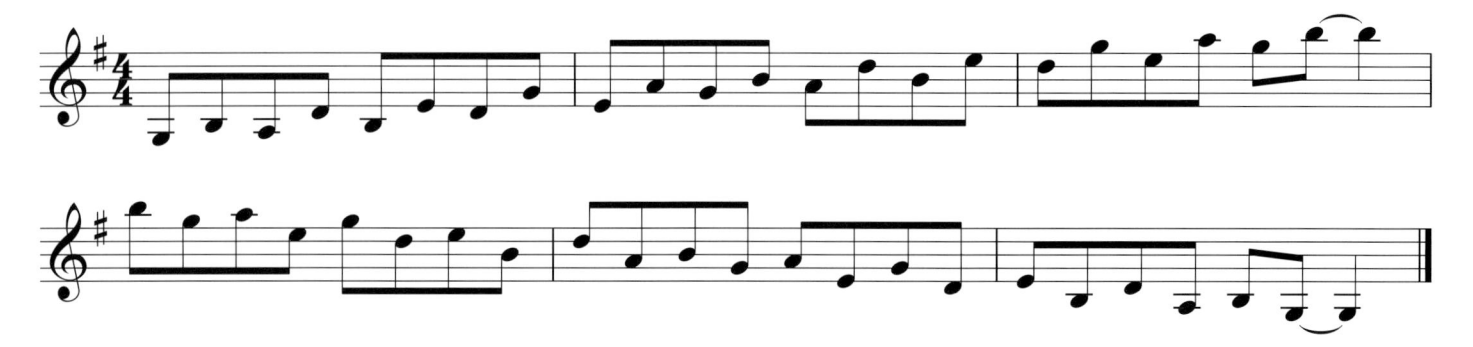

Pentatonic Patterns

In order to make the most of the pentatonic scale, your fingers will need to learn the pattern inside out, back to front and upside down.

The first stage is to practise the scale in 1st position and in every key. G major pentatonic, for example, would be:

Fig 3.6 **G major pentatonic – 1st position**

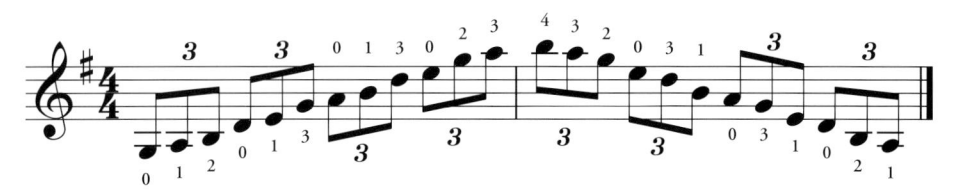

Notice that with this scale, we're using all the available notes on all four strings – that is to say at the top, we continue the pattern up to the note B – the highest note we can reach without changing position. You can, of course, continue upwards by changing position, but since we're using these scales primarily for their ease and simplicity, we'll concentrate on what is available in 1st position to start with.

Work on it string by string, start slowly and then increase the tempo until you are playing as fast as you can; here are examples for the D and A string:

Fig 3.7 **Finger pattern – D string**

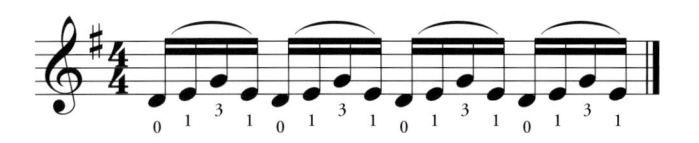

Fig 3.8 **Finger pattern – A string**

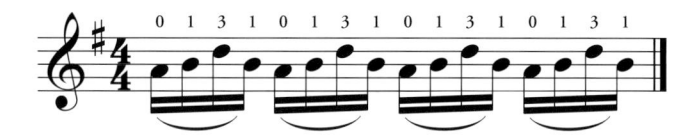

Pay attention to the fingering; with the G major pentatonic, the fingering is the same on the D and A strings (0, 1, 3). So by using this pattern over both the D and A strings you have:

Fig 3.9 **Finger pattern – D and A strings**

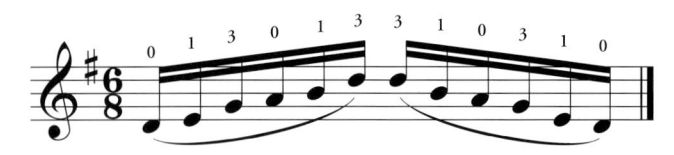

As with conventional scales, there are many patterns that you can use to make the scale more interesting, such as the following examples:

Fig 3.10 **Pentatonic pattern 1**

3: Pentatonic Scales

Fig 3.11 **Pentatonic pattern 2**

A fearless champion of pentatonic scales is Polish-American violinist **Michal Urbaniak**. On his album *Ask Me Now* (recorded in 1999), he used the descending part of this pattern at least three times on every single track, clocking up 49 occurrences in all. Now that's dedication! You could also develop triplet or semiquaver (sixteenth note) patterns:

Fig 3.12 **Pentatonic – triplet pattern 1**

Fig 3.13 **Pentatonic – triplet pattern 2**

Exploring Jazz Violin

Fig 3.14 **Pentatonic – semiquaver pattern 1**

Fig 3.15 **Pentatonic – semiquaver pattern 2**

Here's a simple two-bar 'vamp' or 'turnaround' that you can use to practise the above patterns (a vamp or turnaround is a short, repeated chord sequence, sometimes found at the beginning of tunes or after each solo section):

Fig 3.16 **Two-bar vamp in G major** Backing 21

Although the notes of the G major pentatonic don't exactly match those of the A♭dim chord, they still sound OK because this is simply a passing chord, wedged between two 'safe' chords.

Minor Pentatonics

There are minor pentatonics as well as major ones, but fortunately you don't have to learn a whole new set of scales and patterns. Every major pentatonic has a relative minor which shares all the same notes. So by starting and ending the G major pentatonic on the note E, we get the E minor pentatonic:

Fig 3.17 **G major / E minor pentatonic**

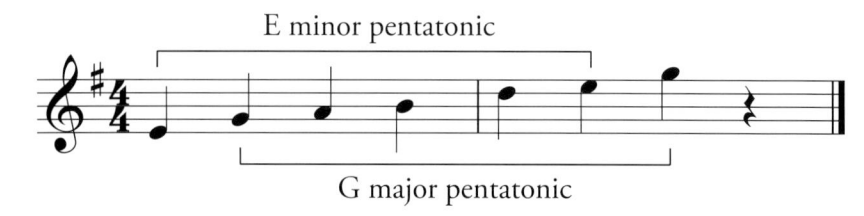

So if you're playing in the key of E minor, you can use all the same notes and finger patterns that you learnt for G major, but just start and end the phrases on an E instead of a G.

3: Pentatonic Scales

Minor pentatonic patterns are particularly useful because they are closely related to the blues scale (discussed in the next chapter). Go to any guitar shop on a Saturday morning and amid the cacophony of 'Stairway to Heaven' and 'Smoke on the Water' you'll be sure to hear some youth picking out the first (and possibly only) scale he ever learnt. Some things never change!

Fig 3.18 **E minor pentatonic descending**

Assignment

Try changing the G major pentatonic patterns to E minor pentatonics and practise them over this vamp.

Backing 22

Fig 3.19 **E minor vamp**

Higher Positions

As well as working on all the pentatonic scales in 1st position, you should also learn them in 'closed' position – using no open strings. Start with A major:

Fig 3.20 **A major pentatonic – closed position**

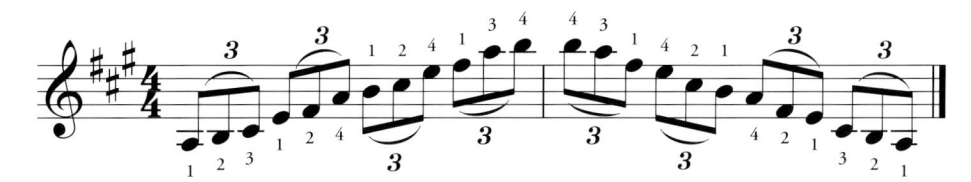

Once you've learnt the fingering for this, you can use it for any key. B major for example, normally a difficult key, is just as easy as A major, providing that:

1. you keep your hand locked in position and
2. you stay in tune.

53

Exploring Jazz Violin

Fig 3.21 B major pentatonic – closed position

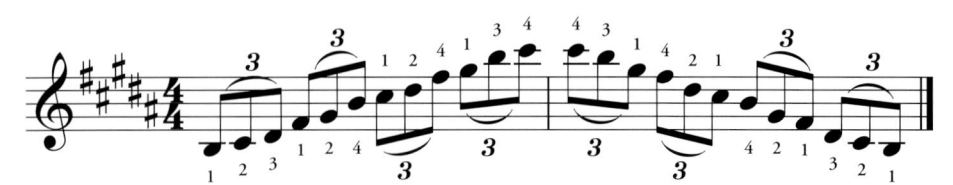

The pentatonic scale now really comes into its own. Playing B major in 1st position is a real headache, but now there's nothing to it. In fact, so long as your fingers are familiar with the patterns, you don't even have to know exactly what notes you're playing all the time – it's like using a capo on a guitar or having a built-in transpose button! Having learnt the fingering without using open strings, it's now easy to take the pattern up to higher positions. Let's say we're starting with the A major pentatonic in 1st position; we can move up to 4th position, replacing your fourth finger with your first:

Fig 3.22 Changing from 1st to 4th position

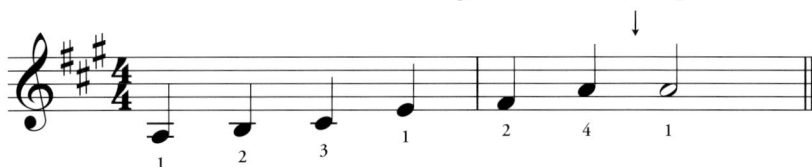

Now use the same finger pattern to play the pentatonic starting from 4th position:

Fig 3.23 A major pentatonic – 4th position

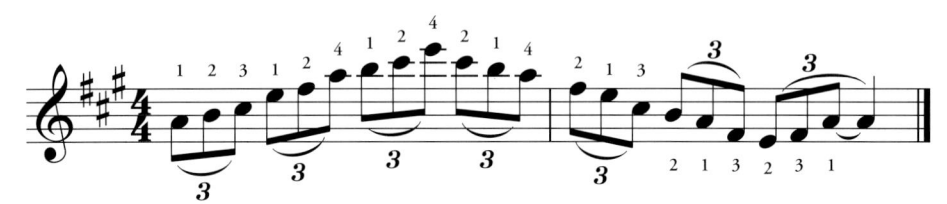

Let's take it higher still. Again, replace your fourth finger with your first to move from 4th to 7th position:

Fig 3.24 Changing from 4th to 7th position

54

Now play the pattern again starting in 7th position.

Fig 3.25 A major pentatonic – 7th position

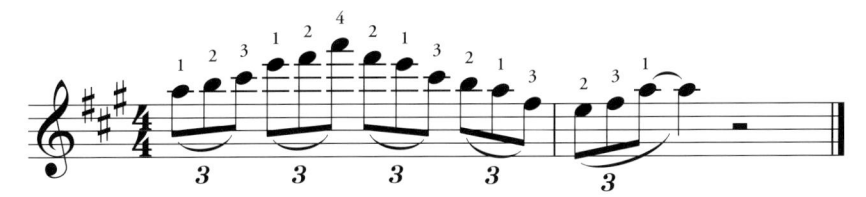

You'll notice that the available notes become fewer as you get higher; if you're not entirely sure what notes you're playing in this position don't worry, just trust in the scale and the pattern to do the work for you. Now you need to try the same exercises in all the different keys. Because you're not using any open strings, it's really not that hard. By using this one simple scale and a couple of finger patterns you now have control of the entire fingerboard, including the dusty end, right at the top.

Checkpoint

Pentatonic scales are one of the fundamentals of improvisation. You'll find them equally useful for country, rock, Celtic and contemporary-folk music. They are a short cut to sounding fluid and confident whilst soloing. At first you'll find them absolutely liberating but eventually, particularly in a jazz context, they can become bland and restricting. So make sure that you don't get to rely on them too much.

Assignment

Play through this next version of 'Mind the Gap' with the backing track. The solo is constructed from pentatonic patterns. Listen carefully to how the scales fit the chords. The uncharitable might place 'fits' in inverted commas and draw parallels with ugly sisters and glass slippers. Certainly, there's no problem with sections like bars 1–8, but with the A^7 and E^7 chords in particular (bars 14 and 28) there are quite a few 'toes' sticking out. A^7 feels 'lost' without the 3rd of the chord (C♯), and likewise the E^7 is 'crying out' for a G♯.

With only five notes to choose from, the pentatonic is able to 'skim' over these chords with a judicious choice of notes, but can never do them justice. We'll delve deeper into chords later on. For now, experiment by trying your own pentatonic patterns, and start the job of training your ear to discriminate between what really fits, what you can get away with (I count myself as an expert in that department!) and what will mark you out forever as a charlatan.

Exploring Jazz Violin

Mind the Gap (solo version)

Chris Haigh

© 2010 Schott Music Ltd, London

'Mind the Gap' had a simple chord sequence, but this next tune has much more complex (chord) changes and will demonstrate the full value of the pentatonic scale.

The Glass Slippers (head)

3: Pentatonic Scales

Demo 24 | Backing 25

Chris Haigh

© 2010 Schott Music Ltd, London

Take a good look at the tune and the chords. There are lots of them! And instead of the tune being in just one key, it moves through three, so the melody is built around three different pentatonic scales. Your first thought is probably despair that it changes from the 'people's key' of D to the 'highfalutin'' key of E♭, then to the 'who do you think you are anyway?' key of D♭. But despair not! All you need to play the melody and improvise over the chords are the three relevant pentatonic scales, each played in a different position on the neck:

Exploring Jazz Violin

Fig 3.26 **D major pentatonic**

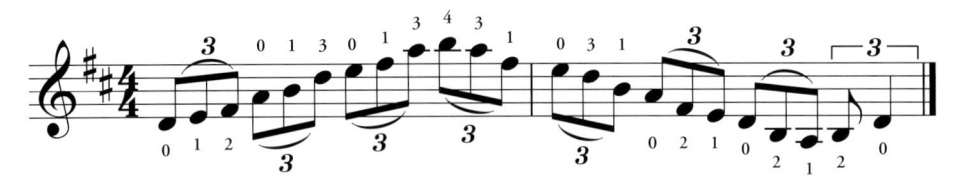

Fig 3.27 **E♭ major pentatonic**

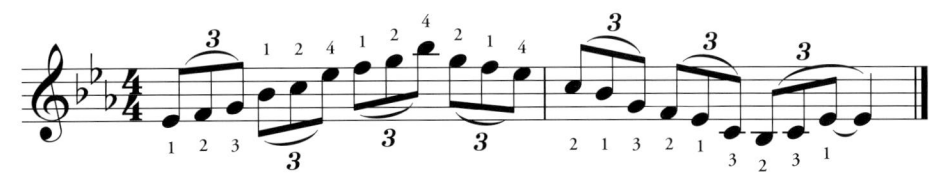

Fig 3.28 **D♭ major pentatonic**

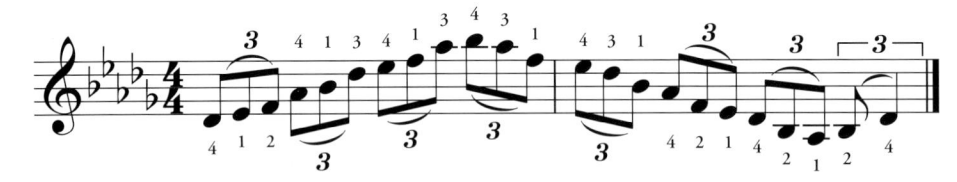

Spend some time on each scale, familiarizing yourself with the finger patterns.

You might find it easier to play the D♭ pentatonic in 4th position, starting with your first finger on the G string; that way you can use the same fingering for both the E♭ and D♭ pentatonics. You'll notice that using 4th position also gives you more notes at the top of the scale.

Fig 3.29 **D♭ major pentatonic – 4th position**

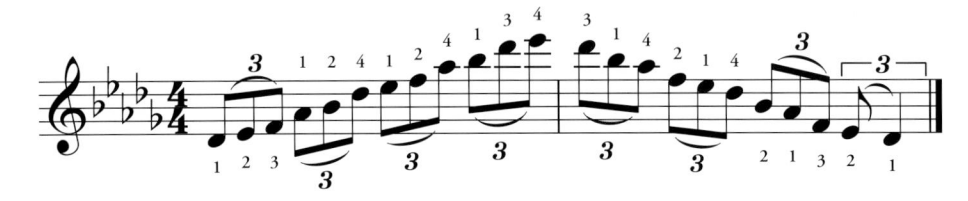

Looking at the whole tune, you'll see that the 'A' section is all in D major; the melody stays completely within the D pentatonic scale, and you can stay on this scale whilst improvising through this section, despite the numerous and fairly complex chords.

There are numerous tunes where the same pentatonic scale will work all the way through, e.g. 'Dinah', 'Lady be Good', 'Autumn Leaves'. With this one, however, at the 'B' section you need to change to E♭ pentatonic for four bars, then D♭ pentatonic for four bars, before returning to D pentatonic for the last 'A' section.

There's nothing about this or any other tune, which says that you have to stick to the pentatonic scale, but it certainly makes dealing with the complex chords and difficult keys a whole lot easier. Also the use of pentatonic scales allows you to be able to find melodic phrases which are readily available to you by using adjacent notes from the scales. Have a look at the solo version.

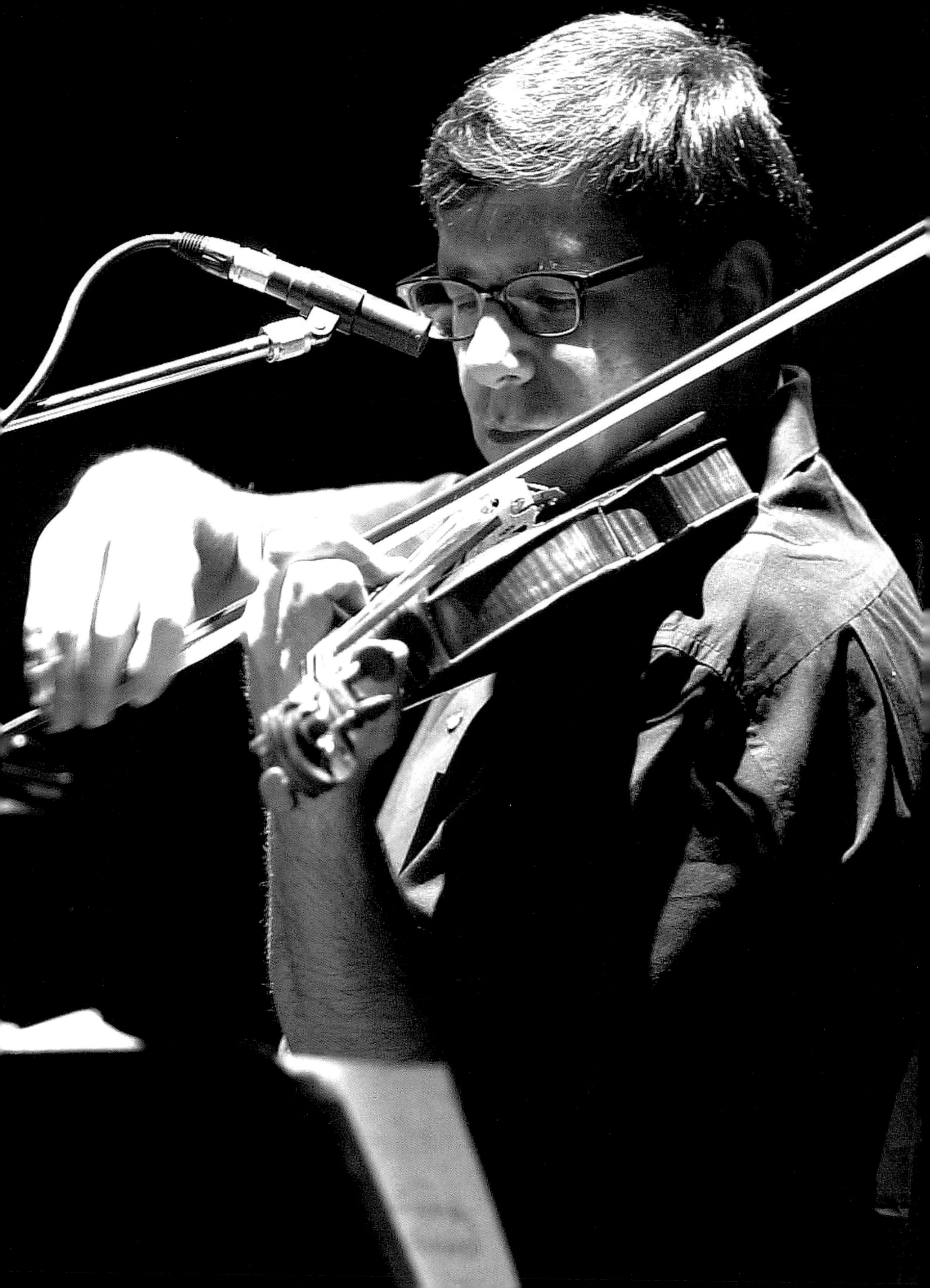

Demo 26 Backing 25

The Glass Slippers (solo version)

Chris Haigh

And the award for best solo goes to… somebody else. OK, basing a solo like this entirely on pentatonic scales is never going to produce a masterpiece, and it will be full of compromises. However, it will at least be easy, and at this stage gives you a good chance of sounding fluent and confident. Let's do a brief post-mortem on 'The Glass Slippers' (solo version).

Bars 1–4
The first two bars are simple phrases which work fine until you hit the E♭7 chord. None of the notes in the D pentatonic are going to come out smelling of roses, but the note D has the advantage that if you hold your nerve and keep it going until bar 3, it's suddenly 'sitting proud' over a chord of D – as if you'd planned it all along! We're thinking of the whole of this section as if it was in D major, even though some of the chords are going to sound tenuous. For now, rely on your ear to help you out; when we get to the chapter on chords you'll be able to analyse this more fully. Bars 5 and 6 are the kind of scale patterns we looked at earlier.

Bars 9–16
Bar 9 takes you all the way up the D pentatonic scale, over two octaves. This is where having memorized the scale in advance makes all the difference, allowing you speed and fluency. Bars 10 and 11 illustrate the fact that it's easy to make simple but strong repeatable patterns with a few adjacent notes from the pentatonic scale. Bar 10 also shows that it can sound good to repeat a run or pattern whilst the chords change underneath; this makes what you're playing seem (possibly) more interesting than it really is! Bars 13 and 14 take a run down, mostly but not completely, following the same pattern.

Bars 17–24
Bars 17–20 mark the first real change; we're now in the key of E♭ major, so the whole pentatonic pattern has to move up a semitone. Two bars of a descending-step pattern are followed by two bars of 'homing in' on the new tonal centre – E♭. The next four bars are in the key of D♭ major; too many flats for comfort here, but the pentatonic scale deals with it easily; you can even play it in 1st position without much trouble. Bar 21 echoes the same descending pattern we had in bar 17, giving a good sense of continuity.

Bars 25–32
For the last 8 bars we're back in the key of D major; more step patterns and simple scales bring us safely to the key note in the last bar.

It's useful to realize that as long as you keep a scale or pattern going, you can easily play over chords which your pentatonic scale doesn't technically fit. It's the first and last notes of a run that are really important, so make sure that they sit comfortably within the chord.

Other Pentatonic Scales

I started out this chapter telling you *"this is the pentatonic scale"*. As usual, I was being slightly economical with the truth. Actually there are many different versions, and any five notes from within an octave will make a pentatonic scale. Most will be practically unusable but there are a few gems to be discovered. Before we move on, try this little beauty, up and down and inside out. You'll notice that the flattened 7th immediately evokes a mystical / Eastern feel. In theoretical terms you could call it a 'major dominant pentatonic', but **Graham Clark** described it to me as *"a real Gong scale!"* (**Gong** being a hippy-trippy-jazz-rock-prog band he played in for many years).

Fig 3.30 **D major dominant pentatonic**

Chapter Summary

1. The pentatonic scale is an easy way to achieve pleasant, logical sounding melodic lines.

2. You should practise them in every key, and get your fingers completely familiar with the patterns.

3. Also practise them in closed position.

4. Work out and learn step-wise patterns and riffs based on the pentatonic scales.

5. Train your ear to recognize how well the scale fits whatever chord you're playing over. If you're 'ploughing' through a chord which is putting up 'resistance', don't stop until you hit a 'safe' note!

In the next chapter we'll move on to an even more useful scale: the blues scale.

4: The Blues

The blues is an essential element of jazz, but a rather complex and elusive one. There are three different aspects to the blues. Firstly, it's a sequence of chords, usually 12 bars in length. Secondly, it's a scale containing certain 'flattened' or 'blue' notes and thirdly it's a feeling which can be applied to music – a passion and angst which finds its expression through playing the blues.

Most jazz violinists include elements of the blues in their playing, and there are some (**Papa John Creach**, **Don Sugarcane Harris**) for whom it is a speciality.

The Blues Sequence

The blues sequence typically has 12 bars which are repeated throughout the tune. We've already seen that most jazz pieces follow an 'AABA', 32-bar structure, so in this sense the blues is quite a departure. In the key of G major the simplest blues chord sequence (where each chord lasts for 1 bar) would be:
G, G, G, G
C, C, G, G
D, C, G, G

Playing this as arpeggios, we get:

Fig 4.1 **Basic blues in G – arpeggios**

Demo 27

The three chords in use are G (the tonic or chord **I**), C (the subdominant or chord **IV**) and D (the dominant or chord **V**).

By referring to the chords as Roman numerals, rather than letters, the sequence becomes 'universal', and can be applied to any key. Here's the basic blues sequence expressed as Roman numerals:

I, I, I, I
IV, IV, I, I
V, IV, I, I

The arpeggios above gave an outline of the basic blues chord sequence, but sound staid and not very bluesy. We can spice things up in several ways:

63

Exploring Jazz Violin

1. We can add a 'flattened' 7th note to each chord (for the chord of G this would be an F♮)

2. Stretch the arpeggio across two bars – going up and then down

3. Replace the last chord in the sequence with a chord of D^7 (V^7, which helps to lead back to the start of the sequence)

4. We can add a bit of swing to the beginning of each phrase.

This results into something like a piano boogie:

Fig 4.2 Blues boogie

Demo 28

Here's what the sequence now looks like when described as Roman numerals:

I^7, I^7, I^7, I^7
IV^7, IV^7, I7, I^7
V^7, IV^7, I^7, V^7

Over this we can superimpose a double-stopped chord part, which sounds like a horn (brass) riff:

Fig 4.3 Basic blues with double stops

Demo 29

The finger shapes are arranged to give minimal movement; shifting one finger by just one semitone (from B to B♭) gives us a change from G^7 to C^7. The note G acts as the root of the G^7 chord and then as the 5th of the C^7 chord, whilst the B is the 3rd of the G^7 chord, this becomes B♭ – the 7th of the C^7 chord.

We will come across many more uses of this idea with blues licks later on. Here's a melody to go over the top of this sequence. Notice again the economical use of notes – the same 4-bar phrase occurs three times with only small variations to accommodate the changing chords; this is typical of many blues melodies.

Fig 4.4 **Blues melody – minimal changes**

Demo 30

Assignment

Listen to some blues music; either with or without violin. Count the twelve bars to get to know the form, and try to identify the chords as being I, IV or V. You will notice that some blues tunes may have variations on the chords, but the basic structure should remain pretty well the same.

Try the four blues tunes above in a few different keys; C, D, A and E to start with. The melody lines are easy enough that you should be able to transpose them by ear without writing them out.

Be warned that not every tune with the word 'blues' in the title is necessarily a blues; there was a time when blues was a 'buzz word' which songwriters would adopt to make any old Tin Pan Alley song sound modern and commercial.

Also a blues is not always 12 bars long, for example, 'Fulsom Prison Blues', by that leading light of the jazz scene, **Johnny Cash**, is conspicuously missing a bar and 'Limehouse Blues' is 32 bars long and certainly not a blues.

Exploring Jazz Violin

Finding the Blues

Now let's look at what makes the blues, 'bluesy'. First a quick bit of theory. In a major scale, arpeggio or chord, the 3rd is two tones above the root; in the key of G major the 3rd then is B♮:

Fig 4.5 G major scale, arpeggio and chord

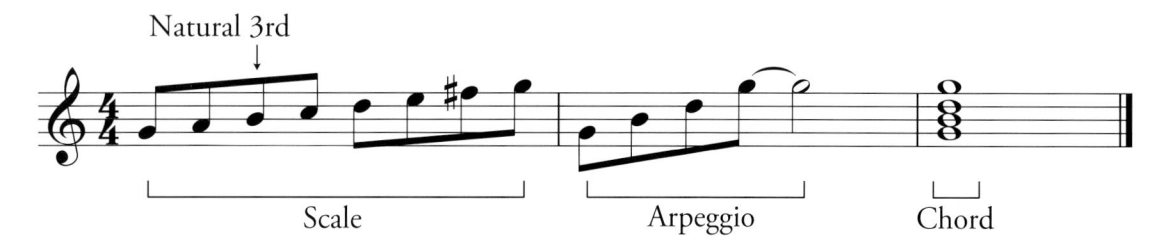

In a minor scale, arpeggio or chord, the 3rd is one and a half tones above the root; in the key of G minor the 3rd is B♭.

Fig 4.6 G (natural) minor scale, arpeggio and chord

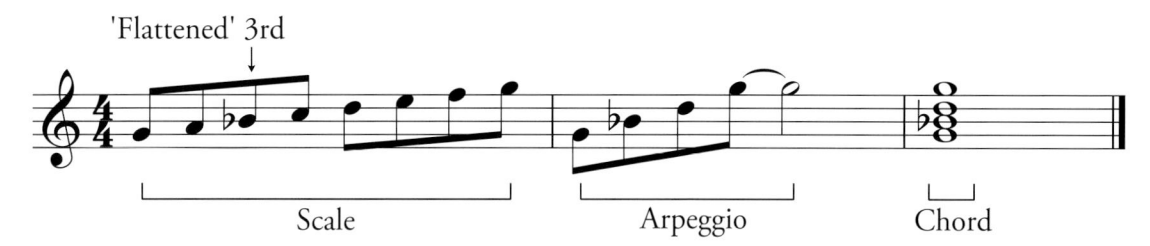

So the 3rd defines whether a scale, arpeggio or chord is major or minor; this in itself is important because we tend to think of major as being happy, and minor as sad. The 3rd then is like a switch, that can change one mood into another. Perhaps the single most important element of the blues is that it can use both the minor and major 3rds together.

Let's take the standard pentatonic scale and make it a little more 'bluesy':

Fig 4.7 G pentatonic blues scale

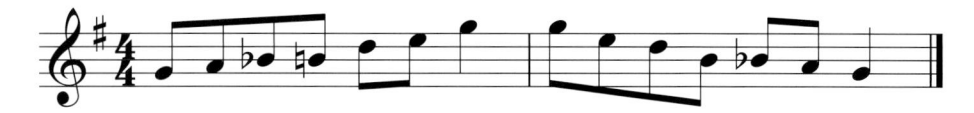

The alert among you will realize that this isn't technically a pentatonic scale, as it comprises of six degrees. It's actually a pentatonic major scale, with an added 'flattened' 3rd (B♭) which is a 'blue' note (a note that sounds bluesy).

For the purposes of this book I shall refer to it though as the pentatonic blues scale as this is what it's most closely related to. (Sometimes it's called the major blues scale but I feel this would confuse matters at this stage.)

For a jazz violinist, this is the most straight-forward and useful way to approach the blues. It's the most useful because it enables you to play blues riffs easily in a major key, and over any kind of song, not just a blues.

66

Violinist **Mike Piggott** who, despite also being a blues guitarist, uses this as his 'default' blues scale.

On the fiddle it's possible to slide between two notes – in this scale between the flattened and natural 3^{rds} is a nice place to do it. Pianists can't do this; they have to hit the two adjacent notes simultaneously, as if trying to get the note in between the cracks.

Get very familiar with this scale. With just a few twists and turns the scale can effortlessly transform itself into some very handy riffs:

Fig 4.8 **Blues riff 1**

Fig 4.9 **Blues riff 2**

Fig 4.10 **Blues riff 3**

Here's a typical **Grappelli** style blues lick:

Fig 4.11 **Grappelli style blues lick**

When playing blues licks over a chord sequence, the same phrases will often work over all three chords.

Here's a melody which makes use of this idea, again using the simple pentatonic blues scale.

Demo 31

Fig 4.12 **Blues with repeating riff**

Exploring Jazz Violin

An alternative approach to using the same riff throughout a sequence is to transpose the riff up a 4th and then a 5th, as the chords change:

Fig 4.13 Blues with transposing riff

Demo 32

Assignment

Create some of your own 2-bar riffs making use of the 'flattened' 3rd 'blue' note. Try playing them over the blues backing sequence, firstly using the idea of changing as little as possible, and secondly by transposing the riff up by a 4th and a 5th.

As with the standard pentatonic scale, to make the most of the pentatonic blues scale, learn it in 3rd position as well as in 1st; as it uses no open strings, it can easily be moved up or down the fingerboard allowing you to play blues licks in any key.

Fig 4.14 Pentatonic blues scale – 3rd position

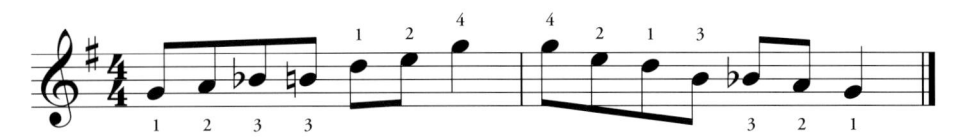

Practise it both with separate notes on the flattened and natural 3rds, and sliding between them. Practise it over and over again. Then practise it some more; it's perhaps the most useful pattern in the whole book. This is born out by the following example – so long as you stay in position F# major, for instance, suddenly becomes as easy as G major:

Fig 4.15 Pentatonic blues scale in F# major

Here are some licks you might use in 'closed' position (any position above 1st position, not using open strings).

Let's change to the key of F major. With this one you can slide between the A♭ and A♮ using your third finger.

Fig 4.16 Blues riff 1 in F major

Fig 4.17 Blues riff 2 in F major

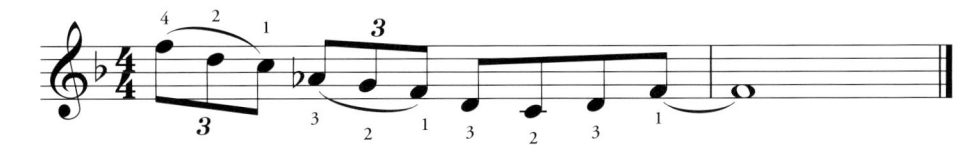

This one stays in the same position, but takes the pattern up higher.

Fig 4.18 Blues riff 3 in F major

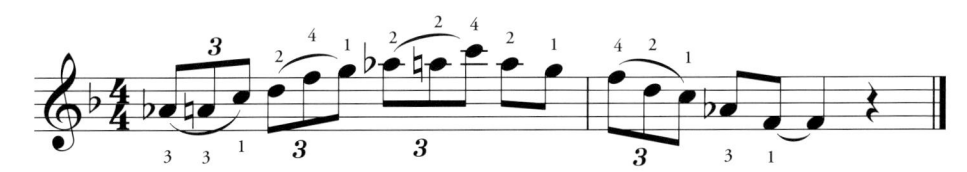

Exploring Jazz Violin

Here's a solo using some of these ideas. It's our old friend 'Head First'; not a blues but a **jazz** tune in G major. For this we can use the G pentatonic blues scale.

Head First (Blues Pentatonic version)

Demo 33 | Backing 6

Chris Haigh

Medium Swing ♩ = 160

© 2010 Schott Music Ltd, London

Bars 1–4

This solo contains at least one blues lick per stave; that's a reasonable average for a swing solo. Bar 2 uses the fourth finger to slide up to the flattened 3rd (B♭) and then down to the A. At the end of bar 4 the first finger slides from the natural 3rd to the flattened 3rd and back again.

Bars 5–8

Bars 5 and 6 are quite interesting; they start a climbing, step-like scale. As we approach the chord of G in bar 7 it becomes clear that the target note is the high B, so there's a scramble to get there with a triplet from F to A, leaving just enough time to slip in the 'blue' note B♭ before reaching the B♮.

Bars 9–12

Bar 9 is a very violinistic blues riff, 'rocking' between the flattened and natural 3rd, and the open E string. This could equally well be played with a first finger slide, but I prefer this one with first and second fingers. Bar 11 is a long fourth finger slide up to and down from the flattened 3rd.

Bars 13–16

There's another 'string-rocking' pattern at bar 13.

Bars 18–21

In bars 18 and 19 the flattened 3rd is like a passing note, but it features as a strong note again in bar 21.

Bar 22

In bar 22, just as a reminder that the flattened 3rd is not compulsory, we have a natural 3rd.

Bars 25–26

Bars 25 and 26 introduce two 'new kids on the block'– the flattened 5th and flattened 7th. Both are 'blue' notes in their own right as we'll see shortly, though they feature much less often in a solo based on a pentatonic blues scale.

More Blue Notes

We already know that the flattened 3rd can be considered a 'blue' note, but there are two others that I'd like to introduce to you, the first is the **flattened 5th**:

Fig 4.19 Flattened 5th

You might use this in licks such as:

Fig 4.20 Flattened 5th riff 1

Exploring Jazz Violin

Fig 4.21 Flattened 5th riff 2

Here's a typical **Joe Venuti** kind of lick where the flattened 3rd (B♭) is used with the flattened 5th (D♭):

Fig 4.22 Venuti lick with flattened 3rd and flattened 5th

The other 'blue' note is the **flattened 7th**:

Fig 4.23 Flattened 7th

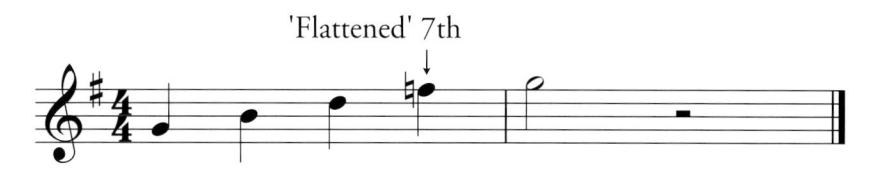

And a couple of riffs:

Fig 4.24 Flattened 7th riff 1

Fig 4.25 Flattened 7th riff 2

This one combines the flattened 7th and flattened 3rd:

Fig 4.26 Flattened 7th and 3rd riff

4: The Blues

The Blues Scale

What happens if you combine all three 'blue' notes – the flattened 3rd, flattened 5th and flattened 7th?

Fig 4.27 Flattened 3rd, 5th and 7th (G blues scale)

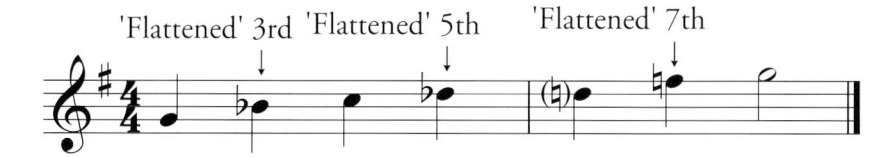

Here's where things could get confusing. This is the scale most commonly taught as 'the blues scale', and it is the first scale that most aspiring lead guitarists will learn. Notice that whilst it has a flattened 3rd, it does not have a natural or major 3rd. This means that, when played in a major key, there will be constant tension and conflict against the chords. It is sometimes referred to as the 'minor blues scale', though this doesn't necessarily imply that it is played in a minor key, over minor chords.

Assignment

Try playing the G blues scale over the chords of 'Head First'. This won't sound altogether too pleasant, but it will illustrate the point of using the wrong scale at the wrong time.

Whereas in the pentatonic blues scale you could slide between the adjacent flattened 3rd and natural 3rd, in this blues scale you can slide between the flattened 5th and natural 5th:

Fig 4.28 Blues scale with flattened / natural 5th

Pentatonic Blues or Blues Scale?

So isn't it inconvenient, the fact that there are two different blues scales? Well actually no, look what happens when you compare them.

Take the B♭ pentatonic blues scale: the G blues scale uses the same pitches. If you start on a B♭ instead of a G you get:

Fig 4.29 B♭ pentatonic blues / G blues scales

Exploring Jazz Violin

Just like when we looked at the G major scale and its relative minor – E minor, here we have two blues scales which share all the same notes, and therefore all the same finger patterns. Proof, if you're looking for it, that there is a God!

Fig 4.30 G blues scale / B♭ pentatonic blues scale

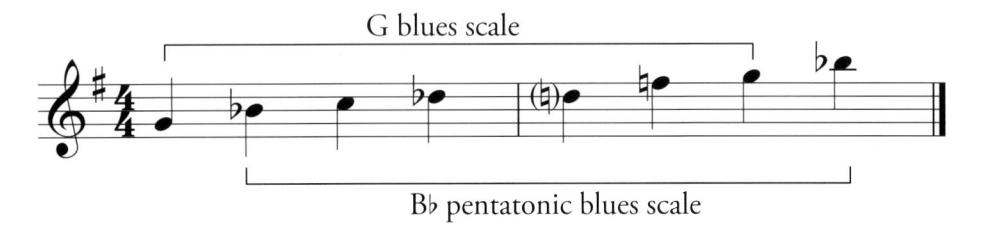

Here's a melody to give you an idea of how the blues scale sounds over major chords.

Fig 4.31 Blues scale melody over major chords

Demo 34

Notice that all the major chords are 7ths. This is one of the features that defines a 'real' blues, and it's part of the reason why the blues scale is the one that works.

I have to apologize on behalf of generations of bluesmen for the fact that when you write down a melody like this, it's bound to be full of accidentals, unless you change the key signature, which would then be readable but way too confusing…

Here's a typical blues-scale lick in the style of **Papa John Creach**:

Fig 4.32 Blues-scale lick (Papa John Creach)

This now sounds really bluesy. Use this blues scale whenever you're either playing on an actual 12-bar blues, or occasionally use it as an effect in a jazz tune in a major key (i.e. not a 12-bar blues); it also works well in a bluegrass setting. I wouldn't recommend that you use it throughout a major tune; the pentatonic blues scale is far more flexible for general use.

The Minor Blues

What happens when you're playing a minor blues – i.e. when the chords are in a minor key? It's pretty straightforward; for the key of E minor, use the E blues scale. If you start the E blues scale on a G, you will effectively be playing the G pentatonic blues scale, if it's easier for you to think in those terms.

Likewise for an A minor blues, you can use the C pentatonic blues scale, or for a G minor blues, use the B♭ pentatonic blues scale.

Fig 4.33 G pentatonic blues / E blues scales

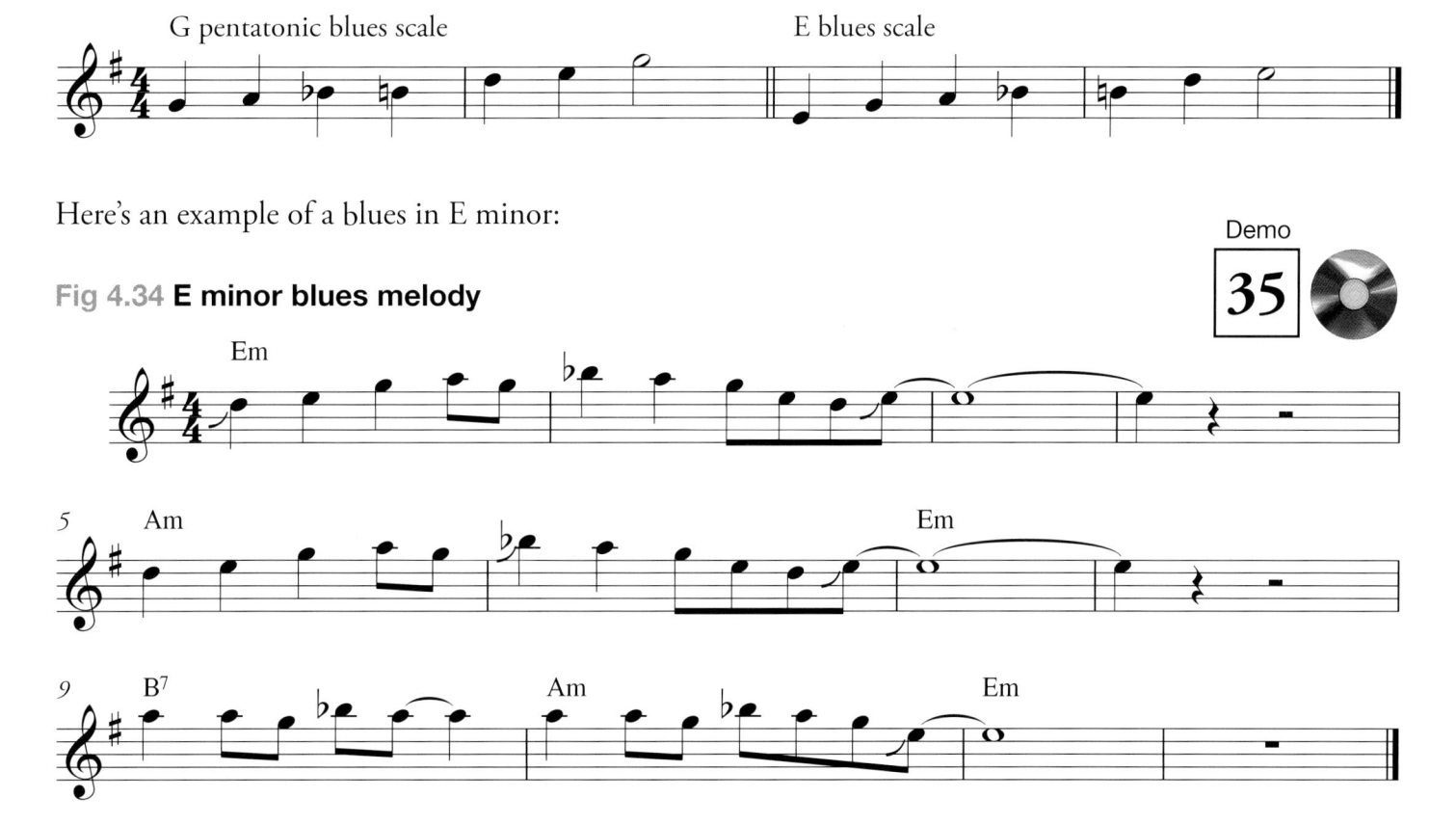

Fig 4.34 E minor blues melody

Here's an example of a blues in E minor:

You can see that the first four bars of melody work perfectly well when repeated over bars 5–8, even though the chords are different in bars 5 and 6. You can use this device extensively in your soloing. Let the chords do some of the work – the (chord) changes will make you sound more interesting. Indeed repetition, whether of large or small fragments of melody, is an essential element of much blues playing.

Exploring Jazz Violin

Checkpoint

OK, maybe your eyes glazed over a little when I started talking about different kinds of blues scales and you just want a simple set of instructions. Here it is:

1. If you're playing a jazz tune in a **major key**, and you want to add a bluesy feel, use the **pentatonic blues scale of that key** (the major pentatonic scale plus the flattened 3rd). You can add a flattened 5th or flattened 7th occasionally as well. So for a tune in G, use the G pentatonic blues scale.

2. If you're playing a 'real' **12-bar blues in a major key** (especially when the first chord is a 7th chord), use the **blues scale of that key**. So for a 12-bar blues in G, use the G blues scale. (This has the flattened 3rd, flattened 5th and flattened 7th, but does not have the natural 3rd).

3. If you're playing a tune in a **minor key**, whether it's a blues or not, use the **blues scale of that key**. So for a tune in E minor, use the E blues scale. (This will have all the same notes as its relative pentatonic blues scale – the G pentatonic blues scale.)

Repetition

Blues licks often use the same two or three notes repeatedly, such as this one, where you can either slide up repeatedly between the B♭ and B♮, or else play them as separate notes using your first and second fingers.

Fig 4.35 Repeated triplets

Here's a similar idea in 3rd position:

Fig 4.36 Repeated triplets – 3rd position

You can also repeat longer phrases, up to 4 bars long; the phrase will sound different as the chords change (as we saw in fig 4.34). It will give your playing a feeling of continuity and decisiveness; most of the 12-bar melodies we have looked at have in fact been largely a simple repetition of 4-bar phrases. Here's the kind of line you might hear from **Papa John Creach**, where he uses the same simple riff repeatedly with great effect. Slide up to the first B in each triplet:

Fig 4.37 **Papa John Creach style blues line**

You'll see how the same lick works happily on both the chords of the dominant (B⁷ or V⁷) and subdominant (A⁷ or IV⁷); we could easily have held it over the tonic chord (E or I) as well.

Other Blues Sequences

By now you've looked at a whole raft of blues licks. Here are two more chord sequences to try them out on. First there's a **jazz blues**. Here the basic 12-bar, three-chord sequence has been embellished to make it more interesting for jazz players; such sequences have been popular from the 1930s onwards.

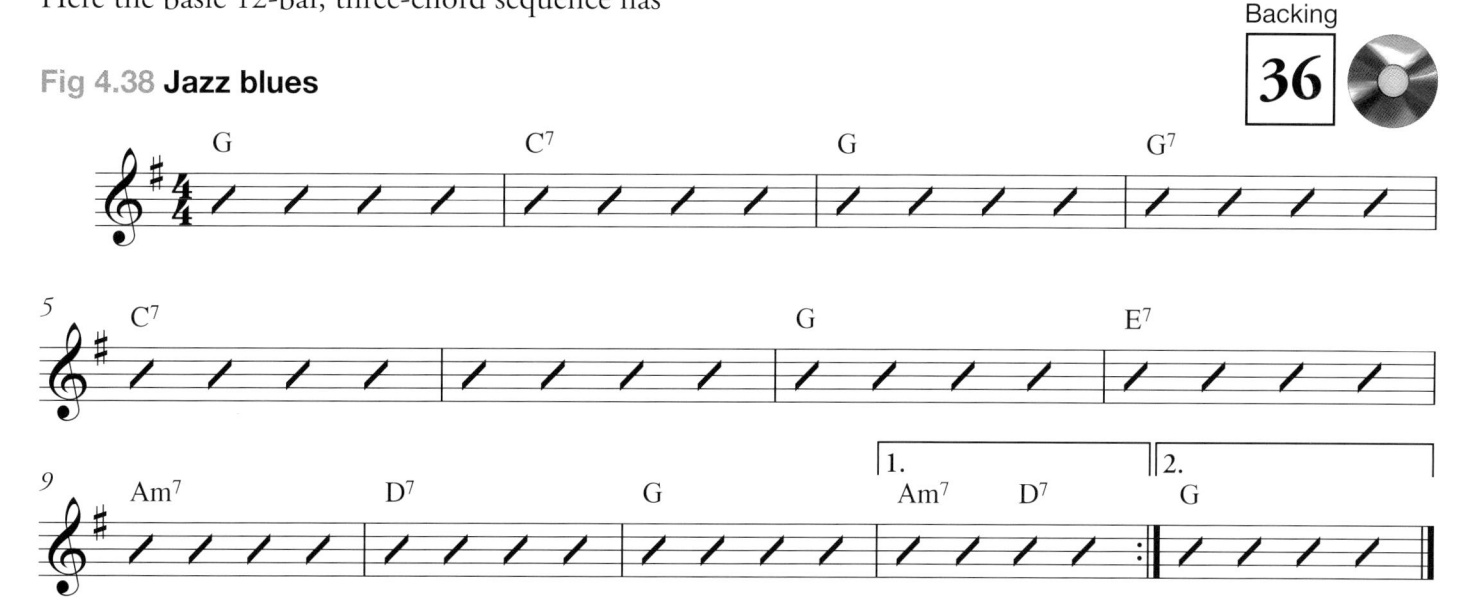

Backing **36**

Fig 4.38 **Jazz blues**

Let's see what changes have been made. In bar 2, instead of staying on the chord of G, we move up to C⁷ before dropping back to G. The G⁷ chord in bar 4 signals the change to C⁷. Bar 8 might take you by surprise with a move to E⁷, and the last 4 bars are replaced by two II-V-I sequences (explained in the next chapter). Try both the pentatonic blues and the blues scales over this sequence and you'll find that there's nothing dangerous about these chords. They will make your lines sound more interesting without any extra effort on your part. Nice!

Exploring Jazz Violin

Second there's the **bebop blues**:

Fig 4.39 **Bebop blues**

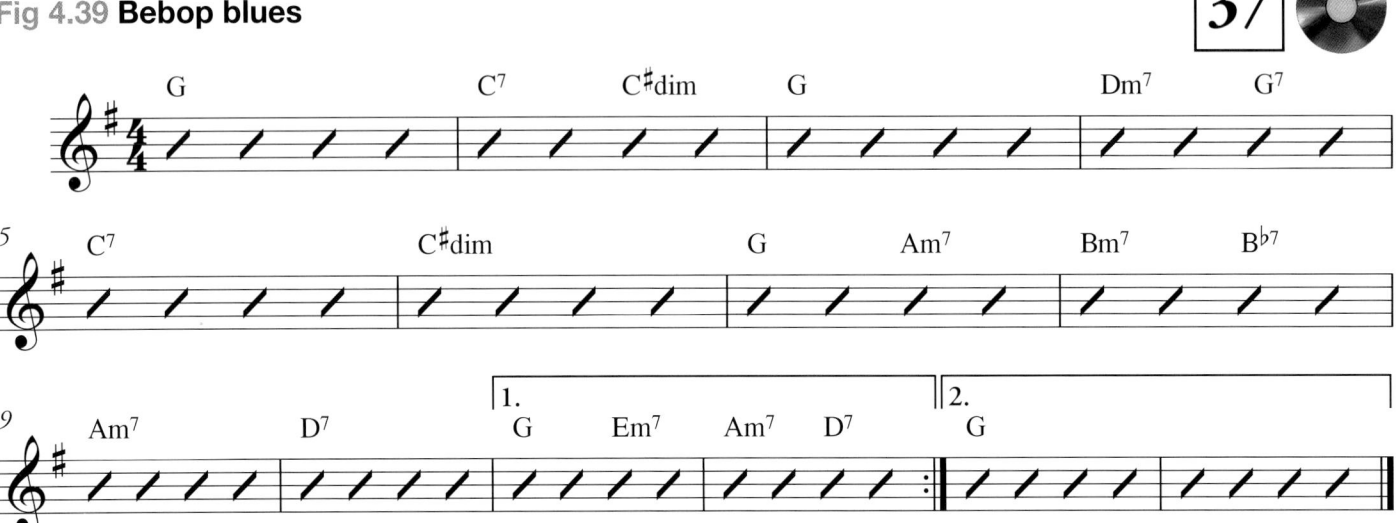

Backing 37

Bebop was the cutting edge of jazz in the 1940s and 50s. Sequences became increasingly more complex and players began to engage ever more closely with the chords and their changes. The 12-bar blues remained a popular format but the new chords provided a far more colourful and challenging backdrop for improvisation. Nevertheless, because of the powerful simplicity of the underlying structure, it is still possible to play a simple major or blues scale all the way through. Chords like C#dim and Bb7 act as passing chords and at this stage we can merely admire them in passing.

So if a bandleader shouts out "Blues in F", don't show your ignorance by asking "Excuse me chaps, but is that the jazz blues, bebop blues or blues blues?" Even if every member of the band has a different idea what to play, it will still fit together surprisingly well.

Chapter Summary

Different players make different use of the blues in their playing. Here's a reminder of the essentials:

1. The blues sequence is 12 bars long, and consists of three basic chords: the tonic, subdominant and dominant (I, IV and V). Any other chords can be considered as variations or substitutions of these.

2. The simplicity of the blues chord sequence allows you to play repeated phrases which will work even though the chords are changing underneath.

3. The pentatonic blues scale is a pentatonic scale with one extra note – a flattened 3rd. This scale is easy to use over most chord sequences.

4. The blues scale has a flattened 3rd, flattened 5th and flattened 7th. It is best to use this only in an actual blues setting.

5. Learn these scales in 1st position and in higher positions. Build yourself a library of licks based on them.

5: Chords Part I

We've finally come to the point where we can't avoid it any longer. Sooner or later you're going to have to improvise over chords such as Am$^{7(\flat5)}$, A$\flat^{7(\sharp5)}$ or B$\flat^{7(\flat9\flat13)}$ and actually have some idea of what's going on. Two words will suffice:

DON'T PANIC!

As violinists, we're particularly prone to chord phobia because, unlike saxophonists for example, we almost certainly didn't start playing our instrument with jazz in mind. More likely we were classical or folk players, for whom chords had little meaning. And unlike pianists or guitarists, our instrument is not designed to play chords – that's my excuse anyway.

So far in this book we've glibly and nonchalantly sauntered through our improvisations as if the chords were a negligible irritant. In fact jazz chords can be extremely complex and difficult, particularly if you take them too seriously, but there are a couple of points in our favour:

1. Some chord symbols have so many added notes to them they look like a stretched limousine. The fact is that whilst the first couple of characters of information are important, the further you read to the right, the less important it is. So with Am$^{7(\flat5)}$ for example, the Am is really important, the 7 less so and the ($\flat$5) even less so. So don't break out into a sweat when you see this kind of chord coming up – the chances are you'll already be onto the next chord before you've read your way to the end of it.

2. Your job is NOT to create a line that includes every note in the chord. It's simply to find a pleasing phrase which fits somewhere within the chord. Even if the chords are complicated, it doesn't stop you from making your solos simple and straightforward.

3. Many of the more complex chords you'll come across will be substitutions; that is to say they're doing the same job as a different, usually simpler, chord. What's more, the accompanist is very likely to be creating his own substitutions, without even telling you. So if you're agonizing about the $\flat$9 on a chord, he's just as likely to be playing a $\sharp$9 instead.

Having said all that, let's get down to basics and explain what chords are and where they come from. If you are already fairly experienced in jazz, you may want to skip a few pages at this point. If you have a good grasp of music theory, but from a classical point of view, then read on, as jazz musicians think about chords rather differently.

What is a Chord?

In this section we're going to explain chords from first principles, so that you can understand the notes, the intervals and the naming of chords. This is easiest to explain with reference to a piano keyboard as you will soon see.

A chord is a group of notes that harmonize with one another and a simple chord will contain three notes, known as a triad. The notes of the triad comprise of the root, 3rd and 5th of the scale. So the chord of C major is built up of the notes from the C major scale: the root – C, the 3rd – E and the 5th – G. (Many chords also have a 7th, and possibly more notes beyond, but we'll come to that later.)

Exploring Jazz Violin

Checkpoint

Chord names and chord symbols (the abbreviations of chords that you will see above a melody line) can be confusing, not least because there are various different systems in use, and some chords can have alternative names and symbols. Occasionally you may come across charts (tunes) that only refer to the chords as Roman numerals, such as IVm^7, V^7 and so on. This requires more thought on your part, but has the advantage of being readily transferable to any key, and moreover draws attention to their relationship with one another. French jazz-sheets have the added peculiarity of sometimes using the solfège (or sol-fa) system, where the symbols *do*, *re*, *mi* etc. are used instead of chord symbols, but you are less likely to come across this.

Where do Chords Come From?

To make a pleasing harmony, notes of a simple chord are a 3rd apart. On the piano, in the key of C major, that means playing every other note (as shown below). Let's look at each note of the chord in turn:

Fig 5.1 C major chord

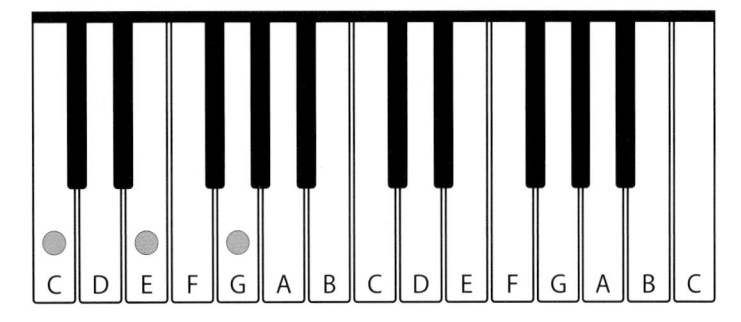

When related to the C major scale, C is the root note of the chord.

E is the 3rd. This is an important note because it defines whether the chord is major or minor.

Because C to E is an interval of a major 3rd (two tones), this is a major chord. If the 3rd of our chord was an E♭, this would be an interval of one and a half tones – a minor 3rd, and this would be a minor chord.

The G is the 5th, which is an interval of a minor 3rd above the note E.

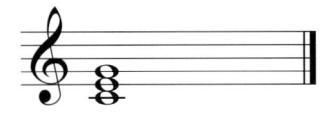

So here's a simple rule: *a major 3rd with a minor 3rd above it forms a major triad or chord.*

Incidentally, as the fiddle is tuned in 5^{ths}, the 5th of a chord is easy to find – it's always one string higher than the root note; so if the root is the third finger on the G string, the 5th will be third finger, same position, on the D string, the next string up.

5: Chords Part I

Understanding Chord Symbols

Chord symbols can be a little tricky when you start out, but there are some basic rules which may help:

1. A major chord doesn't usually have 'major' written after it, i.e. C major is just C.

2. A '7' on it's own, after a chord letter, means a minor 7th, e.g. C7 means the chord of C major with a minor 7th (B♭).

3. A minor chord will be distinguished from a major chord in some way; in this book C minor will be denoted as Cm.

4. Chord symbols could be thought of as having two aspects, the first being the chord's quality and the second being any additional or altered notes e.g. $Cm^{7(b9)}$ could be thought of as C minor (the chord quality), with a 7th and a flattened 9th (additional notes).

5. The chord qualities are usually lower case and the additional or altered notes are usually superscript (written above slightly and smaller).

6. Sometimes minor and major elements are denoted in the same chord e.g. $D♭m^{(b5,\ maj7)}$ means D♭ minor, with a flattened 5th and a major 7th.

7. There are different ways to represent chord symbols (some are shown in parenthesis below).

Chords Based on Degrees of the Major Scale

We said earlier that a chord can also often include a 7th, this involves adding a note a 3rd (two degrees) above the simple triad.

Now, let's construct 7th chords based on each degree of the C major scale, only using the notes available from that scale.

Fig 5.2 **Chord I – C major 7 (C^{maj7}, $C^{\triangle 7}$)**

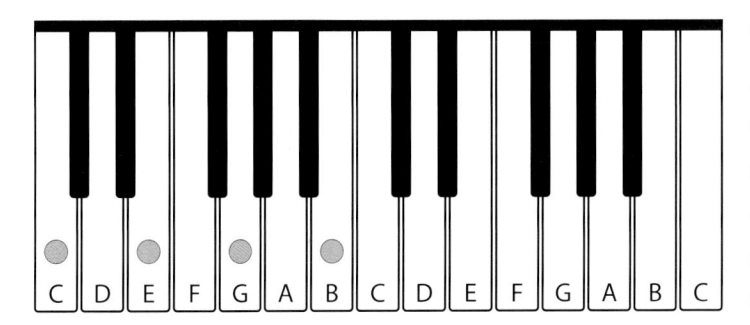

The chord based on the 1st degree (C) will be called **chord I**, the lower three notes are a straightforward C major triad. The 7th degree of a major scale is a semitone below the root, e.g. in C major, the 7th degree is a B. A major chord that includes this type of 7th note is called a **major 7th chord**; there is also an interval of a major 3rd between the 5th and 7th.

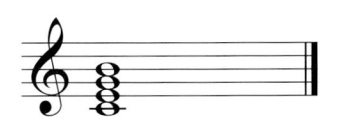

81

Exploring Jazz Violin

Fig 5.3 Chord II – D minor 7 (Dm⁷, D-⁷)

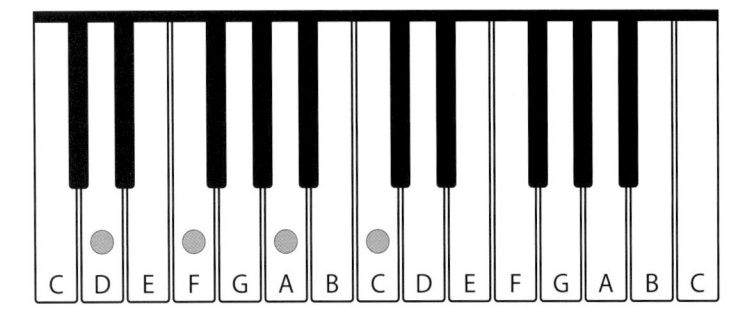

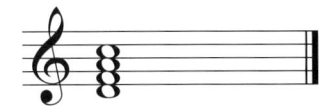

Chord II is based on the 2nd degree of the scale (D), so this is some sort of D chord; to find out whether it's major or minor, let's check out the other notes in the chord.

The 3rd is an F♮, which is an interval of a minor 3rd above the root, and the 5th is an A, a major 3rd above the F. From this we can work out that it's a minor chord and a rule to remember would be: *a minor 3rd with a major 3rd above it forms a minor triad or chord.*

The 7th is flattened (one tone below the root, which is also a minor 3rd above the 5th). We call this a **minor 7th chord**.

Fig 5.4 Chord III – E minor 7 (Em⁷, E-⁷)

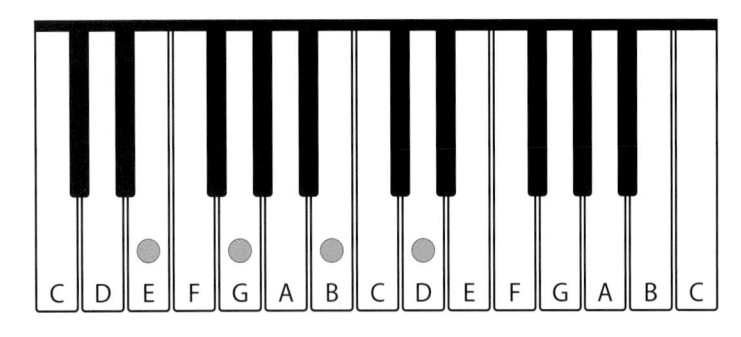

Chord III is based on the 3rd degree, an E in this case. The intervals of this chord are exactly the same as for chord II and so contains a root (E), minor 3rd (G), 5th (B) and flattened 7th (D) so it's another **minor 7th chord**.

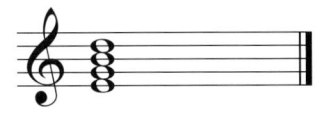

Fig 5.5 Chord IV – F major 7 (F ᵐᵃʲ⁷, F△⁷)

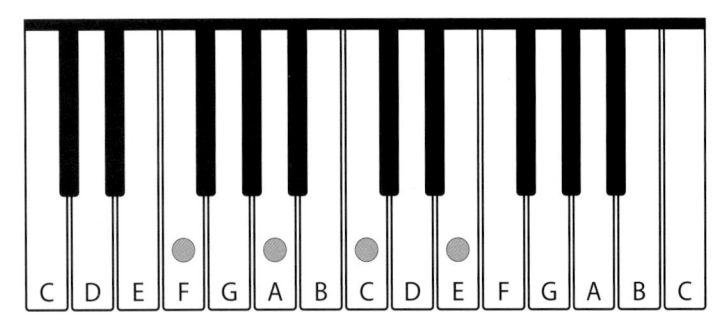

Let's look at the next one, based of the 4th degree – **chord IV**. This has a root (F), a major 3rd (A) and a 5th (C). The 7th is a semitone below the root (or a major 3rd above the 5th) making this another **major 7th chord**.

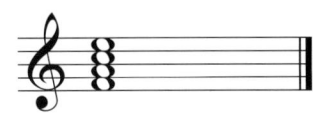

Fig 5.6 Chord V – G7, (G⁷)

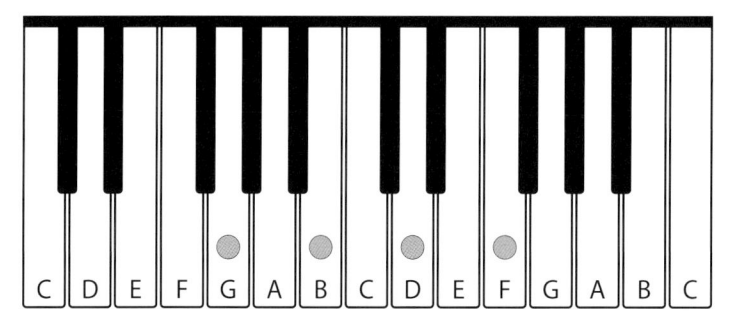

Next is **chord V** which has the root (G), a major 3rd (B), making this a major chord. The 5th is D, and the flattened 7th an F (a minor 3rd above the 5th).

This is the chord of G⁷ – a **7th chord** – not to be confused with either G minor 7th or G major 7th.

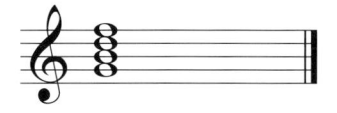

Fig 5.7 Chord VI – A minor 7 (Am⁷, A-⁷)

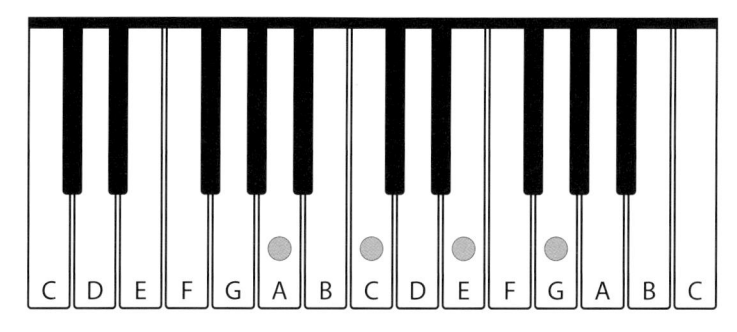

Chord VI is another **minor 7th chord**. The root is an A, the 3rd (C) is a minor 3rd above; the 5th is an E and the flattened 7th a G (a minor 3rd above the 5th). That makes this chord of A minor 7th.

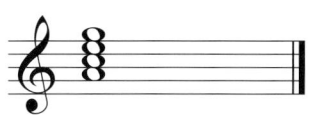

Fig 5.8 Chord VII – B minor 7 flat 5 (Bm⁷⁽♭⁵⁾, B half diminished, Bø)

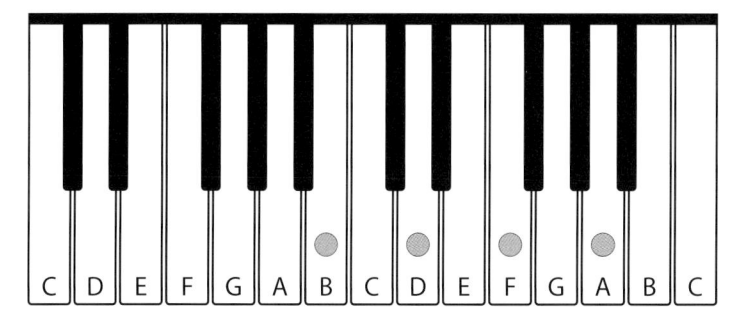

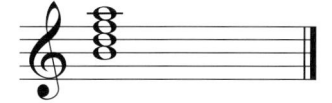

The last one, **chord VII**, is a different type of chord, which we haven't yet seen.
The root is a B. The 3rd (D) is a minor 3rd above the root, making this some sort of minor chord. If it were a chord of B minor, you would expect the 5th to be an F♯. But remember we are only using notes available from the C major scale, so we have to use an F♮, which is a flattened or lowered 5th (♭5). The 7th (A) is one tone below the root, making a minor 7th. All together we have B minor 7th flattened 5th, sometimes called B **half diminished**. I'll explain more about diminished chords later. It's worth noting that in a chord symbol the 7th will always be written before any other added or altered notes (as with the ♭5 of this chord).

Exploring Jazz Violin

So we've now been through the whole of the C major scale, and shown which chords can be made up from it. To summarise, they are:

I C^{maj7}
II Dm^7
III Em^7
IV F^{maj7}
V G^7
VI Am^7
VII $Bm^{7(\flat 5)}$

Fig 5.9 Chords based on each degree of the C major scale

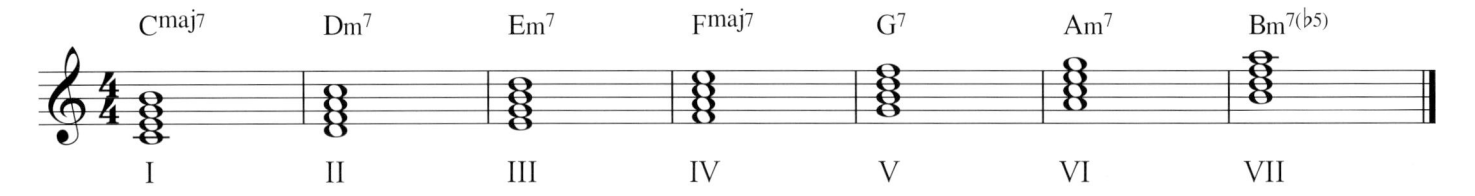

We could have used any major key but C is the easiest one to follow because it has no sharps or flats and is the clearest to show a piano diagram. The use of Roman numerals to describe chords is helpful because it refers to the relationship between the chord and its key. In other words, if you have a chord sequence of C, F, G, you can refer to the chords as I, IV and V. If you decide to change the key of the tune during a rehearsal, you can still refer to them as I, IV and V, no matter what key you're in.

The chords that we have been discussing are the **diatonic** chords – those based on the notes of the scale. If you take a melody that stays within this key, these chords are all you need to provide an effective accompaniment.

Looking at it another way, if you have a chord sequence which is diatonic, then when improvising, all of the notes of the scale of the key you are in will fit over any chord, as we discovered in Chapter 2.

Having explained how chords are constructed, we should point out that they are not just some mathematical abstraction or different random ways of putting notes together. Each chord type in isolation, in some complex and almost magical way, has a different affect on our emotions. Chords can express joy, sadness, triumph, calm, tension and mystery etc. Treat them with respect!

Checkpoint

So here's what we've learned so far:

1. A chord is usually made up of a root, 3rd and 5th, often with a 7th.

2. The 3rd note determines whether the chord has a major or minor quality.

3. The 5th is always the same (7 semitones above the root) unless the chord name specifies otherwise.

4. The 7th is referred to as simply a '7th' in a major chord (or a minor 7th in a minor chord) if it is a tone below the root and a major 7th if it is a semitone below the root.

5. There are many other chord types; these are created by altering some of the above notes, or by adding extra notes.

6. Chords that are created by only using the notes of a single scale are called diatonic chords. These are easy to deal with when improvising, as a single scale will work over every chord.

7. Non-diatonic chords contain notes that are not in the scale suggested by the tune's key, and are therefore harder to deal with.

Dealing with Chords

Now that we have some idea of where chords come from and how they are constructed, let's start to look at how to deal with them. Chapters 2, 3 and 4 showed ways of avoiding the problem, using different scales that will work on all the chords within a tune. Unfortunately these techniques are quite limiting. Many tunes contain some non-diatonic chords, and as we move away from the safety of Hot Club and blues styles into mainstream, Latin, bebop and beyond, 'difficult' chords become increasingly common, and the bluffer's method starts to look very inadequate.

In this section we're going to get much more familiar with individual chord types, talk a little about their function within a sequence, and look at shapes, patterns and licks which can be applied to them.

Major / Major 7th (G^maj7, GMa7, G△)

A major chord in jazz functions as a 'home' chord with a 'settled' feel to it. Both the major and major 7th chords are pretty well interchangeable. The major scale has a 7th note a semitone below the tonic (e.g. F♯ in the scale of G major). As a result, the scale you would play over the chords of G or G major 7th are the same. If you want to emphasize the 7th note, you could play a phrase such as this, where you use the F♯ as a **leading note**, up to the G.

Fig 5.10 **G^maj7 lick 1**

Exploring Jazz Violin

Or you could launch straight into the major 7th note:

Fig 5.11 G^maj7 lick 2

Or alternate between the 8th and 7th degrees:

Fig 5.12 G^maj7 lick 3

The arpeggio of a major chord is one that you'll be familiar with. Here's the fingering starting on an open string, and then starting on a first finger:

Fig 5.13 Fingering for major arpeggios

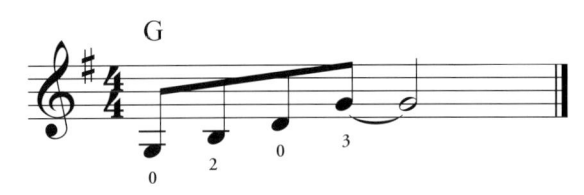

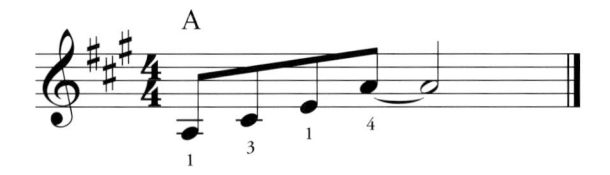

It's useful when dealing with chords, especially when they get more difficult, to get as familiar with these finger patterns as guitarists are with chord shapes. Then, when you see a new chord coming up, you just play the root note and your fingers should be able to deal with the rest.

For a major 7th chord the shape is different from the major-chord arpeggio. Here it is from an open-string root and from a first-finger root:

Fig 5.14 Fingering for major 7th arpeggios

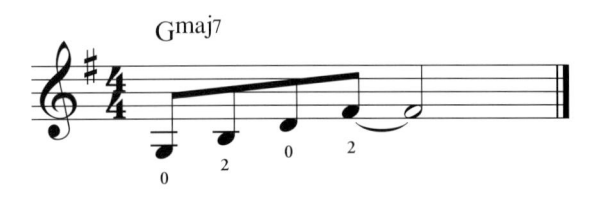

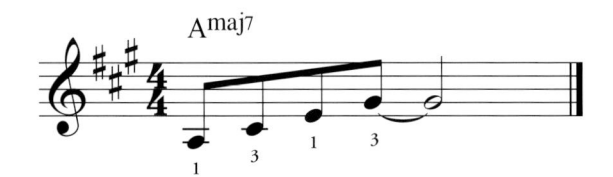

The fingering pattern, starting on an open string, is 0, 2, 0, 2 with a spacing of two tones on each string. Starting on a first finger we get 1, 3, 1, 3 again with the same spacing. With a bit of position changing, these two shapes will cover you for any major 7th chord.

86

For each of the chord types discussed in this section, there's an audio track with a repeated single chord. This lasts for eight bars.

G^{maj7} backing track — Backing **38**

Minor 7th (Amin^7, Am^7, Ami^7, A-^{7})

Most minor chords are played as minor 7^{ths} in jazz. They have a feel of movement, of being ready to travel somewhere else. The arpeggio of a minor 7th chord is an easy pattern to play on the fiddle. It uses the same fingering as the major 7th arpeggio, but with a one and a half tone stretch instead of two tones.

Fig 5.15 Fingering for minor 7th arpeggios

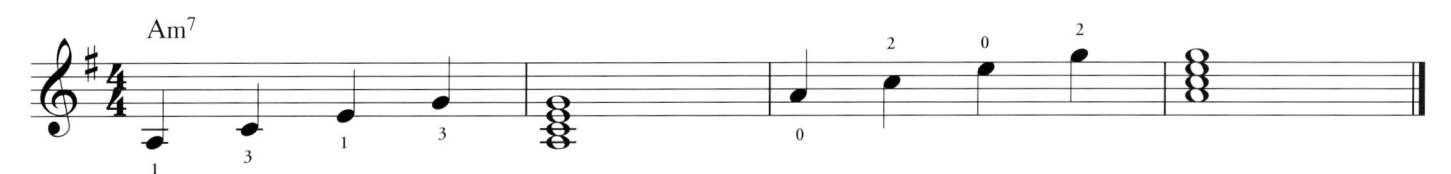

A scale to use over this chord would be:

Fig 5.16 Am^7 scale (A dorian)

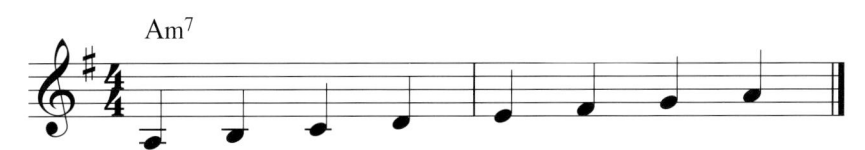

You may have come across a number of different minor scales. This one has a raised 6th (an F♯ in this case); it is also known as the **dorian mode**. We'll look more at modes in Chapter 10.

Remember the bebop scale we looked at earlier, with an added 'passing' note to make it feel smoother? There's a bebop scale for minor 7^{ths} chords, which has an extra note between the 3rd and 4th degrees:

Fig 5.17 Am^7 bebop scale

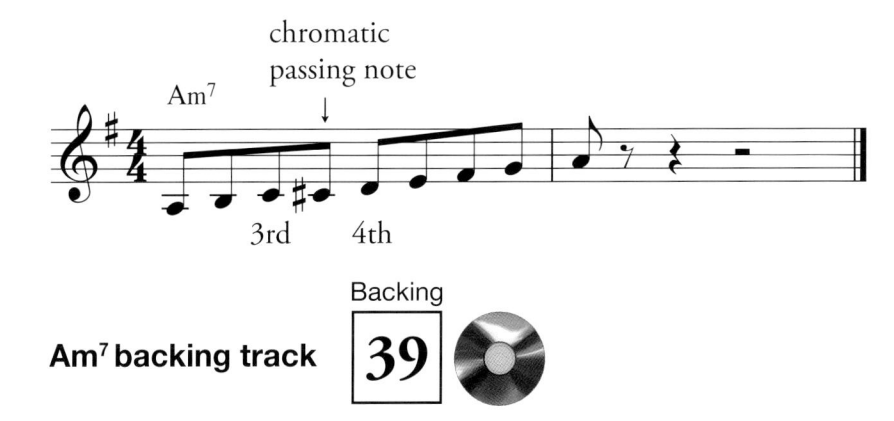

Am^7 backing track — Backing **39**

Exploring Jazz Violin

7th Chord (D⁷, D flattened 7th)

This chord is sometimes called the dominant 7th (when, as it often is, it's based on chord V), and may also be referred to as a flattened 7th (since the 7th note is lowered or 'flattened' by a semitone from its usual position in a major scale). But don't be confused by the term 'flattened 7th'. If you see the symbol D♭⁷, it is referring to the chord of D♭ with a lowered 7th, not D with a lowered 7th.

The 7th chord has a powerful sense of urgency and instability about it, and wants to resolve back to the tonic chord. This property of the (dominant) 7th chord makes it one of the most important 'drivers' of jazz chord-sequences.

The arpeggio of the 7th chord is:

Fig 5.18 Fingering for 7th arpeggio

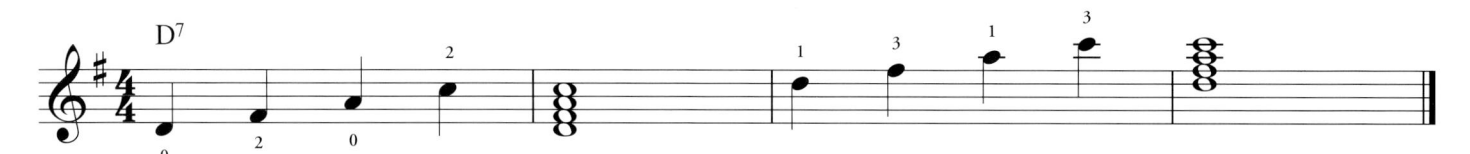

The fingering is very similar to the major 7th chord fingering (0202, 1313 or 2424), except that on the 7ths you move your finger down a semitone from the position it had on the lower string. So, unlike the major and minor 7th patterns, this one is not quite the same on both strings. Here's a scale to use over a D⁷ chord (again it's actually one of the modes – **mixolydian** this time):

Fig 5.19 D⁷ scale (D mixolydian)

The bebop scale to use over a 7th chord has an extra note between the 7th and 8th degrees:

Fig 5.20 D⁷ bebop scale

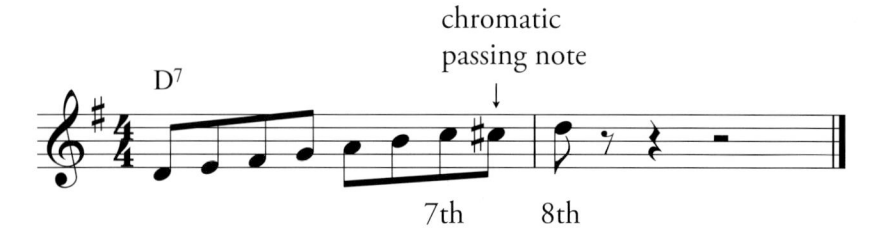

The flattened 7th note always wants to resolve downwards, so when a chord of D⁷ is followed by a chord of G, the natural tendency is for the note C (the flattened 7th) to resolve down a semitone to the B (the 3rd) of the chord of G. This is a move from 'instability' to 'stability':

5: Chords Part I

Fig 5.21 Resolution from D⁷ to G (flattened 7ᵗʰ to 3ʳᵈ)

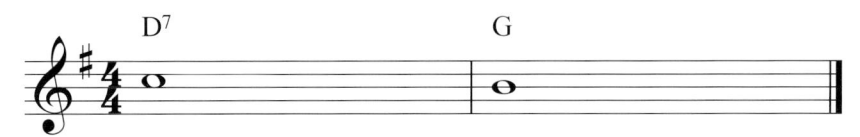

Here's a neat **Grappelli**-type lick to use over a 7ᵗʰ chord. It starts on the 7ᵗʰ note (C), then runs down the arpeggio, with a little scale up from each note of the arpeggio:

Fig 5.22 Descending D⁷ lick 1

You could also play a descending arpeggio by preceding each note with a semitone below:

Fig 5.23 Descending D⁷ lick 2

Notice that the arpeggio notes have been placed on the 'strong' beats of the bar, with the leading notes in weaker positions. But if you're feeling a little bolder, it will work the other way round:

Fig 5.24 Descending D⁷ lick 3

You might want to emphasize just the 7ᵗʰ note:

Fig 5.25 Descending D⁷ lick 4

D⁷ backing track — Backing 40

Exploring Jazz Violin

II-V-I sequences

We've looked at three chord types so far; the major (or maj 7th) (chord **I**), minor 7th (chord **II**) and dominant 7th (chord **V**). These three chords have a very important function in jazz as they are frequently grouped together as a **II-V-I** (said 2-5-1) progression, for example in G major a II-V-I would be Am^7-D^7-G. Look at the chord sequence of almost any jazz tune and you'll find a II-V-I progression in there somewhere. If you compare the scales of the three chords, you'll see that they all coincide:

Fig 5.26 Scales based on the chords of I, II and V (in G major)

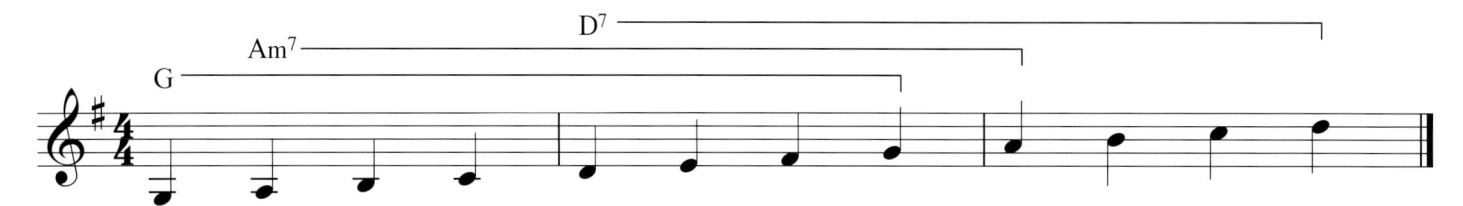

This is good news! As II-V-Is are the very backbone of numerous jazz tunes, it means that they are easy to spot and therefore playing by ear becomes a bit easier. You can create a phrase, or run, which moves smoothly through all three chords.

You can either start on the roots, hitting each new root note as it arrives, or else start on the 3rd each time (in which case the last note of each arpeggio – the 7th of each chord – resolves to the 3rd of the next chord as shown in fig. 5.28):

Fig 5.27 II-V-I descending scales (emphasis on root notes)

Fig 5.28 II-V-I descending scales (emphasis on 3rds)

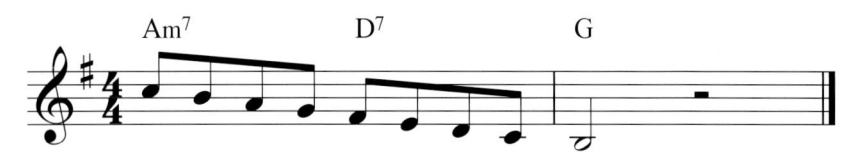

But there are countless other ways of approaching a II-V-I progression. An arpeggiated phrase for the three chords could be:

Fig 5.29 II-V-I arpeggios 1

These phrases aren't particularly exciting, but they do serve to outline the chords. We'll look at some more interesting II-V-I licks later. Now what happens when we combine the bebop scales we used earlier for chords II (minor 7th) and V (7th)? Again they coincide neatly; the added chromatic note is the same in each:

Fig 5.30 **Bebop scales of chord II and V**

It's a good idea to practise and memorize a string of licks that you can use over a II-V-I; let's look at a few more ways to approach the progression. The most simple way to deal with a II-V-I is by playing arpeggios, up from the roots. But to create a more fluid and interesting phrase we could make the middle arpeggio descend:

Fig 5.31 **II-V-I arpeggios 2**

There's no reason why the first arpeggio has to start on the root; it could just as easily start on the 3rd, 5th or 7th. If you begin on the 3rd, it's very convenient to keep the same shape going, up to the 9th:

Fig 5.32 **II-V-I arpeggios 3**

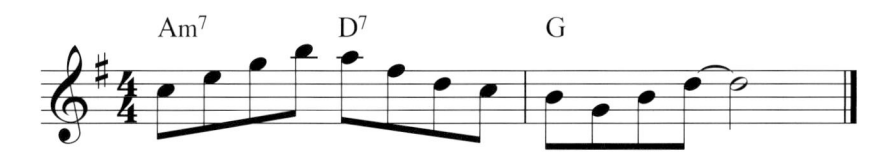

The 9th note is the high B. It's 'outside' the chord (much more about the scary concept of 'outsider notes' later!) Suffice it to say that notes 'outside' the chord are usually more interesting and sound more modern than those 'inside'.

Notice how in the above example we've modified the arpeggios of D7 and G in order to give a smooth movement from one to the next. Having three arpeggios in a row is rhythmically uninteresting, so it's common to only arpeggiate the minor 7th (particularly as on the violin it's such a neat and easy pattern).

Here's a simple lick, again starting on the 3rd of the minor 7th arpeggio, and finishing on the 9th:

Fig 5.33 **II-V-I lick 1**

Exploring Jazz Violin

To go further 'outside', you might start on the 5th of the minor 7th chord, followed by the 7th, 9th and 11th, continuing the movement up through the D7 chord:

Fig 5.34 II-V-I lick 2

Stuff Smith loved syncopated licks like this:

Fig 5.35 II-V-I lick 3

You can add some extra movement that is not implied by the chords, such as the example below, where there's a chromatic downward movement from the note A, through A♭ and G to F♯. We'll come back to this idea in the next chapter.

Fig 5.36 II-V-I lick 4

Or, as we said before, because the three chords of the II-V-I are diatonic, you can use a single scale all the way through, effectively ignoring the chord changes. **Grappelli** often used a G pentatonic blues scale over a II-V-I progression:

Fig 5.37 II-V-I lick 5

You can buy whole books full of II-V-I licks – they're something you can never have too much of. Practise these licks over the following backing track, which goes through the sequence four times.

II-V-I in G major backing track — Backing 41

The Minor II-V-I

The II-V-I is not restricted to major keys. In a minor key, chord II becomes a half diminished ($m^{7(b5)}$) chord (we'll meet up with this chord again shortly), chord V remains the same and chord I can be either a straight minor or a minor 7th. So in the relative minor key of G major, namely E minor, a II-V-I progression would be:

Fig 5.38 Minor II-V-I

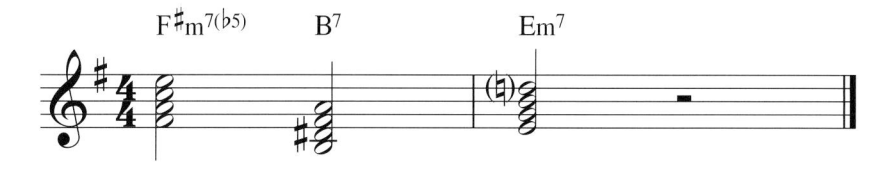

Running down the scale from the 3rd of F♯m would give you:

Fig 5.39 Minor II-V-I descending scale

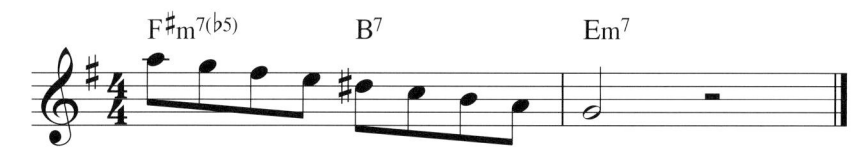

This uses notes from the E harmonic minor scale. You can use this to build minor II-V-I licks, such as:

Fig 5.40 Minor II-V-I lick

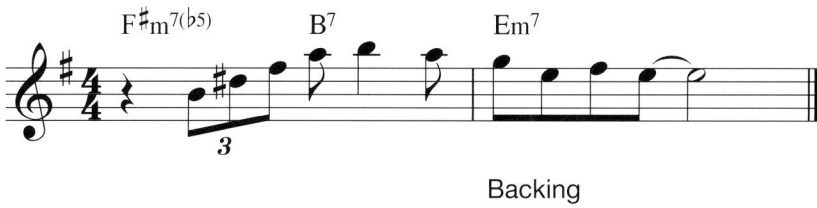

II-V-I in E minor backing track — Backing 42

Temporary Dominants

In a diatonic sequence there are three minor 7th chords (IIm^7, $IIIm^7$ and VIm^7) but only one 7th chord – V^7, which will usually be followed by chord I. However, you may come across other, non-diatonic (dominant) 7th chords from time to time. These can function as '**temporary dominants**' – where they will momentarily act as chord V, leading to a new chord I (also temporary).

If we look at the (chord) changes for 'Mind the Gap', I can demonstrate the point more clearly. The boxes illustrate where there are temporary dominants with a resolution to a new chord I.

Exploring Jazz Violin

Mind the Gap (Temporary Dominants)

Demo 19 | Backing 20

Chris Haigh

At bar 10 we find that the chord of G^6 (chord I), is followed by G^7 (I^7). It is no longer 'at rest'. As soon as you see or hear this chord you can predict that it is usually acting as a new V^7 chord and will want to resolve to a chord a 5th below – in this case C major (the temporary chord I).

At bar 14 you will see an A^7. Normally chord II is a minor 7th chord, but as it's now a 7th chord it acts as chord V^7 – a temporary dominant – leading (via Am^7) to a new chord I, in this case, D^7.

At 22 you get another G^7, this time acting as the middle chord of a temporary II-V-I progression in C major (Dm^7-G^7-C).

At bar 27 we have another G^7, but just to teach us not to be complacent it leads, not to a chord of C, but is raised a 6th to E^7, yet another temporary dominant that resolves down a 5th to Am^7.

At bar 30 the $A\flat^7$ chords functions as a substitute for D^7 (the original chord V), which finally leads us back to G (chord I).

Checkpoint

Understanding and recognizing 7th chords is essential to 'joined up' soloing. Temporary 7^{ths} provide surprise within a sequence, taking the ear away from the predictability of diatonic chords. If you listen carefully to the above progression you should be able to 'feel the ground shifting' as each temporary dominant occurs.

These are the kind of changes that you shouldn't try to bluff your way around or duck out of by avoiding the non-diatonic chords. Instead, emphasize them, particularly the 3^{rds} and 7^{ths} of each chord. As a soloist you should aim to sound startling, not startled.

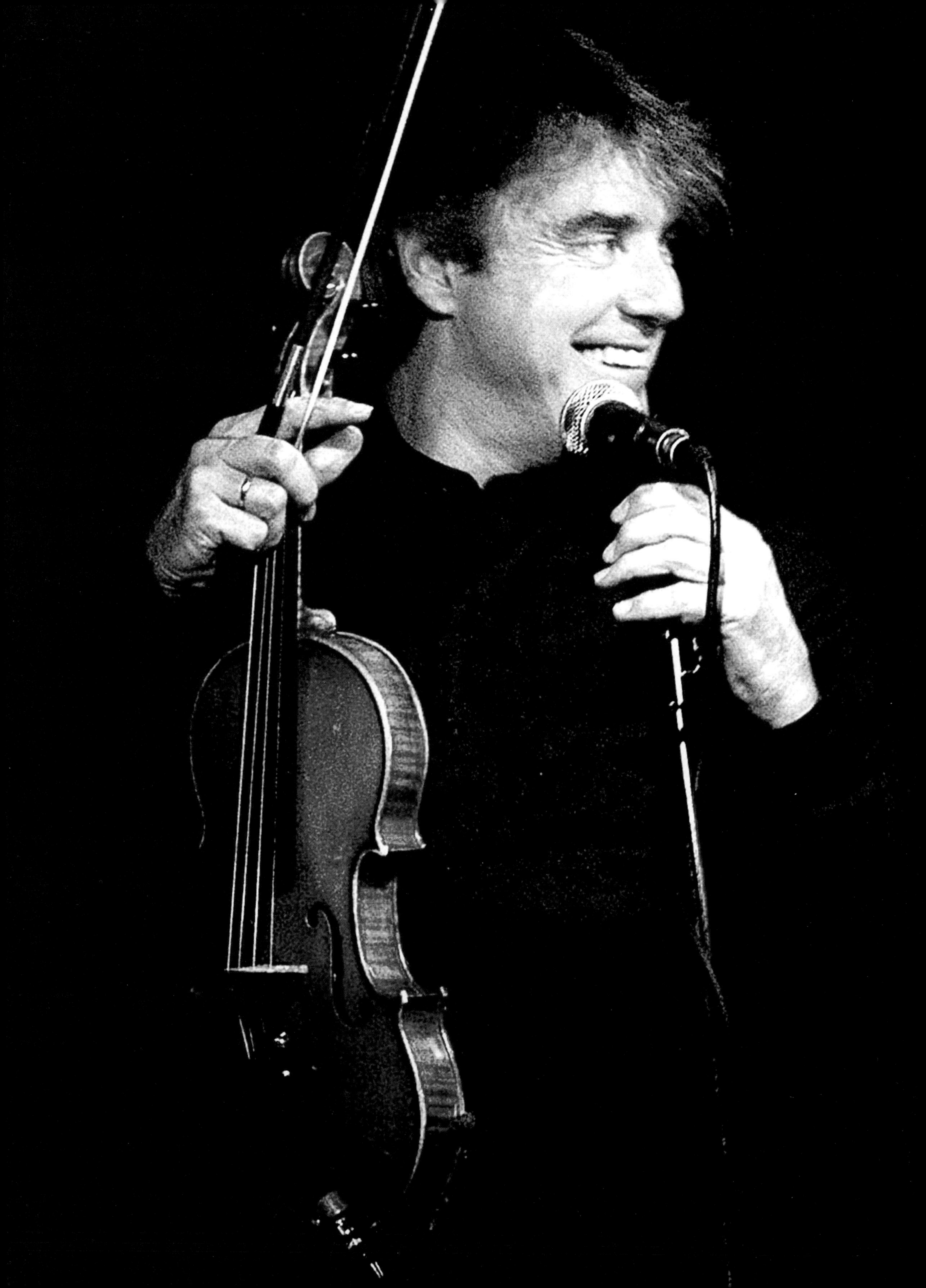

6: Chords Part II

In this chapter we will extend our knowledge of different chord types and how to deal with them, but first we need to look at one of the most important foundations of jazz theory.

Cycle of Fifths

Chemistry has the 'Periodic Table', biology has the 'Tree of Life' and the 'Double Helix'; jazz has the 'Cycle of Fifths' – a simple diagram that brings sense and order to what would otherwise be a hopelessly confusing and seemingly random jumble of information. It defines the relationship between the keys, the sharps and flats they contain, the association between major and minor, and the driving force of jazz chord sequences.

This explanation starts out as pure theory, but it also has many uses in jazz practice and improvisation.

At its simplest, it's the twelve major keys arranged in a circle, with C major at the top. Moving anticlockwise you pass through the flat keys; F, B♭, E♭, A♭, D♭ and so on – each new key is a 5th below the last. At the bottom of the circle you have G♭, (or F♯); you then move through the sharp keys until you get back to C.

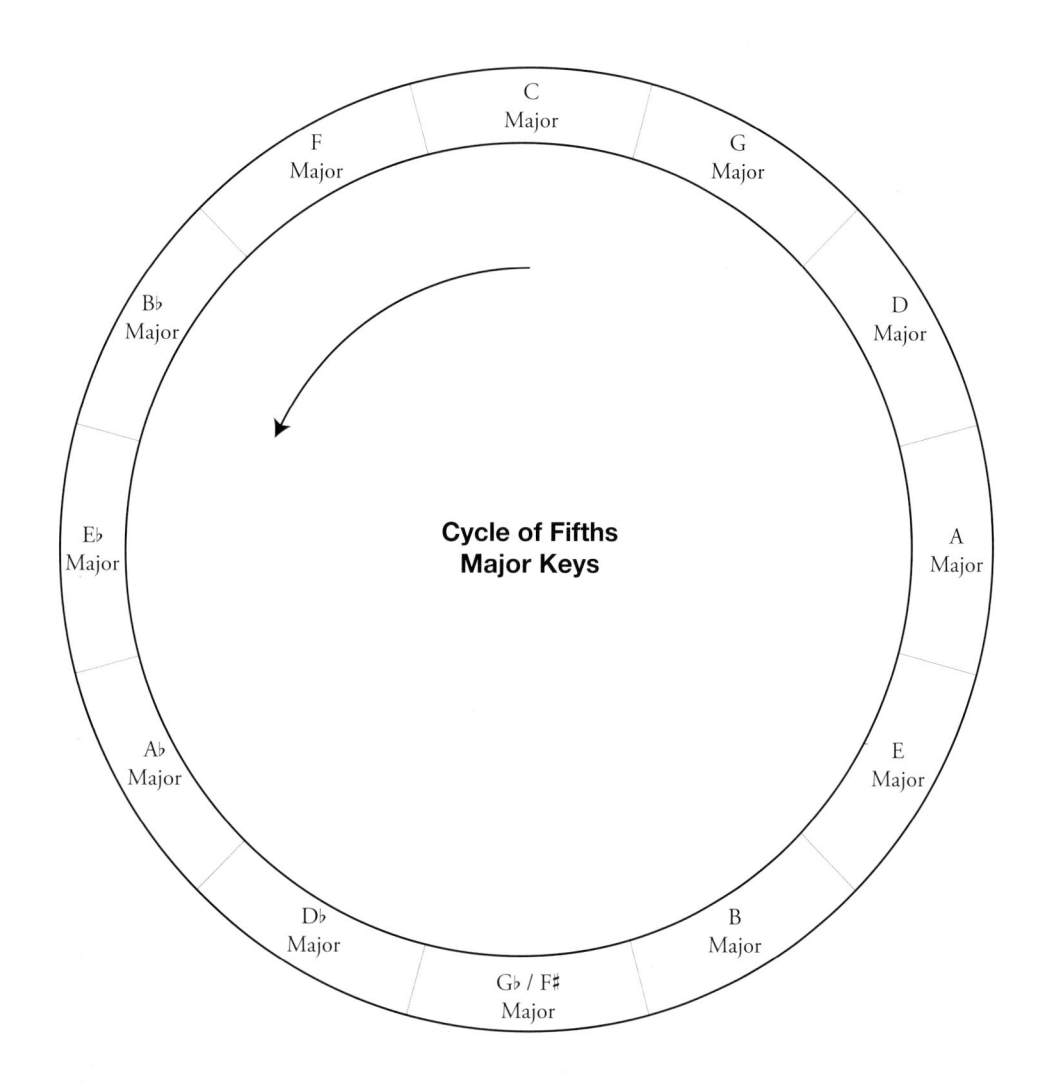

Cycle of Fifths
Major Keys

- C Major
- F Major
- G Major
- B♭ Major
- D Major
- E♭ Major
- A Major
- A♭ Major
- E Major
- D♭ Major
- B Major
- G♭ / F♯ Major

Exploring Jazz Violin

This starts to make a bit more sense when you add information about the number of sharps and flats in the keys. Starting at C again, each time you move round an extra flat is added to the key signature.

C has no sharps or flats; F has one flat, B♭ has two, and so on down to G♭ which has six flats, or six sharps if you think of it as F♯. You then lose one sharp each time as you go through B, E, A, D, G back to C.

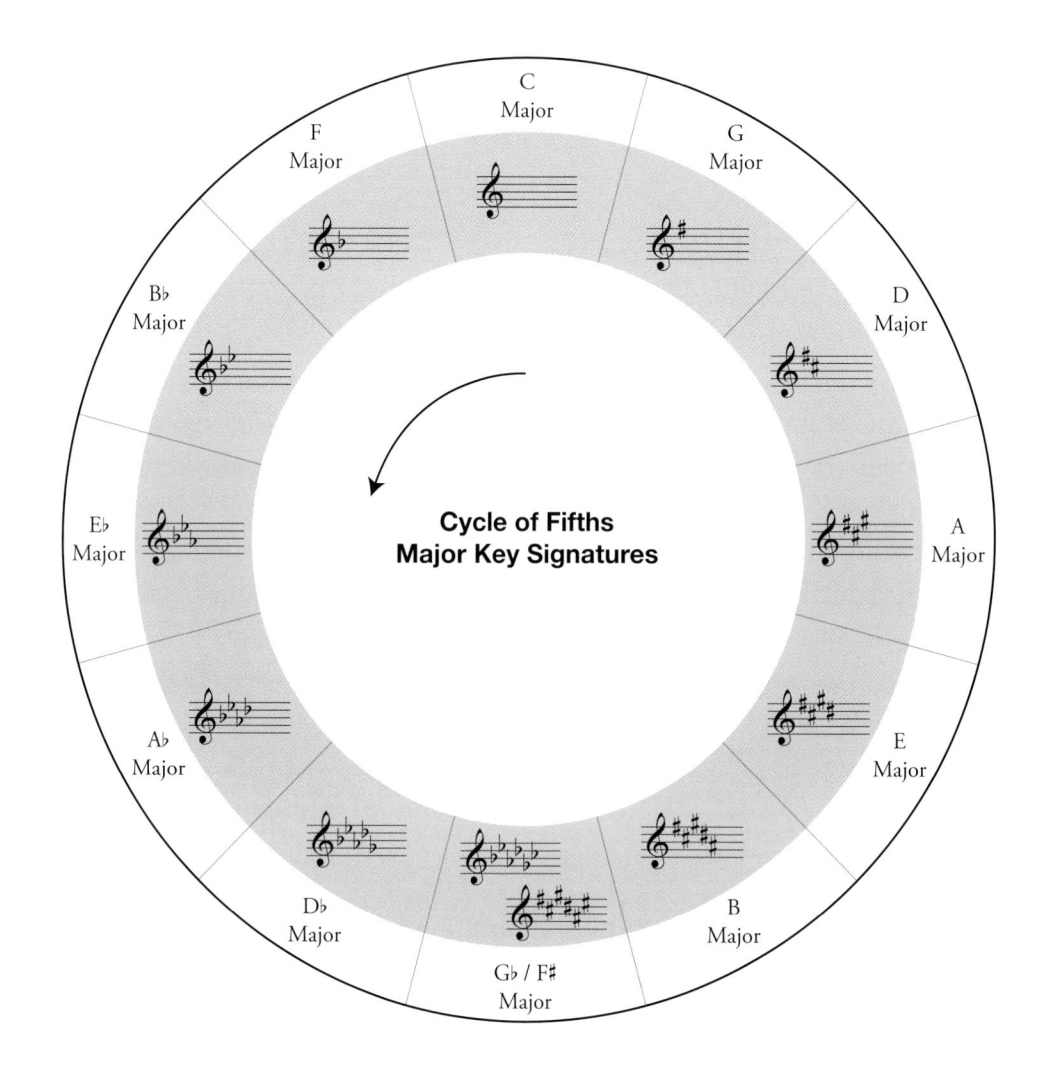

Finally let's add some information about the minor keys. We can form an inner circle with A minor at the top – the relative minor of C major. It's a close relative of C because it has no sharps or flats. F has Dm as its relative minor; both keys have one flat. And so on round the circle.

6: Chords Part II

Cycle of Fifths Major / Minor Key Signatures

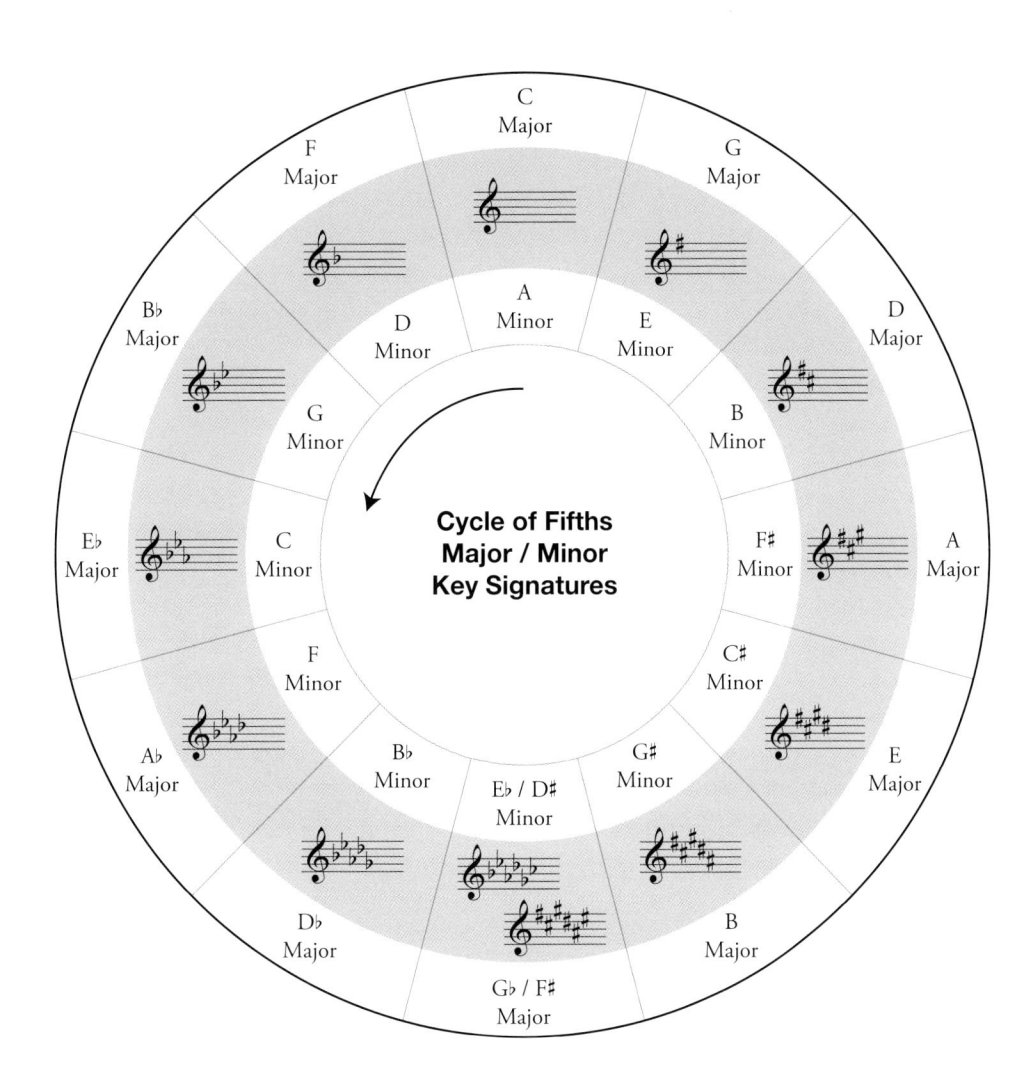

Now let's look at it briefly from a fiddler's point-of-view. The first thing you might consider is that the easy keys are all bunched together at the top and right of the circle. Everything between C and E is pretty easy. More than four sharps starts to get hairy, unless you've already been working with a lot of wind players, in which case you may be more used to the flat keys.

The arrangement of the violin strings is very convenient in navigating the cycle of fifths, since they are themselves a 5th apart. This means that it's easy to visualize what comes next in the cycle, simply by imagining the fingering of a note and then moving that finger position over to the string below.

The relationship of relative major and minor keys is also valuable. Many keys which initially sound scary can be thought of in a different way. C♯ or F♯ minor may be intimidating keys until you think of them as E or A major; now they seem like old friends.

So let's see how you can make use of the cycle of fifths as it appears in chord sequences. The first thing to point out is that because of the relationship of chord V to chord I, chord progressions tend to move anticlockwise around the cycle, as in the II-V-I sequence. The notes referred to in the cycle of fifths are the roots of chords, and don't imply that each is a major chord; in the next diagram we see how a II-V-I sequence in the key of E♭ relates to the cycle.

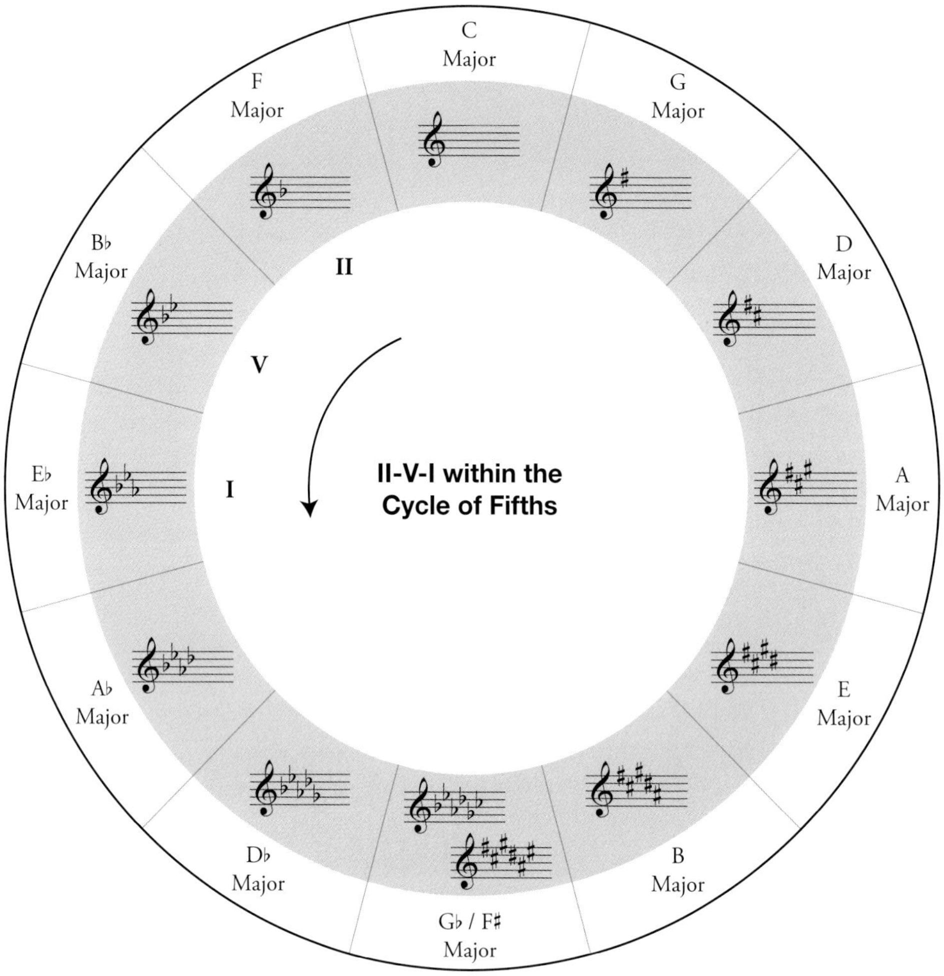
C
Major
G
Major
D
Major
A
Major
E
Major
B
Major
G♭ / F♯
Major
D♭
Major
A♭
Major
E♭
Major
B♭
Major
F
Major
II
V
I
II-V-I within the
Cycle of Fifths

Sometimes there can be a much longer sequence of chords moving down in fifths around the cycle. One of the clearest examples of this is the jazz standard 'Sweet Georgia Brown'. Here's a tune named 'Cycle Ride' that uses a similar idea.

Demo 43 Backing 44

Cycle Ride (head)

Chris Haigh

Medium swing ♩ = 186

E7
5
A7

© 2010 Schott Music Ltd, London

It starts at E major on the cycle and moves round until it gets to G, incorporating the chords E[7], A[7], D[7] and G[maj7]. This situation is sometimes called the 'V of V'; that is to say, a chord which is a dominant to another chord which is itself a dominant chord. This tune is also useful as an example of a sequence which, although very simple and straightforward, is not diatonic. Try bluffing your way through it with a G blues or pentatonic scale and right from the start you'll come unstuck because the G♮ will sound painful against the E[7].

The first option for dealing with this tune is to play phrases based on the first chord, and then transpose them down a 5th for the next chord.

Fig 6.1 Option 1 – transposition of bars 1–4 to 5–8

Exploring Jazz Violin

This kind of transposition is easy, as you just move the whole pattern over one string. It gives some logic and coherence to your playing to move a phrase like this with the chords, but as this is a 4-bar phrase you may be better off repeating the first part of the phrase, perhaps two bars, and then adding a variation. With four chord changes in all, it would certainly be over-egging the pudding to transpose the entire phrase four times. At the very least you'd want to modify the phrase based on G^{maj7} to give it more finality.

The second option, as used in the melody itself, is to repeat a phrase without transposition, but modifying one or two notes as necessary. Thus the phrase can be treated as shown below:

Fig 6.2 Option 2 – bars 1–4

Fig 6.3 Option 2 – bars 1–4 modified for bars 5–8 (without transposition)

G♯ is the 3rd of the E^7 chord. Bring it down by a semitone and it becomes the 7th of A^7. Again we've achieved continuity with a minimum of effort. The same idea won't work a third time, unless you bring the whole phrase down by a tone:

Fig 6.4 Option 2 – bars 1–4 down a tone to create bars 9–11

Here's a sample solo:

Cycle Ride (solo version)

Demo 45 | Backing 44

Chris Haigh

Medium swing ♩ = 186

Bars 1–4
We start with a strong two-note motif based on the 3rd and flattened 3rd of E7.

Bars 5–8
Here we use the same motif but with both notes transposed down by a semitone. The rest of the phrase is different.

© 2010 Schott Music Ltd, London

Exploring Jazz Violin

Bars 9–12
By bar 9 we have a new idea – an ascending arpeggio with leading notes one semitone below each chord note. The line ends with a descending run that clearly telegraphs the target note of G, as it hits the home chord.

Bars 17–20
Bars 17 and 18 open with the same phrase as bars 9 and 10, but transposed to E and starting on the 3rd instead of the root of the chord. It pays to remember what you've just played!

Bars 21–24
The familiar phrase is back for a third time, using the easy drop of a 5th, and bars 23 and 24 echo bars 18 and 19, but with the G♯ lowered by a semitone.

Bars 25–28
Having four consecutive bars of one chord is a bit of a luxury, you can use it for fancy runs or arpeggios which go through several octaves; the last D^7 phrase gives you a fairly modest example.

The most often read, and least welcome phrase in any jazz tutor book must be "Now try this in every key". You've got away pretty lightly up till now, but having learnt about the cycle of fifths and the II-V-I progression, now is the time to do it for real. You might reasonably ask. Why? Why can't I just play everything in G? The problem is that you can't perform jazz fiddle on your own. You need to play with other musicians, who will expect you to play tunes in the standard keys which everyone is used to, be it G, F or A♭. And unfortunately, whilst string players love keys with a few sharps, wind players, who have dominated jazz right from the start, tend to dislike them and prefer to wallow in flats.

So your goal is to be able to play with equal autonomy in any key, and to free yourself from the dependency on patterns that rely on open strings. Whenever you practise a new lick, take it all the way round the cycle of fifths. Even if you've chickened out when I've harangued you before about this try it now, even if it's only to experience the full horror of the task before you.

On this next track we have a II-V-I progression in every key of the cycle of fifths. We start at G with the corresponding chords of Am^7, D^7, G^{maj7}. Then it moves round the cycle anticlockwise with a II-V-I in C and so on.

Backing 46

Fig 6.5 **II-V-I phrase in every key**

© 2010 Schott Music Ltd, London

So what did you discover, apart from a new-found and undying respect for the profession of the jazz musician? It's a lot easier if you don't think about each individual note you're playing. Think of the first note, the root of the minor 7th arpeggio, think of the rest in terms of patterns or relationships.

There's also the problem of octaves. If you're ending a pattern on the G or D string, you're probably going to have to jump up an octave for the next one, and it makes sense to do that on the descending chromatic run itself rather than the start of the next phrase. When there's an octave shift involved, you may find it helpful to think of it as up a 4th rather than down a 5th and then up an octave. Use this backing track whenever you come to a phrase you want to 'take around the houses'. Now we'll continue looking at the different chord types.

Exploring Jazz Violin

Diminished (G dim, G°)

The diminished chord symbol can be denoted in two ways, for example Gdim or G°. A diminished chord is symmetrical, in that every interval is the same – a minor 3rd:

Fig 6.6 G diminished arpeggio / chord

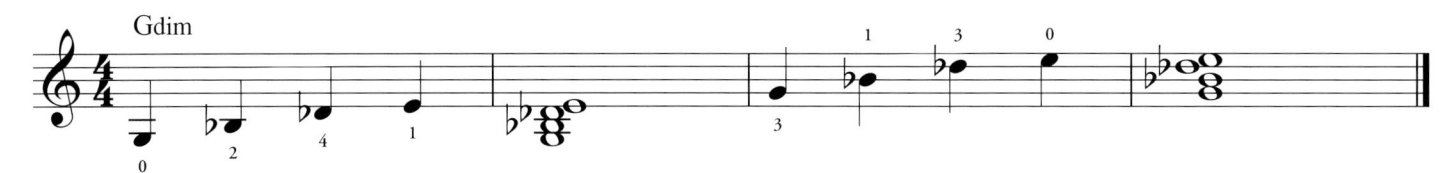

One result of this is that instead of there being twelve diminished chords (G, A♭, A, B♭, B etc), there are in fact only three different ones.

If you look at B♭dim you'll see it has the same notes as Gdim, but with a different root:

Fig 6.7 B♭ diminished arpeggio / chord

So **Gdim** is the same as B♭dim, D♭dim and Edim:

A♭dim is the same as Bdim, Ddim and Fdim:

Adim is the same as Cdim, E♭dim and G♭dim.

Another way of looking at it is that any note in a diminished chord can act as the root. This is good news, as it saves you learning a lot of tricky patterns.

Here's the scale of G diminished:

Fig 6.8 G diminished scale

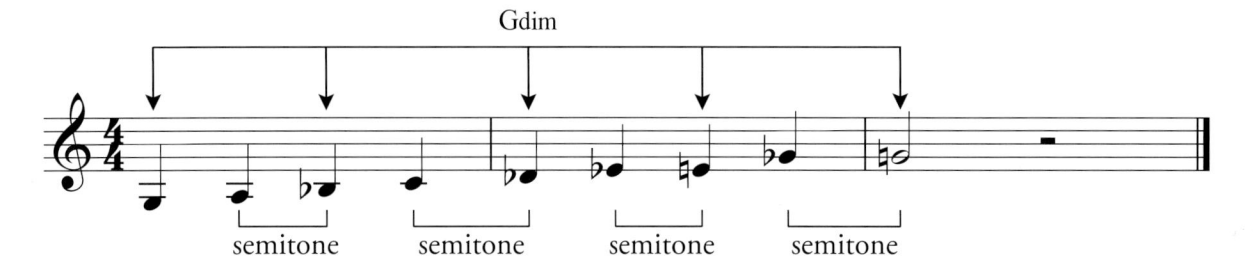

106

You'll see that the scale consists of the G diminished arpeggio (G, B♭, D♭, E) plus 'leading notes', one semitone below each arpeggio note. If you look at your fingers as you play the scale, you'll see a pattern emerge. The finger pattern on the D string is the same as on the G string, but a half position lower. Open strings complicate this pattern, but if you play in a higher position it's easy to play the scale over all four strings. Start in 4th position:

Fig 6.9 G diminished scale – changing position

Simply play the same pattern on each string, moving down by a half position each time. One of the easiest and most convenient ways of dealing with a diminished chord is to make a step pattern with the arpeggio, such as:

Fig 6.10 G diminished arpeggio – step pattern

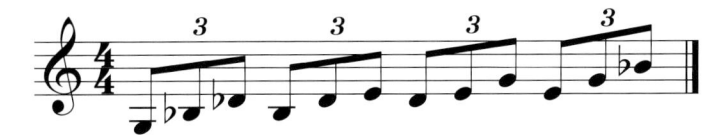

If you want to be more adventurous you can make a pattern using the scale rather than just the arpeggio. This one's a real beauty:

Fig 6.11 G diminished scale pattern

As in the previous chapter, below is a backing track to use with the above examples and really immerse yourself in the diminished sound.

G diminished backing track Backing 47

Finally, a brief look at the function of diminished chords within a sequence. Diminished chords have a strong tendency to resolve up to a chord one semitone above. A G dim chord would therefore resolve to A♭, and B dim to C.

The most common use of a diminished chord is as a passing chord between chords I and IIm⁷. Here, for example, is a 'turnaround' (a sequence that leads back to itself and can be endlessly repeated). The A♭dim chord allows a smooth semitone movement between G (chord I) and Am⁷ (chord IIm⁷):

5Fig 6.12 A♭ dim in a turnaround

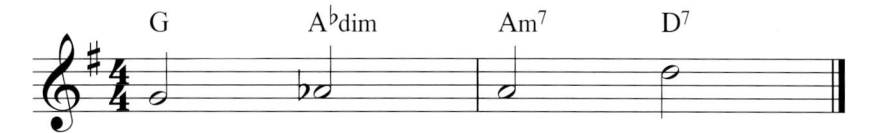

In this context, unless it's very slow, you can virtually ignore the diminished chord when soloing and play notes from the G major scale, as you would over a II-V-I sequence. For example, here's a phrase that skims over the diminished chord:

Fig 6.13 Phrase over diminished chord

Augmented (G aug, G⁷+, G⁷♯⁵)

The augmented chord is rather exotic in sound and, like the diminished chord, is symmetrical, but this time each interval is a major 3rd. The chord symbol is denoted as either (for example) Gaug, G+ or G♯⁵. It's very common to see an augmented chord with a 7th (this is a minor 3rd above the 5th). The scale that fits best over G⁷ augmented is a whole-tone scale.

Fig 6.14 G⁷ augmented / G whole-tone scale

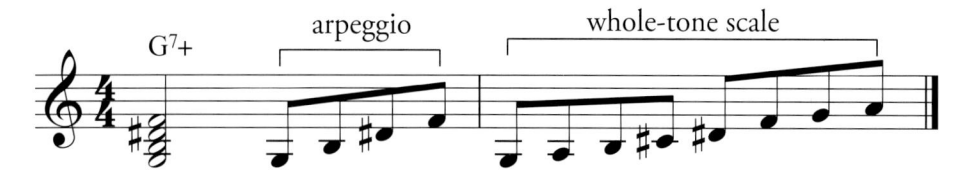

You'll immediately hear that this sounds strange, dreamy and unsettled. It's a device much loved by film composers when a character goes into a daydream, but it's also a powerful motif in jazz soloing, when handled carefully.

The scale we're using for G⁷aug is similar to the one we used for G⁷ but with two notes altered: the 4th degree (C) is raised to C♯ and the 5th degree (D) is raised to D♯.

6: Chords Part II

Again like the diminished scale, there are not twelve scales to learn – in fact, there are just two; the **G whole-tone scale** will also work for G, A, B, C♯, D♯ and F, whilst the **A♭ whole-tone scale** will deal with all the others (A♭, B♭, C, D, E, G♭). Over an augmented chord, any phrase can be repeated up or down any number of whole tones:

Fig 6.15 **Augmented chord – repeated phrase**

Here's a descending whole-tone scale pattern. It makes an interesting run, but you'll see that the fingering is quite tricky.

Fig 6.16 **Descending whole-tone scale pattern**

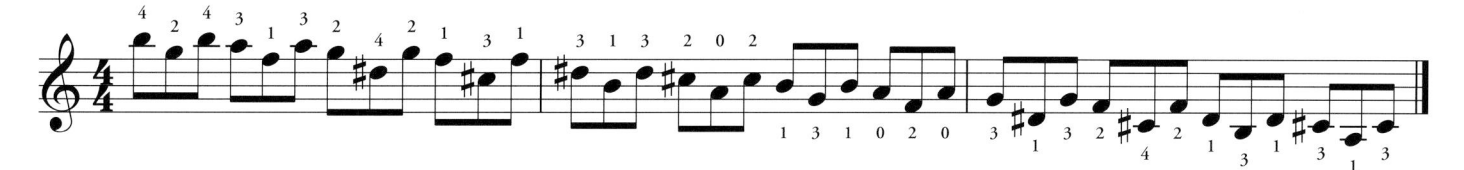

When creating scale patterns, an easy way to change strings is to move your hand position up a semitone for each string as you ascend the scale. In this way you can keep the same fingering for each string.

Fig 6.17 **Ascending whole-tone scale pattern**

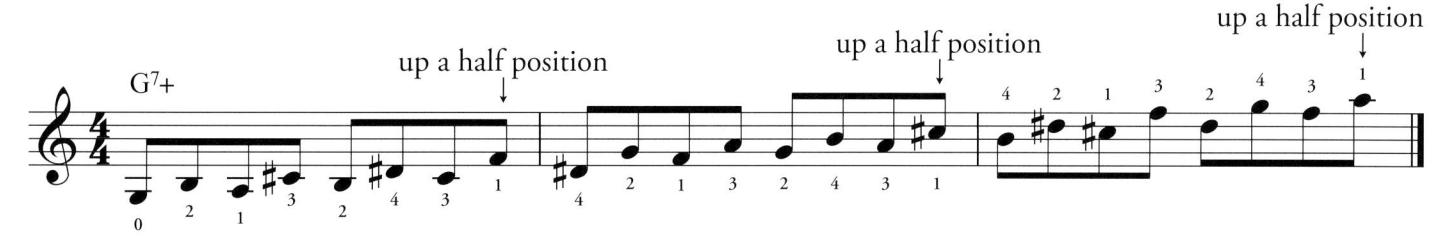

Here's another example, using just two fingers:

Fig 6.18 **Ascending whole-tone scale pattern – two fingers**

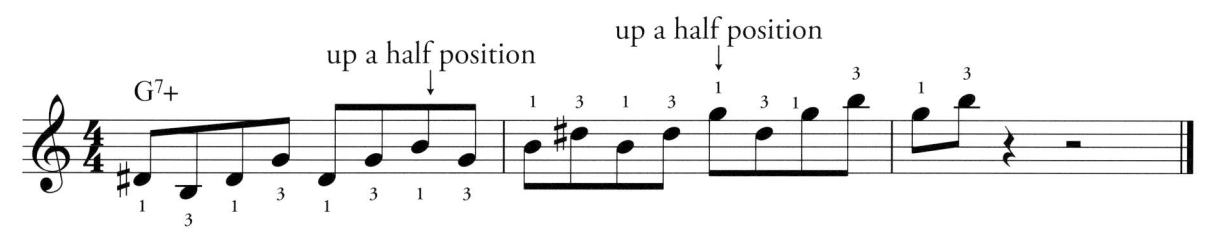

Augmented chords are not common in chord sequences. They most often occur as the last chord of a section or at the end of a whole sequence.

G⁷ augmented backing track

Backing **48**

Exploring Jazz Violin

Checkpoint

The '+' sign

You may see the '+' sign used with other chords. If no note is specified (as in C+), you will assume that it the 5th which is being raised or augmented. But if you come across C^{7+11}, this means that the 11th is raised; it could also be written as $C^{7\#11}$.

$m^{7\flat5}$ / $7^{\flat9}$ ($Am^{7\flat5}$ / $D^{7\flat9}$)

Here are a couple of scary looking chords. Like a pair of villain's sidekicks, you'll frequently find them hanging around together, lurking menacingly in otherwise inoffensive tunes such as 'Autumn Leaves' or 'Black Orpheus'. Like most altered chords, they're actually a lot easier to deal with than you might first expect.

They usually form part of an altered II-V-I so for example, Am^7-D^7-Gm could become $Am^{7\flat5}$-$D^{7\flat9}$-Gm.

Let's look at them individually. Here's $Am^{7\flat5}$, otherwise known as A half diminished. An alternative symbol for the half diminished chord is a circle cut in half by a diagonal line ( ).

Fig 6.19 $Am^{7\flat5}$ **chord / scale for** $Am^{7\flat5}$

We've simply taken the Am^7 chord and flattened the 5th. The associated scale has a flattened 2nd, 5th and 7th plus a raised 6th (the Locrian mode has similar properties but without the raised 6th; more on modes later in the book). All of these clues point to the fact that we're in the key of G minor, and that this chord is acting as a IIm^7 chord.

We've already seen how the arpeggio on a minor 7th chord is a simple finger pattern with the same fingers on two adjacent strings. To play a minor 7th with a flattened 5th chord, you simply lower the 5th down by a semitone, so it's no longer a symmetrical pattern:

Fig 6.20 $Am^{7\flat5}$ **arpeggio fingering**

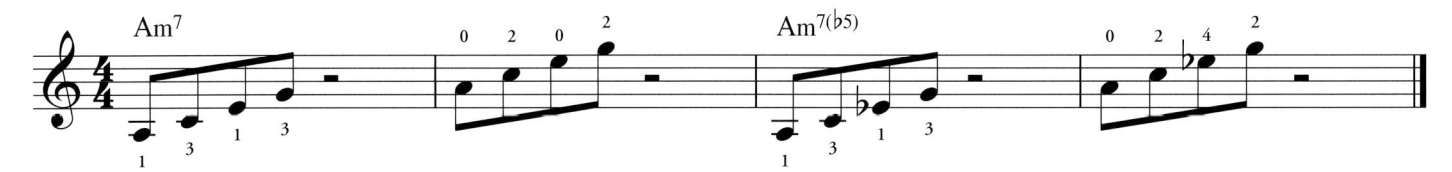

As mentioned above, this chord can also be called 'half diminished'. Why? It's because it's not fully diminished. To be a fully diminished chord you would also need to flatten the 7th, as in the next exam-

Fig 6.21 A (fully) diminished

Now here's $D^{7\flat 9}$.

Fig 6.22 $D^{7\flat 9}$ chord / scale for $D^{7\flat 9}$

This is simply a dominant 7th chord with an extra note – the flattened 9th (E♭). This note has a strong tendency to resolve down by a semitone. Chord $V^{7\flat 9}$ can often be followed by chord Im. So in this case the ♭9th (E♭) resolves to the 5th (D) of Gm.

With both the chords we're looking at I've provided a scale to go with the arpeggios. These are not necessarily the only scales that you can use with these chords, but they come heavily recommended – the reason being that they completely coincide. They are the same scale but starting from a different place.

This is why the two chords are often found together and why, as promised, they're a lot easier to deal with than you may have first thought.

Fig 6.23 Coinciding scales based on $Am^{7\flat 5}$ and $D^{7\flat 9}$

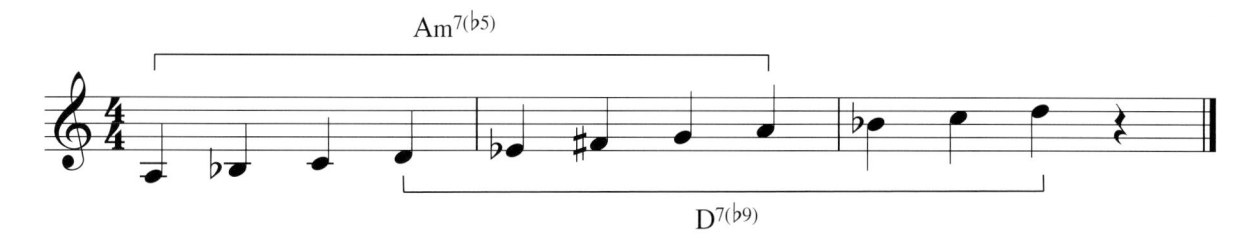

Here's the kind of riff you might use, based on the above scale:

Fig 6.24 $Am^{7\flat 5}$-$D^{7\flat 9}$-Gm riff

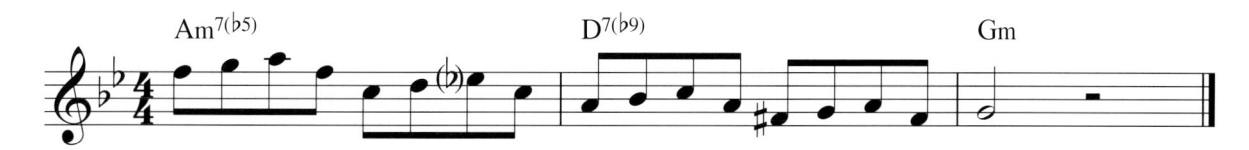

Finally, and fairly briefly, there are a couple more chord types that you might come across, one of which is the **sus** chord:

Sus (G^sus, G^(sus4), G^7(sus4))

Sus is short for suspended; it's a device originally used in contrapuntal music where a note is carried over from a previous bar, creating a dissonance, which is then resolved. In a sus chord the 3rd is absent, replaced by a perfect 4th, which can then drop a semitone to provide the resolution. Sus chords can be denoted (for example) as G^sus or G^(sus4).

Fig 6.25 G^(sus4) - G

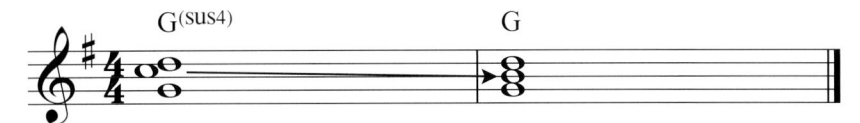

Perhaps the best-known use of the sus chord in popular music is the guitar introduction of 'Pinball Wizard' by **The Who**.

In jazz, sus chords are usually dominant 7ths, in which case there will be a further resolution to the tonic chord:

Fig 6.26 G^7(sus4) - G^7 - C

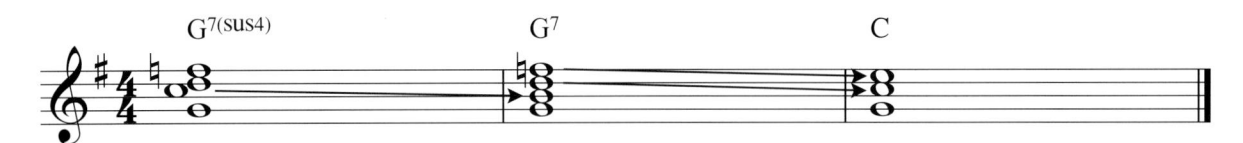

For a soloist there is nothing tricky about sus chords. You can either emphasize the resolution (i.e. play the 4th then the 3rd), or else ignore it altogether, and just play as if it were a G^7 chord. In mainstream jazz the sus chord, because of its instability, will always resolve. In modal music however, (which we'll look at in more detail later), the ambiguity of such chords is seen not as a temporary dissonance, but a permanent state of flux that need never resolve. Check out **Herbie Hancock**'s 'Maiden Voyage' as an example.

Slash Chords (B♭/D)

Slash was the top-hatted lead guitarist with the heavy rock band **Guns N' Roses**. These are not his chords. Instead they are chords where the root or bass note is not that implied by the chord name, but is specified by the note after the slash.

So B♭/D (said B♭ over D) would be a chord of B♭ with a D at the bottom. It's a way to denote inversions and more complex chords. Here's a short sequence involving some slash chords.

Fig 6.27 Slash chords

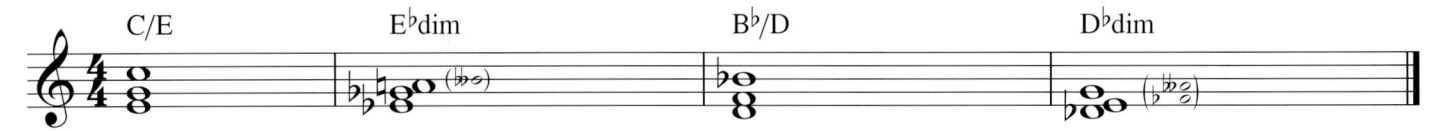

6: Chords Part II

Here the slash chords are being used to define a descending bass line. Some slash chords have a note, which is not normally part of the chord. If you were to analyse such a chord in isolation, you could give it a completely different name, based on the root note. So B/C could also be named $C^{maj7\sharp4\natural9}$. It's often better to describe chords as simply as possible. As with sus chords, they are not a problem for the soloist. You can either choose to emphasize these notes, or else leave them for the accompanist to play.

Checkpoint

We've looked at all the most common chord types, summarized below:

Fig 6.28 Chord summary

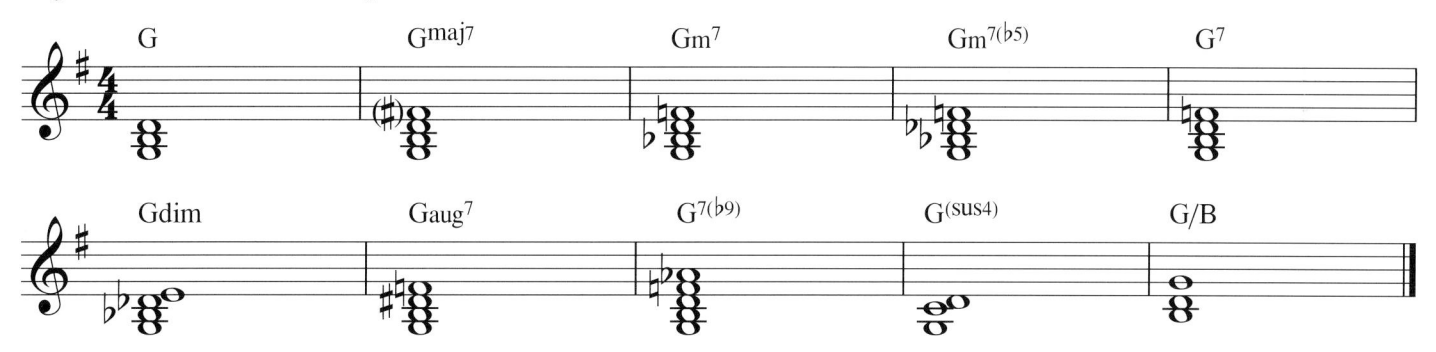

Playing Outside

The first part of this book we spent as a tearaway, irresponsible youth, going to any lengths to avoid having to think about chords; we then grew up, got a job, took on a mortgage and started the serious work of learning how to act responsibly with chords. Finally the kids have grown up, we've got money in the bank and quite frankly we're bored with sticking to the straight and narrow, we believe we've earned a little fun. It's time to buy a Harley Davidson and take to the open road!

Or, less prosaically, to start learning how to deliberately play 'outside' of the chords instead of staying safely 'inside' them the whole time.

The concept of playing outside has to some extent been with us almost as long as jazz itself, starting with the idea of leading notes or passing notes, which were already being used in the 1920s and 30s. In the 1950s the bebop era saw an important move towards 'outsidedness', followed by jazz-fusion and free jazz, by which time outside had already become the new inside.

We can consider a spectrum of 'outsidedness' ranging from 1–6, starting at the safe end, passing through exciting, dangerous and finally risky madness.

Exploring Jazz Violin

1. Chromaticism
We've already seen many examples of the use of chromatic notes not native to the scale. These can be 'leading notes', one semitone below the melody note which follows, or they can be part of a chromatic scale, where only the first and last notes have to be 'in'.

2. Extending the duration of a chord
When a chord changes, you would normally change the scale or mode of your solo at that point. By anticipating the change by, say, half a bar, you create tension, which is then released as the chord arrives.

3. Chord extensions
These are all to some extent different ways of looking at the same thing. By chord extensions we mean adding notes such as the 9th, 11th and 13th.

Here's an Am^7 arpeggio; the first bar is the standard arpeggio, whilst the second bar includes the chord extensions (9th, 11th, 13th).

Fig 6.29 **Am^7 with chord extensions**

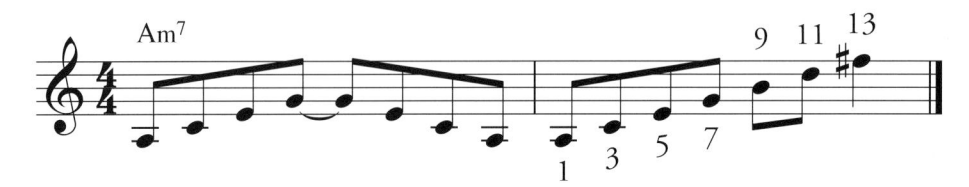

It sounds adventurous, though the B, D and F♯ are all actually 'in' notes; it's merely the placing of them that makes them interesting.

The chord created by the second bar would be Am^{13}. (It's convention not to write $Am^{7, 9, 11, 13}$ as the lower extensions are implied.)

4. Altered Notes
You can really turn up the heat by using 'altered notes' – those that are non-diatonic because they have been sharpened or flattened – so they lie outside of the scale implied by the chord.

Altered notes are usually applied to a dominant (V^7) chord, and the most common are the sharpened 5th, flattened 9th and sharpened 9th. Strictly speaking the blue notes (♭3rd, ♭5th, ♭7th) are also 'altered notes', but the language of the blues has become so ingrained into general musical consciousness that that they no longer sound in any way out of place. In a II-V-I sequence in the key of F, these altered notes are:

Fig 6.30 **Altered notes within a II-V-I in F**

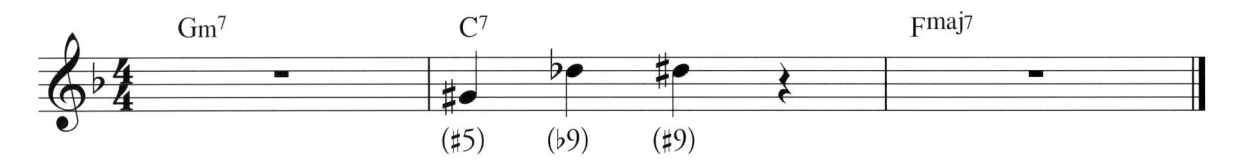

These notes add a great deal of spice to II-V-I licks. Here are some examples; most involve a change of position so take your time working them out.

Because they don't involve any open strings, it's easy to transfer patterns like these to different keys. In the example opposite you will occasionally see the ♭9 or ♯9 creep in ahead of the C⁷ chord (as in bar 4) – this is the C⁷ (with altered notes) being anticipated.

You will also see that some notes have been enharmonically written e.g. E♭ for the ♯9 and A♭ for the ♯5.

Fig 6.31 II-V-I patterns with altered notes

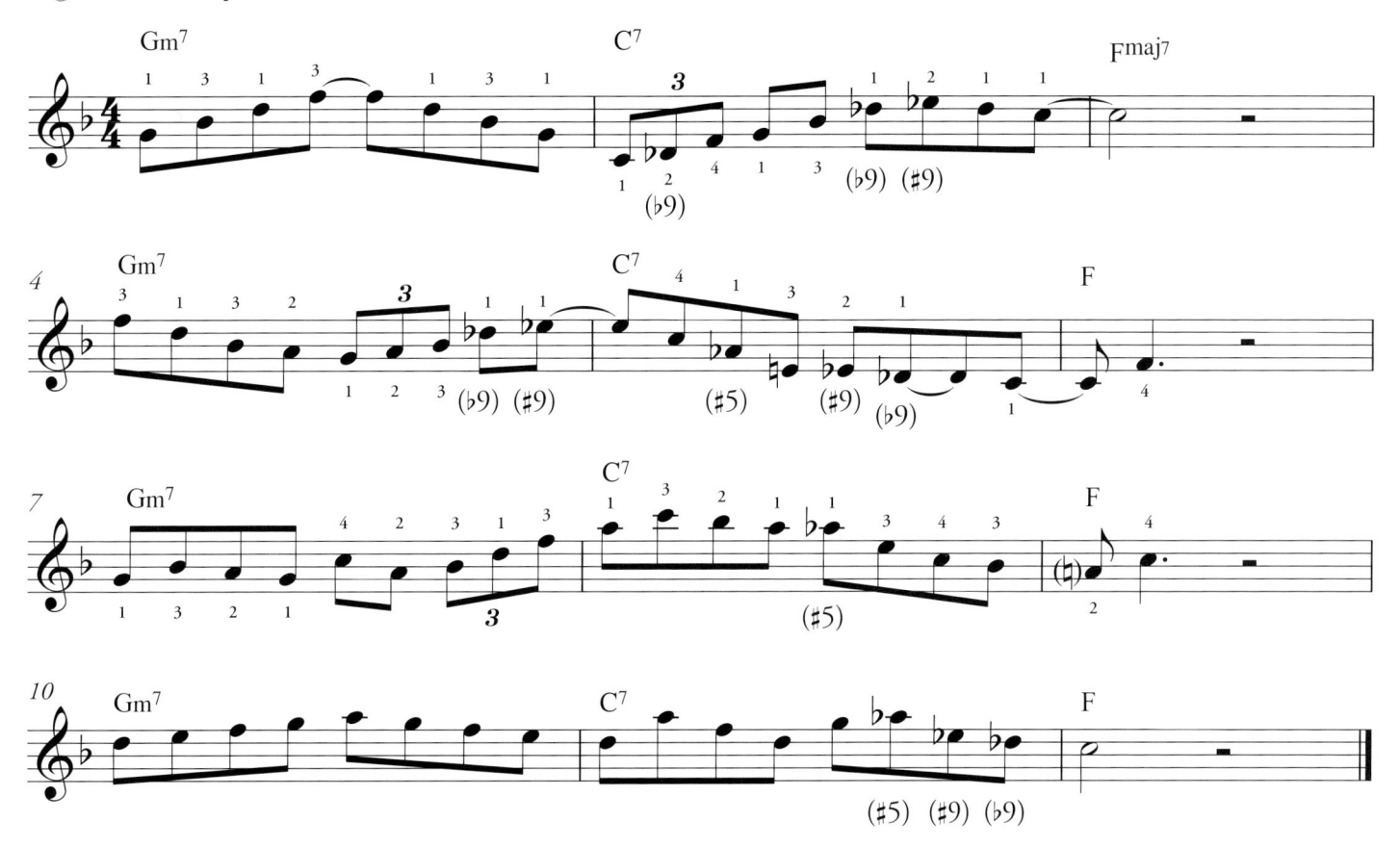

5. Chord Substitutions

Substitutions are usually carried out by an accompanist, who can play an alternative chord to the one written – sufficiently different from the original to add interest and colour, but sufficiently similar that it serves the same harmonic function.

There's no reason why you as the soloist can't do the same thing. **Stéphane Grappelli** often turned a dominant 7th chord into a 7♭9 chord, for example by squeezing a sly E♭ note into a chord of D⁷:

Fig 6.32 ♭9 substitution

Exploring Jazz Violin

The dominant 7th chord is the one most susceptible to substitution. It can easily be turned into an augmented chord by adding a sharpened 5th. Here the idea is used to spice up a II-V-I:

Fig 6.33 **Augmented substitution within a II-V-I progression**

You can also substitute a dominant 7th chord for a diminished chord. You build this not from the root of the dominant chord, but from its 7th. Thus G^7 can be turned into Fdim:

Fig 6.34 **Diminished substitution**

Diminished riffs are also useful in dealing with the $m7\flat5 / 7\flat9$ pair we looked at earlier. For example, a Ddim riff will fit neatly over $Dm^{7\flat5} / G^{7\flat9}$.

Fig 6.35 **Diminished substitution over $m^{7\flat5} / {}^{7\flat9}$**

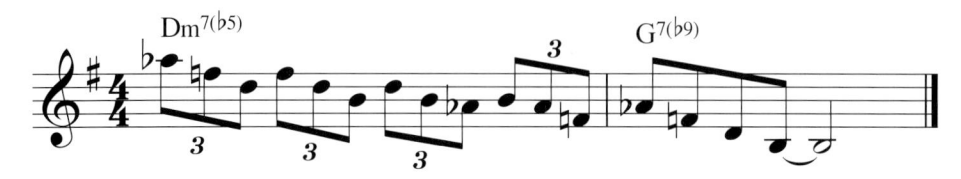

Here's a blues in G where the backing chords are standard, but diminished and augmented chords have been substituted in the solo line; a B♭dim riff is played over each C^7 chord and a Daug riff over each D chord.

Fig 6.36 **Blues with substitutions**

Demo 49

6. Moving Riffs

One of the boldest (and riskiest!) ways of playing outside is to play a simple, strong lick, which is definitely inside, and then move it up a semitone. This is sometimes referred to as sidestepping or sequencing. Some, or possibly all of the notes will now be outside, but because you prepared the ground with your first lick, there will still appear to be some musical logic to what you're doing. If you can smoothly get back 'inside' at the end of the phrase, you've pulled off a neat trick and deserve a round of applause. If you leave the phrase 'hanging out' you'll be greeted by confusion and suspicion that you've entirely lost the plot.

Here's a very versatile little lick, which is ideal for this purpose:

Fig 6.37 Inside / outside lick

Players such as **Jean-Luc Ponty**, **Didier Lockwood** and **Michal Urbaniak** frequently make use of this technique; we'll see more examples in the Ponty chapter. It's an exciting but dangerous game to play.

As **Graham Clark** explained to me, "You need to have some internal logic…playing outside isn't just playing any old nonsense!" Here are a few simple rules to help you pull it off:

1. Start with a strong, simple 'inside' lick. Pentatonic phrases usually work well; it's best not to use open strings.

2. Play it several times to establish it in the listener's ear.

3. Shift it up a semitone (preferably by changing your hand position), at this point most of the notes will be outside.

4. The safest way to finish is to shift it back down again; alternatively shift up, though you may have to modify one or two notes to get it back 'in'.

5. If your intonation is at all shaky, the whole exercise will be a disaster. You have to make the 'out' notes sound totally convincing!

Exploring Jazz Violin

Whole-tone Scales

We've already seen how a whole-tone scale works over an augmented 7th chord, and how it will act as a substitute for a dominant (7th) chord. You can also use it as a vehicle for getting 'outside' over a regular major chord. Here's a **Jean-Luc Ponty** style scalar lick which starts inside the key of D, moves down through a whole-tone scale and stops when it gets back inside.

Fig 6.38 **Descending whole-tone lick**

Conclusion

One of your biggest single challenges in learning to play jazz is to be able to follow the changes – to hear and understand the chords, and to be able to play inside them. Modern jazz, however, offers the further challenge of playing outside them. This absolutely does not mean ignoring the chords, but it means your relationship with them will be more complex and tempestuous.

7: Masters of Swing

Having studied the basic techniques and theory of jazz violin playing, we'll now investigate the work of some of the great players. Don't be hesitant about borrowing licks and stylistic approaches from other people; it's how all jazz players learn and develop, and sooner or later your own style will emerge. In this chapter we'll begin with a look at the first of our master swing violinists – **Joe Venuti** and then at the highly influential but much under-rated **Stuff Smith**.

Joe Venuti (1903–78)

Joe Venuti was a larger-than-life character; an abrasive, fast-talking, wise-cracking Italian-American who was legendary, not just for being the first great swing violinist, but also for being one of the greatest pranksters in the jazz world. Tales of his madcap antics and practical jokes abound, many of them exaggerated in the telling, not least by himself. The victims were often his fellow musicians; he is said to have silenced the annoying foot-tapping of a pianist by nailing his shoe to the floor, and thrown **Bing Crosby** into a Lake on a golf course, filled a tuba player's instrument with five pounds of flour, and to have sent trumpeter **Wingy Manone** on a 200-mile trip to a gig which was just around the corner. His one-time bandleader **Paul Whiteman** not only had his bath filled with Jello, but had his violin eaten live on stage.

Perhaps most notorious of all was the tale that he once invited 37 New York bass players to a non-existent gig, just to see the ensuing mayhem when they all showed up at once. Typically, this is one story that changed in the telling. **Bill Crow** describes in his book, *Jazz Anecdotes*, that in fact it was a crowd of Hollywood tuba players that he had booked for a gig at Sunset and Vine. He was reported to the Union and ended up having to pay them ten dollars a head. But the story didn't end there. Of their own accord, 26 double bass players later turned up at a Venuti gig in Chicago, to show him that he wasn't the only one with a sense of humour.

Venuti was born in Philadelphia in 1903 (though he claimed at various times to have been born in Italy and on the ship on the way over). He had classical training on the violin and at school met guitarist **Eddy Lang**. They began playing together, trading tunes and licks, and they soon found themselves playing hot jazz. Either as a duo or as the core of various small bands, the pair were soon popular performing and recording artists. Venuti's wacky humour carried through into the music which was always lively and brimming with invention. They recorded titles such as 'Pretty Trix', 'Wild Dog', 'Kickin' the Cat' and 'Add a Little Wiggle', and recording credits include such unconventional instruments as kazoo, fountain pen, and goofus – a saxophone-like instrument that uses harmonica-style reeds, also known as a couesnophone or queenophone.

Venuti became famous for his unconventional use of the bow. As a party piece he would disconnect the frog from the bow stick so that he could place the stick under the fiddle, with the hairs wrapped around the strings. This enabled him to play four-note chords, an otherwise impossible trick on the violin. You can hear the rather startling effect on such numbers as 'Four String Joe'. He also pioneered the double shuffle, a complex, syncopated bowing pattern which rocks backwards and forwards on the string; this was later adopted as a staple of the country and bluegrass fiddling fraternity.

Exploring Jazz Violin

As well as his work with **Eddy Lang**, throughout the 1920s and 30s Venuti was much in demand as a featured artist with names such as **Bing Crosby**, **Jack Teagarden**, **Paul Whiteman** (with whom he appeared in the film *King of Jazz*), **Benny Goodman** and the **Dorsey Brothers**. On a trip to Paris in 1935 he proved to be a great influence on the young **Stéphane Grappelli**.

The premature death of **Eddy Lang** in 1933 was a major blow to Venuti, and as jazz moved into the swing era, with its increasingly smooth and sophisticated textures, his 1920s-style music began to sound twee and dated. His career went into a slow decline; he moved to Hollywood, where he survived largely on anonymous session work. One of the few highlights of this period was his regular appearances on the **Bing Crosby** radio show in the early 1950s, where his quick-fire repartee and tall tales made him a popular guest. A 1954 recording with guitarist and fellow Italian-American **Tony Romano** demonstrates that despite his absence from the jazz scene, he was playing better than ever, with flawless technique and a gorgeous tone.

1967 brought a comeback in fortunes for **Joe Venuti** and for the last decade of his life he was once again a successful performer, working with such artists as saxophonist **Zoot Simms**, guitarist **Bucky Pizzarelli** and pianist **Earl Hines**.

The Playing Style of Joe Venuti

He used lots of blues licks but few 'outside' notes. He was far less prone to repeating the same licks than some other players I could mention, but there is one in particular that he used again and again. It rapidly passed into the armoury of country and bluegrass players, who named it the 'double shuffle'.

The double shuffle sounds complex, but is just a simple rhythmic pattern. Once you've got the hang of it it's easy to play and elaborate on, and is a guaranteed crowd pleaser that sounds far harder than it really is. Here it is in its simplest form:

Fig 7.1 Double shuffle rhythm

The bow rocks between two strings, and because it's mostly three-note phrases in four-four time, the emphasis of the pattern changes constantly. This is what makes it so confusing to the ear. Put an accent on the beginning of each three-note phrase, and use short bows. Don't be disheartened if you're not able to master this straight away. Trust me – it'll be worth it in the long run!

Once you've got the hang of this, you can make it more melodically interesting by experimenting with the top notes:

Fig 7.2 Double shuffle – moving top note

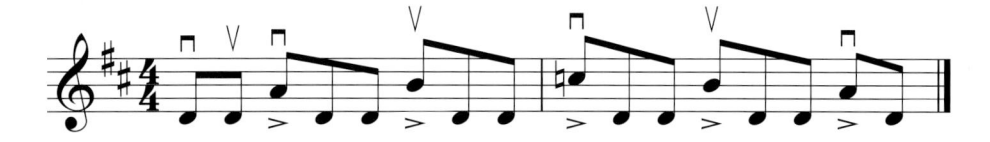

You can further elaborate it by changing one of the lower notes, creating an arpeggio effect.

At the beginning of bar 2 you need to bring your first finger up to play the C.

Fig 7.3 Double shuffle – arpeggio

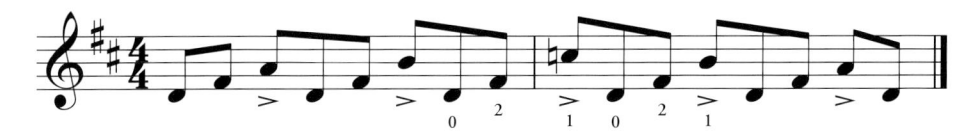

With this trickier fingering it is best to add some slurs:

Fig 7.4 Double shuffle – arpeggio plus slurs

Venuti builds a phrase similar to this into his tune 'Pretty Trix'. You'll find it easiest to play the lower notes by sliding your first finger up each time from the D♯ to E:

Fig 7.5 Double shuffle – 'Pretty Trix' style

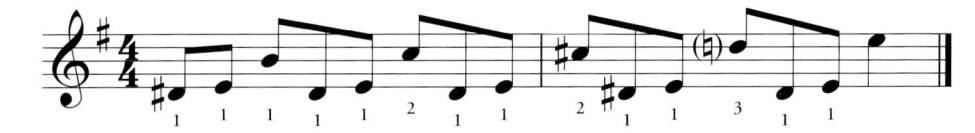

An extension to the double shuffle involves double stops. Here the pattern changes as the chord changes.

Fig 7.6 Double shuffle – double stops

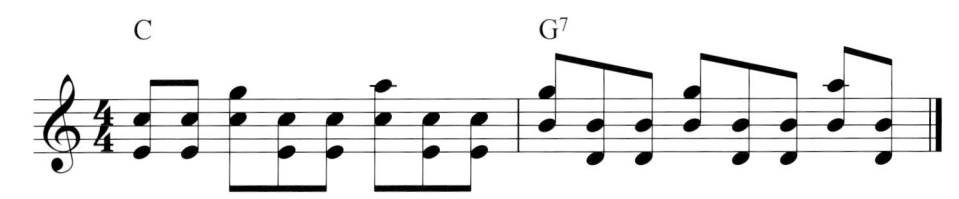

Exploring Jazz Violin

Here's an even more elaborate construction built on a double shuffle. It's made of arpeggios where, instead of keeping at least one note constant, all three ascend together. Not only that, but the pattern extends beyond the usual two bars, making it much harder to find where you are at the end. Fortunately you can play it all in 1st position.

Fig 7.7 Double shuffle – ascending arpeggios

If you slur it differently, it will have quite a different feel and sound:

Fig 7.8 Double shuffle – ascending arpeggios, alternative phrasing

There's no limit to how long you can keep the double shuffle going; listen to Venuti's recording of 'Goin' Home' and you'll hear it for a full 16 bars!

Assignment

The double shuffle is a great effect which is pretty well unique to the fiddle, since it's designed around the idea of rocking between adjacent strings. Get the rhythm firmly into your repertoire, then try creating your own licks. It should be possible to improvise freely using the double shuffle. Go back to some of the previous tunes we've worked on and try to find a place for it.

The Yodel

This brings us on to a type of riff you might call a 'yodel'. It's based on a scale where you follow the melody a 6th below on the string below. Here's a scale of G major in 6ths:

Fig 7.9 G major scale in 6ths

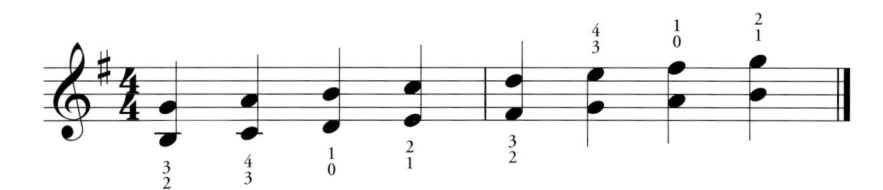

122

Once you've got your fingers round this it's easy to develop interesting riffs:

Fig 7.10 Yodel riff

Here's a fine Venuti-style yodel:

Fig 7.11 Venuti yodel

Most yodels have descending patterns, but here's an exception:

Fig 7.12 Ascending yodel

Here's a 'blue' yodel, much beloved by the country singer **Hank Williams**.

Fig 7.13 Blue yodel

For this one, in D major, each lower note is preceded by one a semitone below:

Fig 7.14 Yodel with chromatic steps

Double Stops (Joe Venuti)

Double stops (playing two notes together, on adjacent strings) are another Venuti trademark, particularly those built around a particular second and third finger shape.

Below you can see the second–third finger shape being constantly returned to throughout this fancy way of moving through the chords of D and G:

Fig 7.15 Double stops lick 1

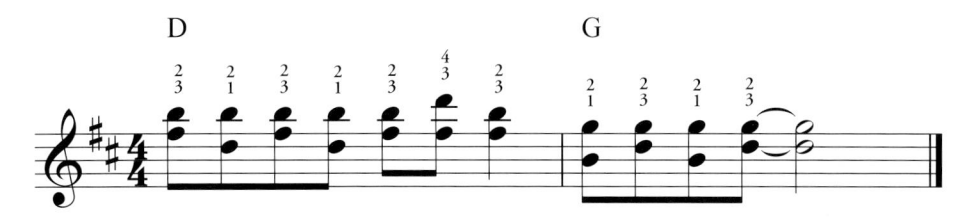

The same lick could also be condensed into two trills. For the first bar, use your third and first fingers to trill between F♯ and D; on the second bar, use your first and third fingers to trill between B and D. (Technically these are 'shakes' and not trills, as the interval is greater than a 2nd.)

Fig 7.16 Double stops – trill lick

Here's a few more double stop phrases:

Fig 7.17 Double stops lick 2

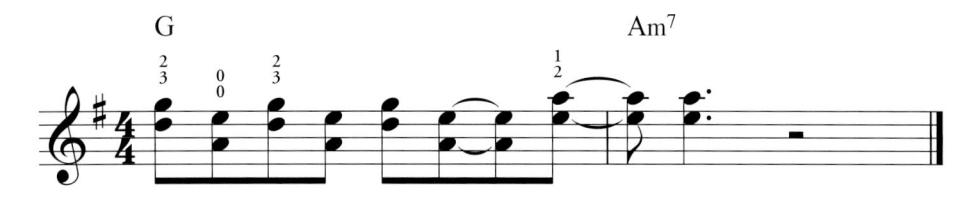

Fig 7.18 Double stops lick 3

For the next one you need to be in 3rd position. The second and third fingers slide up a semitone and down again in the middle of the lick.

7: Masters of Swing

Fig 7.19 **Double stops lick 4**

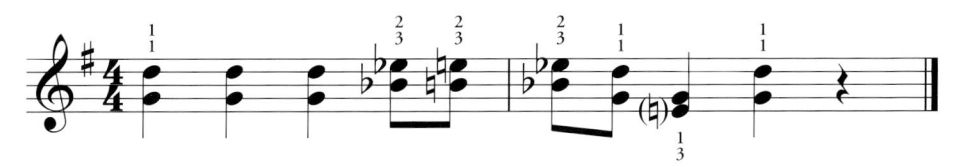

Parallel 5[ths]

Venuti was also keen on parallel 5[ths], where the finger lays across two adjacent strings. Always think of the lower note as being the melody and the upper note the harmony.

Fig 7.20 **Parallel 5[ths] lick 1**

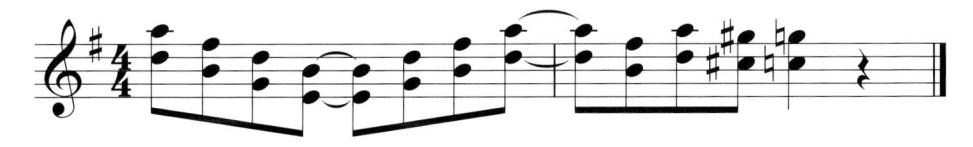

Fig 7.21 **Parallel 5[ths] lick 2**

A descending chromatic scale of parallel 5[ths] makes a dramatic ending, especially in G major.

Fig 7.22 **Parallel 5[ths] ending lick**

Harmonics

Venuti makes extensive use of harmonics, both natural and artificial. There are several ways to notate harmonics, below is a guide for this book.

Natural harmonics

These are produced by lightly fingering an open string at a harmonic node (indicated by a diamond note head) and are notated with an 'o' above.

Artificial harmonics

These are produced by firmly fingering a note (the fundamental) with the first finger whilst lightly touching the string with the fourth finger a perfect 4th above – the resultant note sounds two octave above the fundamental (other intervals will produce different harmonics). A diamond note head above the fundamental indicates where your fourth finger should be placed.

Here's the kind of lick Venuti would use which mixes both kinds of harmonics. I've included a second stave which gives you the pitch that you will actually hear.

125

Exploring Jazz Violin

Fig 7.23 Harmonics – example 1

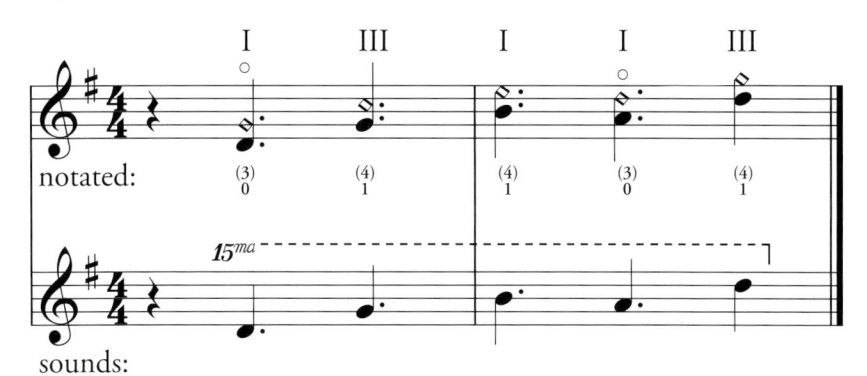

As these artificial harmonics are produced with the first and fourth fingers, there may be a lot of position changing involved in these kind of licks. This one, however, stays in 3rd position.

Fig 7.24 Harmonics – example 2

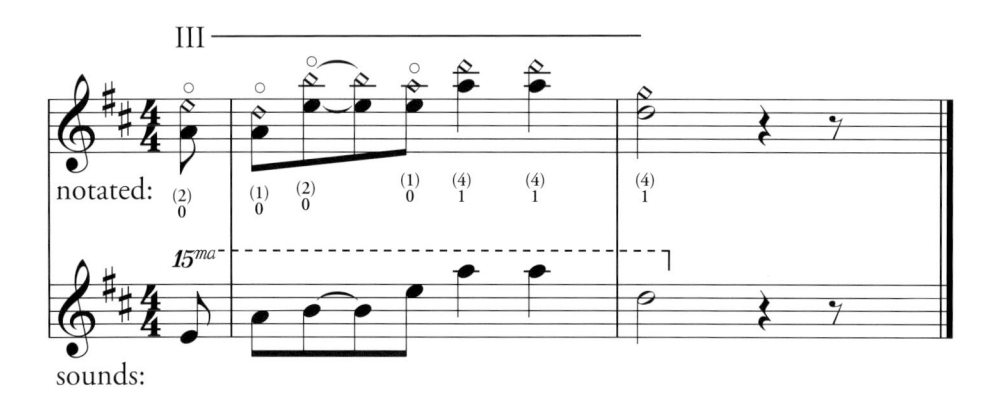

One of Venuti's most distinctive trademarks was his 'four string' technique. This involved removing the frog from the bow, wrapping the hair over all four strings whilst the bow stick went underneath the violin. It was then possible to play all the strings simultaneously, creating big, fat harmonies which would otherwise be impossible on the violin.

Finally here's a tune which includes a selection of Venuti-type licks.

Demo Backing
50 51

Jumpin' with Joe

Chris Haigh

Medium swing ♩ = 170

© 2010 Schott Music Ltd, London

7: Masters of Swing

Assignment

Work through 'Jumpin with Joe' slowly and carefully. Practise this until you can play it cleanly all the way through. Then use the backing track to try swapping around the licks, trying each one over different sections of the piece. Here's some points to watch out for:

Bars 1–8
At bars 1–5 there is a selection of artificial harmonics. When you get confident with these it should be possible to achieve a sweet vibrato on the longer notes. At bars 6, 7 and 8 you have parallel 5ths.

Bars 9–16
Bars 9–12 have more harmonics, and then at bars 13–16 there's some fairly complex double stops.

Bars 17–24
You get more parallel 5ths in bars 17 and 18, and then an ascending scale pattern in 19 and 20. Notice how in these two bars the pattern continues through the changing chords – a good effect but not always easy to do. There are some natural harmonics in bar 22, play these in 3rd position.

Bars 25–32
Bars 25–28 has a long ascending double shuffle, ending up in 3rd position, whilst from 29 to the end there are over two octaves of parallel 5ths descending chromatically.

Stuff Smith (1907–67)

It is difficult to imagine a swing violinist less like **Stéphane Grappelli** than **Stuff Smith**. They were very much chalk and cheese. Whilst Grappelli was a sophisticated Frenchman, Smith was a tough, 'rootsy' African-American who made his name in New York. Where Grappelli displayed elegance and an effortless flow in his playing, Smith's style was dirty, punchy and explosive. Where Grappelli was polite and reserved, Smith was a wisecracking, consummate entertainer, often flamboyantly attired in a top hat, with a stuffed monkey or parrot perched on his shoulder.

He was born **Hezekiah Leroy Gordon Smith** in Ohio in 1909 and in his youth his main musical influence was the trumpet playing of **Louis Armstrong**. He learned to phrase more like a horn player than a violinist and was perfectly at home among the flat keys, unlike Venuti or Grappelli who always preferred the more fiddle-friendly sharps. From 1927 to 1930 he toured with the **Alphonso Trent Orchestra** and from 1936 to 1939 led a successful quintet at the Onyx Club in New York. Here he wowed audiences with his humour, showmanship, jive singing and fabulous swinging violin. He had hit recordings with numbers like 'I'se a Muggin" and 'You'se a Viper'

In the 1940s he became deeply involved in the beginnings of bebop, jamming regularly with **Dizzy Gillespie** and **Charlie Parker**. His playing was harmonically very adventurous and he would frequently play outside the chords.

He always faced a struggle to make himself heard over the drums and so became a pioneer of the electric violin. At first he tried using s *Stroh* violin – an instrument with a horn like an old-fashioned gramophone, designed to have maximum volume for use in recording studios. In the late 30s he was approached by **Loma Cooper**, a representative of the *Violectra* company; she offered him the use of the company's new electric violin. He took to it like a duck to water, saying "oh, oh, this is it, man!" He appeared in adverts endorsing the instrument.

He continued gigging and recording through the 1940s and 50s, and moved to Denmark in the mid 60s. Apart from his Onyx Club recordings, he also recorded with **Nat King Cole**, **Dizzy Gillespie** and **Ella Fitzgerald**. He appeared with **Stéphane Grappelli** on the album *Violins No End*, and more than held his own at the 1966 violin summit alongside Grappelli, **Svend Asmussen** and **Jean-Luc Ponty**. He also produced several fine solo albums.

He never achieved the commercial success of **Stéphane Grappelli**, not least because his harsh and aggressive tone was never as appealing to audiences, but he is admired among jazz violinists for the drive, intensity and invention of his playing.

His raucous and bluesy approach was characterized by certain tricks and licks that he employed repeatedly. The following will give you an idea of his style.

Fig 7.25 **Repeated roll or turn**

This phrase was often morphed into a descending scale:

Fig 7.26 **Repeated roll – descending**

Sometimes this phrase would be used in an upper position, gradually sliding down with only the first and last phrases strictly in tune.

Fig 7.27 **Syncopated chops**

On his recording of 'You'se a Viper' he slips this in no less than nine times within two choruses. They work either as up bows near the tip, or down bows near the heel.

Stuff was very keen on 'chops' – short, percussive notes played at the heel end of the bow. He often syncopated them, playing three or four in a row:

Another rhythmic idea Stuff used was a three-beat phrase played over a four-beat bar which when repeated, reoccurred at a different place in the bar (effectively playing in 3/4 whilst in 4/4 time).

Fig 7.28 **3/4 phrase in 4/4 time**

Double Stops (Stuff Smith)

Stuff Smith often used double stops, one of which was frequently the flattened 3rd. He would usually slide up to, and possibly down from, these notes:

Fig 7.29 **Sliding double stops**

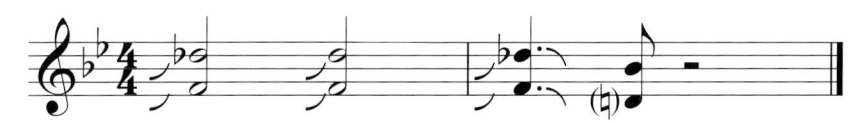

Here the 'chops' are combined with double stops.

Fig 7.30 **Chopped double stops**

Exploring Jazz Violin

Smith sometimes used a double stopped scale, using the interval of a 6th. Think of the upper notes as being the melody; this is the same scale Venuti used for his 'yodel' riffs.

Fig 7.31 Scale in 6ths

He would frequently use parallel 5ths in a chromatic scale, where one finger covered two strings. Always think of the lower note as the melody, with the upper note as the harmony. These double stops could be descending or ascending:

Fig 7.32 Descending parallel 5ths

Fig 7.33 Ascending parallel 5ths

As usual with these licks, they're a lot harder to read than they actually are to play.

Instead of using chromatic movement he would sometimes use wider intervals of 4th or major 3rd between pitches (e.g. in the example below the upper notes move from B♭ to F♯ – enharmonically a major 3rd, then E♭ to B♮ – again a major 3rd). This usually meant building riffs around the first and fourth fingers. Here's one where, typically, the simple phrase is elaborated by playing it in parallel 5ths, and repeating it on the next strings down, or up.

Fig 7.34 Wide interval lick

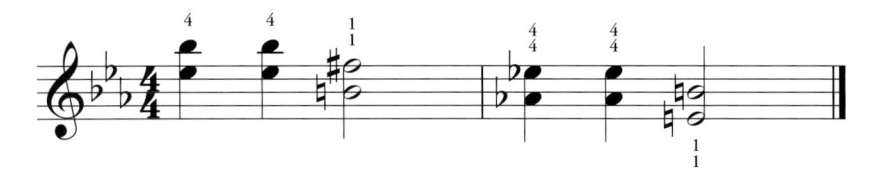

Notice how the notes start off consonant, i.e. inside the chord of B♭7, and soon step dramatically out.

A string of on-the beat downward slides is another common motif:

Fig 7.35 Repeated downward slides

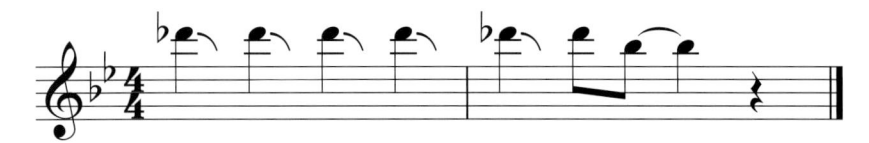

7: Masters of Swing

If he was playing in one of the 'simple' keys (C, G, D, A), **Stuff Smith** had a habit of playing open string, left-hand pizzicatos between phrases (indicated below by a '+' symbol). These served to punctuate the phrases, but really had no musical value. Similarly he would slide up to a harmonic half way up an open string.

Fig 7.36 Left-hand pizz / harmonic

He also loved descending chromatic 'cascades' of notes. Here's a fairly simple one. It's six notes running down first the D string, then the A and then the E. Just to make it more rhythmically exciting it's a three-beat phrase in 4/4 time, so the emphasis within the bar keeps changing.

Fig 7.37 Chromatic cascades 1

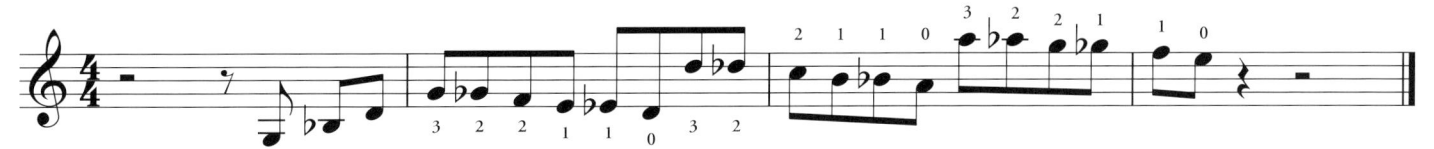

This one looks horrendously difficult, but it's not. Find E♭ with your fourth finger on the E string. Your other three fingers are bunched together below that. After the first four notes, stay in the same position but play on the A string. Bring the whole pattern down a semitone and repeat until you run out of string, or until someone runs at you with an axe!

Fig 7.38 Chromatic cascades 2

No one could accuse **Stuff Smith** of being understated. Here's another one, this time move the pattern up one semitone each time you change string. It's a clever riff to use for a G^7 chord, emphasizing the 7th (F♮) and 3rd (B♮) of the chord.

Fig 7.39 Chromatic cascades 3

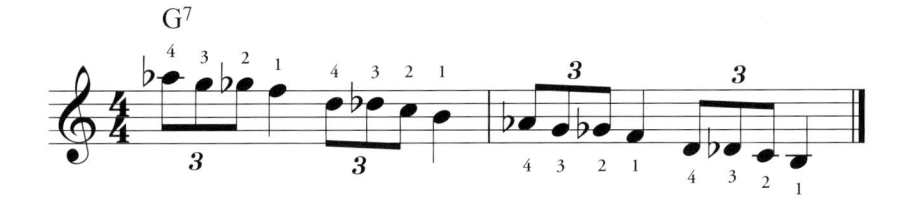

Exploring Jazz Violin

Here's a simpler one, going up and then down again:

Fig 7.40 Chromatic phrase – ascending and descending

Octaves are another **Stuff Smith** hallmark. You need to play a note with your first finger and the same note, but an octave higher, on the string above, with your fourth finger:

Fig 7.41 Octaves

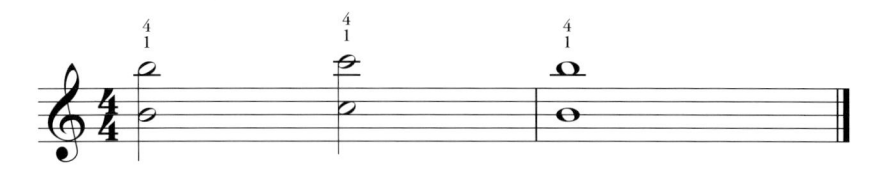

Stuff had a neat trick for creating a chromatic 'internal' melody within a II-V-I progression, using the flattened 5th of chord V, often in octaves:

Fig 7.42 Octaves – descending through a II-V-I in B♭

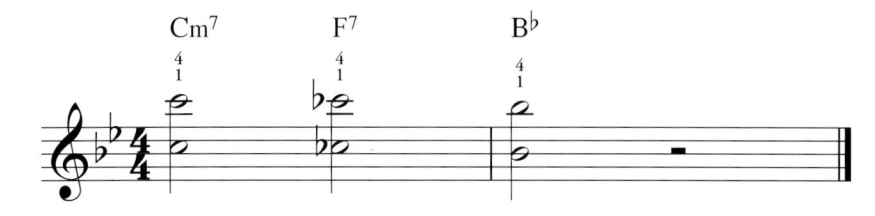

Here's the same thing, but ascending; this time we use the sharpened 5th of chord V.

Fig 7.43 Octaves – ascending through a II-V-I in B♭

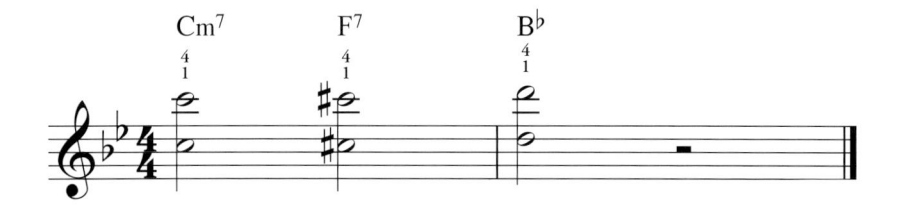

7: Masters of Swing

One of his most exciting octave licks was with the 'Salt Peanuts' rhythm ('Salt Peanuts' is a well known bebop tune). A simple three-note motif is repeated, ascending in semitones:

Fig 7.44 **Octaves – 'Salt Peanuts' rhythm**

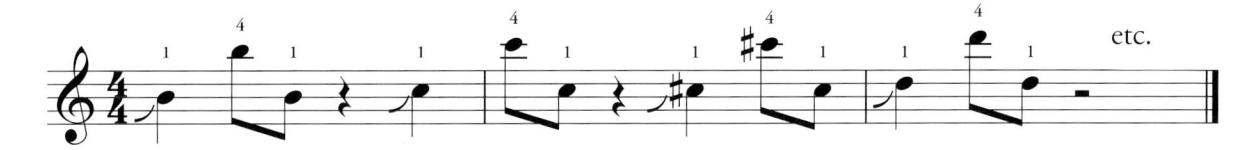

Checkpoint

There's no getting around it; playing octaves on the violin is hard. You might think that your intonation is pretty good until you double the same note with your first and fourth finger together, then suddenly you're not so sure. The fourth finger is inevitably your weakest link, and when you start to change position things just get worse, because the distance between your two fingers gets slightly smaller every time you move up the fingerboard.

So don't be surprised if it takes you a long time to master these kind of licks. On the positive side, a slight discrepancy of tuning is not the end of the world. We're not playing the Mendelssohn Violin Concerto here; we're deliberately creating a fat, dirty sound more akin to a sax or a distorted guitar.

Substitutions

Stuff Smith was no slouch at substitutions. Here's how he might have turned a chord of B♭ into B♭ dim:

Fig 7.45 **B♭ dim substitution**

Here's a stylish whole-tone scale pattern that you can use over an aug⁷ chord. This one can be used for G+⁷, A+⁷, B+⁷, C♯+⁷, E♭+⁷ or F+⁷:

Fig 7.46 **Whole-tone scale pattern**

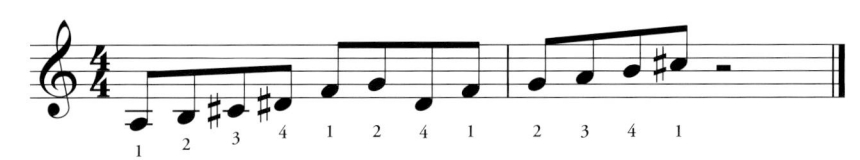

Exploring Jazz Violin

He could also happily play a whole tone scale over a chord of B♭:

Fig 7.47 Whole-tone scale over B♭

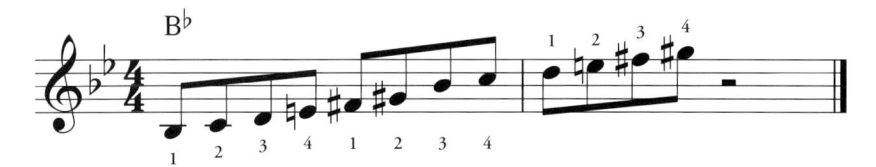

Here's a double stopped, parallel-fifths trill he sometimes used – here over a chord of B♭. Three of the notes in use are altered notes – of the lower notes the C♭ (written here as B♮) is a flattened 9th and C♯ a sharpened 9th, whilst of the upper notes F♯ is a sharpened 5th.

Fig 7.48 Double-stopped trill 1

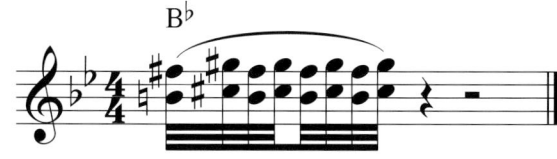

Here's another similar one, the G♭ (written here as F♯) is a spicy flattened 5th. Over a chord of C he might play this simple third–first fingering:

Fig 7.49 Double-stopped trill 2

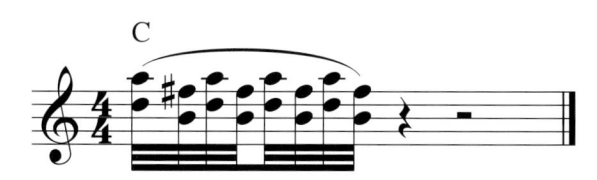

And here's a wacky pattern guaranteed to generate a lot of outside notes. The fourth–first finger stretch creates an interval of a 4th, and every four notes the whole pattern is moved up one semitone:

Fig 7.50 Fourth–first fingers lick 1

This fourth–first finger pattern moves over three strings, descending chromatically:

Fig 7.51 Fourth–first fingers lick 2

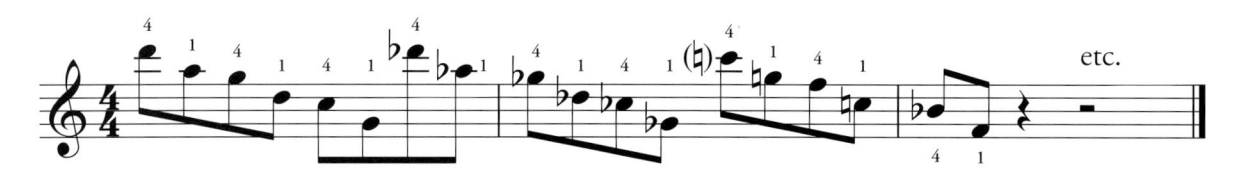

'I Got Rhythm' by **George** and **Ira Gershwin** is a jazz standard, the chord progression of which is known as 'rhythm changes'. The next solo and many other jazz tunes are based on 'rhythm changes' such as 'Anthropology', 'Crazeology', 'Salt Peanuts', 'Serpent's Tooth' so it's a good idea to be familiar with it.

7: Masters of Swing

'Rhythm Changes' presents many of the **Stuff Smith** style licks we've been studying. Once you've played it through, try it again, but this time swap the licks around so they occur at different places in the tune. The backing track version goes three times through the sequence and omits the pickup bar.

Rhythm Changes

Demo 52 | Backing 53

Chris Haigh

Other Swing Players

In the next chapter we'll look at the best known of all jazz violinists, **Stéphane Grappelli**. He has dominated the field to such an extent that to many people it is a surprise to learn that there were, and are, many other significant swing violinists.

The violinist **Eddie South** was a contemporary of **Joe Venuti**. He had a phenomenal technique, and would have been a concert violinist had not racist attitudes made it impossible at that time. He studied in Paris and Budapest, and developed a strong interest in gypsy music, which combined well with his swing playing. He was nicknamed 'The Dark Angel of the violin'.

American born **Ray Nance** played with **Duke Ellington** throughout the 1940s and 50s. He also played trumpet (on which he recorded iconic solos including 'Take the A Train'), sang and danced – for which multiple talents he was nicknamed 'floorshow'.

Somewhat in the **Eddie South** mould was **Paul Nero**, best known for his novelty piece 'Hot Canary' – a show-off composition featuring harmonics, some very high position work and left-hand pizzicato.

In the 1940s **Johnny Frigo** played comedy violin routines with the **Chico Marx Orchestra**, and later worked with the **Jimmy Dorsey Band**. He spent most of his career playing bass, and only in the 1980s did he start to concentrate on jazz violin.

The hottest ticket in contemporary American jazz violin is **Regina Carter**. Like **Stuff Smith** she phrases like a horn player and has a bluesy, punchy style; she also infuses her work with strong elements of soul, funk and Latin.

The Danish violinist **Svend Asmussen** would almost certainly have been much better known had he not predominately stayed in his native country. He was a good all-round musician, singing and doubling on many other instruments. He featured on the famous jazz violin summit in Switzerland in 1966 alongside Grappelli, Smith and the newcomer **Jean-Luc Ponty**, and also on the **Duke Ellington** jazz violin session with Grappelli and Nance in 1963.

Britain has a number of fine swing violinists. Perhaps best known is **Chris Garrick**, whose playing ranges from a Grappelli-style swing (which he performs with ex-Grappelli guitarist **John Etheridge** in **Sweet Chorus**) to his own contemporary and often electric material on his many solo albums.

A good contemporary exponent of the early swing styles of **Joe Venuti** and **Stuff Smith** is **Mike Piggott**. His show is enlivened by such party tricks as the Venuti four-string technique, the occasional use of a *Stroh* (horn) violin, and pizzicato solos.

Billy Thompson was a finalist of the UK's 'Young Jazz Musician of the Year' in 1996 and 98; his playing ranges from gypsy jazz to contemporary (with **Barbara Thompson**'s **Paraphernalia**). Scotland also has a fine swing player in the person of **Alex Yellowlees**.

8: Stéphane Grappelli

December 2nd, 1934 was a big day in jazz violin history. The concert was on a Sunday morning at a Paris music school – L'École Normale de Musique – hardly auspicious, either in timing or venue, for a genre so deeply associated with late-night, smoke-filled bars and cafés. However, this was no ordinary gig – it was the launch of the **Quintette du Hot Club de France**.

The Hot Club was a recently-founded association whose goal was the promotion of the newly-emerging French jazz movement. The Quintette consisted of the brilliant and mercurial gypsy guitarist **Django Reinhardt**, two rhythm guitarists including Django's brother **Joseph Reinhardt**, a double bassist and violinist **Stéphane Grappelli**. Here are the events that led up to that day:

Grappelli's Childhood

Stéphane **Grappelli** was born in 1908 to an Italian father and French mother. His mother died when he was just four, leaving the young Stéphane not quite an orphan, but nevertheless having to largely fend for himself. This first happened when his father was called up to the Italian army and later when his father was often away travelling and eking out a meagre living with occasional teaching, journalism and translation. Buskers would often enter the courtyards of the Parisian courtyard near Pigalle where they lived, playing waltzes and light Classical pieces for coins thrown from the windows. When, as a child, Stéphane was given a violin, it was to these buskers that he looked for inspiration. With a little help from his father and an occasional lesson from a neighbour, he had soon taught himself the rudiments of the instrument and was out on the streets scratching a living.

A rather confusing aspect of his story is that it is often told that he studied at the Paris Conservatoire, suggesting a background of intellectual elitism, privilege and academia. Nothing could be further from the truth. He did indeed attend, but it was from the ages 12 to 15 and it was not a degree course but a basic grounding, mostly in reading music. This was the only formal education he ever had and his playing was largely self-taught.

As well as the violin he also mastered the piano by simply walking into cafés and experimenting on the instruments whenever he could get away with it. Before long he was making a living with one or another instrument, playing in cinemas, as an accompanist in a dance school, and performing at private parties. He had a strong work ethic which remained with him for the rest of his life and was always both driven and haunted by the poverty and insecurity of the early years behind him.

By 1914 Paris was at a turning point in history. *La Belle Époques* – the golden age of Impressionism, Art Nouveau and the carefree bohemian lifestyle of the rich and beautiful – had been brought to an end by the Great War. The arrival of thousands of American troops had ushered in the jazz age and the startling new rhythms and harmonies of **Louis Armstrong** and **Duke Ellington** were starting to displace the musettes, operettas and tangos of the Parisian salons, cafés and night clubs. To most Europeans, jazz was American music, powered by drum kits and lead by trumpets and saxophones. No wonder there was excitement in the air with word of this new home-grown sensation; not only French but a revolutionary new type of string band – 'Jazz Hot'.

Grappelli Discovers Jazz

By 1925 Stéphane had discovered jazz and took to it immediately, saying "it seemed to have been invented expressly for me". Despite by now being a good reader, Grappelli still played largely by ear and was a natural improviser. He heard and admired the music of the American violinist **Joe Venuti**, but did not copy him; he considered Venuti's playing to be something of a novelty – full of tricks and set-pieces, but not real jazz. As a pianist Grappelli joined, what was at the time, the top name in what passed for French jazz – **Gregor and his Gregorians**. This curious outfit was led by an eccentric showman who liked to be preceded at a performance by a young boy who would blow a trumpet fanfare and announce "Gregor! Le roi du jazz!". With this group, Grappelli performed widely, even travelling to South America. It was also to South America that 'Le roi' eventually fled, after having a car accident in Paris, leaving Grappelli once more in search of a job.

He was soon working every night at the Croix du Sud club in Montparnasse and it was here that he was approached one night by a menacing looking figure looking like an American gangster or a Calabrian bandit. At first Stéphane was so alarmed he almost fell off the stage, until the man introduced himself as **Django Reinhardt**, who said he was looking for a violinist to form a band with him. Stéphane had seen Django before – the gypsy had even played in his courtyard years ago, but despite the enviable reputation the guitarist was already establishing, Stéphane was reluctant to give up his secure job at the night club to go off with this unsavoury looking character. Not least among his reservations was the fact that Stéphane still felt more confident on the piano than the violin and was worried that the amplification problems, already bad enough with the violin alone, would be compounded if the other lead instrument was a guitar.

Formation of the Hot Club

Thus it was, that the idea lay dormant for three years until the two found themselves playing the same job, hired by Louis Vola for a regular tango gig at the Hotel Claridge. Django made a habit of staying behind at the interval, practising and improvising while the rest of the band went out to get a drink.

One night Stéphane joined him in an impromptu performance of 'Dinah' and the magic was immediate and striking. With Django's brother Joseph on rhythm guitar they soon had the core of a band. They quickly came to the attention of **Charles Delauney** of the **Hot Club de France**, who saw them as a possible house band and flag bearers for the fast-developing French jazz scene. A recording session was arranged and they put down four classic tracks: 'Dinah', 'Tiger Rag', 'Lady be Good' and 'I Saw Stars'. Extensive publicity led to a full house at their first gig and it was soon clear to the audience, and critics alike, that this was indeed something quite new. For one thing, people came to listen, not to dance – an unheard of thing at the time. They became the regular backing group for visiting American musicians, including the black violinist **Eddie South**, who was in Paris for the 1937 Paris Exposition.

Stéphane and Eddie did several recordings together, including a bold experiment: two versions of the first movement of the **Bach** *Double Violin Concerto*. The first version had 32 bars of the melody which is repeated. The second version had 32 bars of the melody followed by some rather frantic improvisation when Delauncey, who had dreamt up the idea, suddenly snatched away the music to see what would happen. There were mixed feelings about the result. Grappelli later referred to it as "an insult to Bach" (though that didn't stop him from releasing the *Brandenburg Boogie* album in 1980). The 1937 recording resulted in both the BBC and the Nazi party banning it.

A string of successful releases followed, as well as tours throughout France, other parts of Europe and Scandinavia, but it was in England that the band had its greatest success – an initial one-off gig led to a four-month tour. The testing of an air-raid siren in London on 1st September brought things to a sudden halt. Django, in a panic, immediately returned to Paris whilst Stéphane, with fewer family ties, remained in London for the duration of the war.

The classic Hot Club line-up lasted just five years, but in that period they made many recordings. Grappelli went on to have a further fifty years of playing, but his style in later life, as he took to the concert halls of the world, was very different from his early years. Therefore we will analyse his playing in two sections, starting with this earlier period.

Grappelli's Playing Style (1934–9)

The Quintette had a unique rhythm section. When they were joined by **Joseph Reinhardt**, Django didn't think it was fair that Stéphane got two guitars playing rhythm behind him whilst he himself had only one. They therefore added a second rhythm guitar (initially **Roger Chaput**). There was certainly no need for drums with this powerhouse chugging away four-to-a-bar, enlivened by the 'chops' and syncopations of Django. The bass provided a plodding, and often inaccurate, two-to-a-bar but the real action was up front. The two soloists were like two sides of a coin: Django dark, brooding, dazzling in speed, and endlessly inventive; Stéphane charming, elegant, relaxed and effortless.

There are three violinists with whom he can be directly compared. **Joe Venuti** was already well established by the time Grappelli discovered jazz and although the Frenchman would certainly have heard his recordings, there is little sign of a direct influence. The double shuffle, a Venuti trademark, never appeared in Grappelli's playing. Other techniques such as parallel fifths, chromatic runs and harmonics only occasionally appeared at this stage of his career. The 'Dark Angel of the Jazz Violin', Eddie South, we have already mentioned. South had an advanced classical background, "too much!" according to Grappelli. Again there is little evidence that Grappelli attempted to emulate him; indeed when South sat in with the band, Grappelli would take the opportunity to slip out to get a drink at a bar around the corner.

Michel Warlop was a fine fiddler and a good friend of Grappelli's – they shared lodgings for a time. Warlop had a thorough Conservatoire training and though he often shared both stage and studio with Grappelli, his sound on recordings shows that he never really could swing, despite learning verbatim many of Venuti's licks. His playing was too sweet, his vibrato too classical and his soloing always sounding nervous and insubstantial. His friend, Stéphane, said that he "never really understood the meaning of jazz". He died young, an alcoholic and bitterly disappointed that he could not emulate his fellow jazz violinists.

Stéphane Grappelli, then, was one of a kind. The fact that he was self-taught and did not have a classical background almost certainly helped him. He played what he heard and what he felt. The most distinctive single characteristic of his early playing was what he called "my little blue note". He had a stock of blues phrases which he used repeatedly, the same one often occurring repeatedly in a single tune. His playing was largely based on the major pentatonic blues scale, but his use of this scale was very distinctive. Rather than bending from the flattened 3rd up to the natural 3rd, he would almost always slide up to the flattened 3rd itself.

Exploring Jazz Violin

So in the key of C, a typical phrase would be:

Fig 8.1 Slide up to flatten 3rd

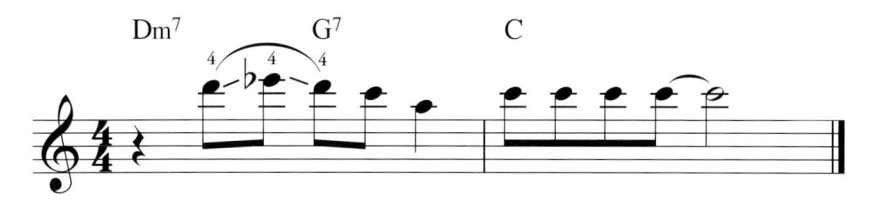

He did this by sliding the fourth finger up from D to E♭ and then down again. He obviously liked the feel of this phrase; if there was space he would sometimes double it up, dropping down an octave for the second one:

Fig 8.2 Double slide up to flattened 3rd

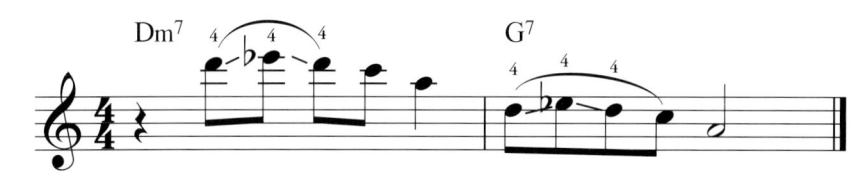

This version is a repeated 3-beat phrase; a rhythmic device that Grappelli was very fond of. For continuity I would stick with the same fingering when you drop down to 1st position.

This riff is clearly designed to emphasize the flattened 3rd, but he would also use exactly the same riff over an Am chord, over Adim (in which case the blue note is now a flattened 5th), or in the key of F, in which case the note you're sliding up to is now the flattened 7th.

The same phrase and fingering can also be transposed to other keys. For G it would be:

Fig 8.3 Slide up to flattened 3rd in G

This could be done by sliding a third finger, but again, in order to keep the same fingering as in the C version, I would recommend using the fourth finger. In almost any Grappelli tune in G, you'll hear something like this at least once, often many times. Here's a slight modification of the C version, which will also work over a chord of A7. In this context we're sliding from the 4th to a flattened 5th and back.

Fig 8.4 Slide up to flattened 5th over A7

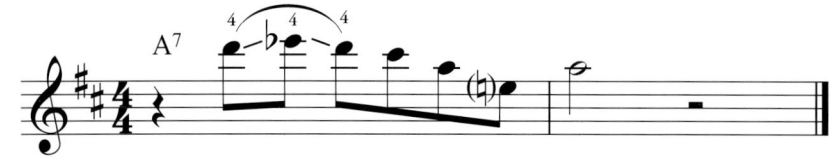

Another blues lick he favoured was a stretch from the fourth to first finger (against the nut) – an interval of a flattened 5th.

Fig 8.5 Fourth- to first-finger stretch 1

Here's a more complex version:

Fig 8.6 Fourth- to first-finger stretch 2

It also works nicely over an E^7 chord in the key of Am; a perfect lick for 'Minor Swing' – one of the best known of all gypsy jazz tunes.

Fig 8.7 Fourth- to first-finger stretch 3

Whilst most of his playing was in 1st position, he was happy to go up the neck without hesitation and with flawless intonation.

He had a fine strident lick in 4th position to use on an E chord; it works well on 'Sweet Georgia Brown'.

Fig 8.8 4th position lick

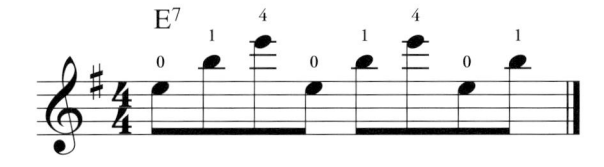

Exploring Jazz Violin

You can repeat this as many times as you like. Without transposing, the same lick will also work nicely over a II-V-I in G.

The lick is often preceded with a long slide up to a high E with a wide vibrato; it can also be embellished with triplets:

Fig 8.9 Embellished 4th position lick

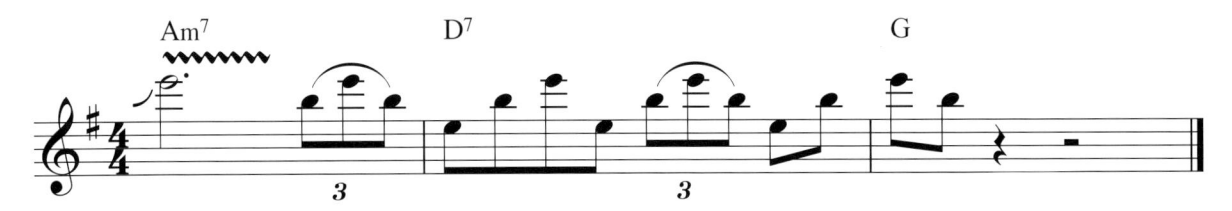

This version is another three-beat phrase (in 4/4 time). He often started a new chord or phrase with a roll; here, there's a roll on each step of a descending arpeggio:

Fig 8.10 Rolls on a descending arpeggio

Here it is ascending:

Fig 8.11 Rolls on an ascending arpeggio

Notice that both of these are three-beat phrases. Arpeggios can also be decorated with triplets, using the note one semitone below from the chord note:

Fig 8.12 Triplets on arpeggio

One of his trademarks in later years was the parallel 5ths run. These rarely appeared in his hot club years, perhaps just the occasional chopped riff like this:

Fig 8.13 Parallel 5th chops

His use of natural harmonics, an essential part of his armoury post-war, appeared only fleetingly at first. Two Django / Stéphane compositions – 'Daphne' and 'HCQ Strut' used harmonics at the start of the melody. These were mostly 3rd position, second-, third-finger harmonics:

Fig 8.14 Natural harmonics 1

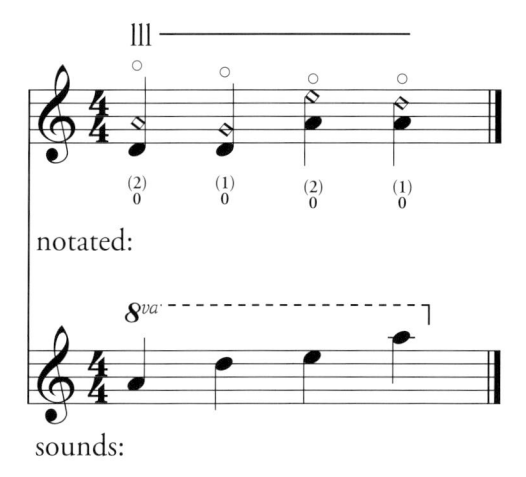

notated:

sounds:

He would sometimes slide to a harmonic halfway up the string with the fourth finger, followed by two higher sounding harmonics on the same string:

Fig 8.15 Natural harmonics 2

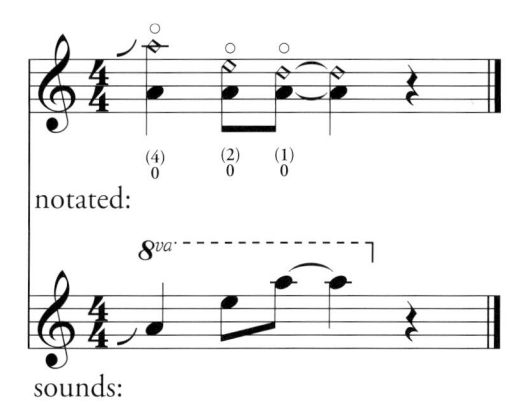

notated:

sounds:

Another important feature of Grappelli's playing is his distinctive vibrato, which is fast and intense. Expert Grappelli stylist **Tim Kliphuis** recommends practising vibrato with a metronome and playing a specific number of 'shakes' per note, going up and down a scale.

A New Vocabulary (1939–71)

Stéphane Grappelli was an out-and-out professional, who took opportunities wherever they arose. The departure of Django from England, though a blow, did little to interfere with the violinist's workload. He began playing with a series of different pianists, starting with **Arthur Young** and then **George Shearing**, when Young was injured in a bombing raid. They had a regular engagement at Hatchett's in Piccadilly, which lasted for most of the war. For all the fire and excitement he had enjoyed with Django, Grappelli found working with these pianists a liberating experience. The broader, more expansive chords and more subtle rhythms encouraged new approaches in his playing and he began to develop a whole new musical vocabulary.

Over in France, the **Quintette du Hot Club** continued with Django now as undisputed leader (the rivalry between him and Stéphane had been an ongoing problem from the start); rather than finding another violinist, he took on the clarinettist **Hubert Rostaing**. Tolerated by the Nazis and idolized by the French, Reinhardt emerged a huge star in the wartime years, becoming something of a symbol of the temporarily-thwarted French nationalism.

In January 1946, Django arrived in London for an emotional reunion with Grappelli. The two men, unable to speak, got out their instruments and broke into a spontaneous performance of 'La Marseillaise'. A new recording session quickly ensued, including a swinging recreation of their national anthem – which did not amuse the French Government.

However, hopes that the partnership could take up where it left off were unfounded. Both musicians had pursued separate paths during the war, both perhaps relishing their independence. The decision was made for them when Django was taken ill and returned home.

Death of Django

Grappelli continued his work in England with **George Shearing**, whilst Django tried his luck in America, on invitation from no less than **Duke Ellington**. This adventure was largely a failure, due in no small part to the gypsy's disorganised lifestyle (he turned up in America without a guitar and arrived catastrophically late for one of the key performances). He never really recovered from this disappointment and, on return to France, went into a slow decline, dying tragically young in 1953 at his home on the banks of the Seine, where he suffered a stroke after a day's fishing.

Grappelli, meanwhile, was steadily working away; he spent the next two decades or so playing in a series of classy hotels and restaurants in London as well as France and Italy. He had financial security, which had always been an important factor to him, and approached these jobs with great professionalism. However, he was playing for dinner dances to a public more interested in the menu than the music and so was gradually descending into a world of schmaltz – waltzes, tangos, ballads and the like. Whilst he continued to make proper jazz recordings, they had little impact on the critics.

As the 50s moved into the 60s he was seen as falling into the unfortunate area in between, on the one hand, the thrusting new world of post-bebop and modal music and on the other, the revival of 'traditional' Dixieland jazz. In France there was a continued interest in jazz, but to be taken seriously you had to be American, black, a gypsy or some kind of anti-establishment radical. Grappelli did not score highly on any of these counts. In 1967 he took on, what many people regard as, the lowlight of his career – a five-year stint at the Paris Hilton. Musicians who visited him at the gig were shocked by the anonymity of his position and the indifference of the diners, completely unaware of the living legend in their presence.

Revival (1971 onwards)

So what brought Grappelli from this low point to the elevated status he finally achieved in his later years? The rise of **Jean-Luc Ponty** in the US, first as a bebop player, then in jazz-rock and fusion, sparked a renewed interest in the violin as a jazz instrument. Among the young, the counterculture were showing a strong revival of interest in all types of 'roots' music, be it folk, cajun or bluegrass. Hot club jazz, with its acoustic string line-up and its by now legendary gypsy guitarist, was seen by many as falling into this roots category. Among an older audience there was an increasing nostalgia for the faded glories of pre-war Paris, with which Grappelli would be forever associated. Meanwhile, despite the lack of serious jazz gigs, Grappelli was playing better than ever, as demonstrated by a series of superb recordings. Two events in the early 70s were the catalyst for his comeback.

The first was in December 1971, when he was approached by the producers of the *Parkinson* TV show to see whether he would be interested in appearing with the classical virtuoso, **Yehudi Menuhin**. The show had a habit of trying to introduce artists of a widely contrasting background, to see if something interesting would ensue. It did. Both men had been excited but apprehensive about the encounter, both seeing the potential to make complete fools of themselves. Menuhin was an undisputed genius on the violin, with the highest possible credentials. He also had great intellectual curiosity about other forms of music, but had no experience whatsoever of jazz or improvisation.

Grappelli, largely self-taught and from the humblest of backgrounds, would have been desperate to prove himself the equal of this musical royalty. As it turned out, the odds were stacked entirely in Grappelli's favour. They performed two numbers: 'Jealousy', chosen by Menuhin as the only 'jazz' tune that he knew the melody for and 'Lady be Good'. Menuhin learned a written solo whilst Grappelli was of course happy to improvise as he always did and remarked "I was frightened of playing with the maestro. However, three bars into 'Lady be Good', tell me who is the maestro?"

Comment among jazz musicians was largely critical; **Svend Asmussen** describing the event as "completely ridiculous". Menuhin, clearly, could neither swing nor improvise to save his life, but on the other hand he was certainly not pretending to, merely opening himself up to a new musical experience and providing some entertainment at the same time. Whatever the artistic merits of the venture, it was a huge success with the public. The chattering classes could hardly stop talking about it and the record industry, which was just beginning to discover the potential for crossover musical ventures, took note. EMI produced what was to be the first of a long series of hit records of the two violinists. For Grappelli it was both financially lucrative and remarkable publicity.

Who's on Piano?

The second catalyst arose out of a meeting with **Diz Disley**, a Djangophile guitarist with extensive experience, first of the short-lived Skiffle boom and then of the British folk scene. He had been booked as a compere at the 1973 *Cambridge folk festival* and suggested to the organiser that Grappelli, who was performing in London at the time, would make an excellent addition to the bill. It was agreed and the violinist duly arrived, somewhat taken aback by, firstly the prospect of playing in a field (hardly the Hilton, mon dieu!) and secondly at performing for so many young people – very few of whom had heard of him. However, things went better than he could have imagined. The band – two guitars and a bass – was a line-up reminiscent of the Hot Club. It was practically the first time he had played without piano and drums in decades. In fact when originally offered the gig, his first question had been "Who's on piano?" He was somewhat alarmed when told there would be no

Exploring Jazz Violin

piano, he thought he'd escaped the massed guitars for good! However it turned out to be the ideal band to present to a folk audience; they were playing acoustic folk instruments, but playing like demons – as fresh and excited as teenagers, but masterful without being schmaltzy.

They were a huge success and subsequent gigs up and down the country were met with equal acclaim.

From then on there was no holding him back and he toured the world almost non-stop, the only concession to increasing age being that he began to perform seated, rather than standing. He was playing right up until his death in 1997. He had proved himself the total master of his instrument, had become by far the best known player of the jazz violin and freed himself completely from the shadow of his former partner, **Django Reinhardt**.

Grappelli's Playing Style (Post Hot Club – 1939 onwards)

His old-world Gallic charm, unfailing politeness and gentility, his remarkable aura of blissful relaxation and enjoyment when playing all contributed to his popularity with the public, but it was his technique and improvisational skill which made him the envy of every jazz violinist that heard him. The Grappelli that came back to the attention of the public in the 1970s was immeasurably richer in musical vocabulary, tone and fluency. Where before there had been a constant sense of urgency, exploration and excitement, now there was an effortless ease and total self confidence.

With the advent of quality microphones and sound systems, he no longer had the need to force out his music against the opposition of tinkling cutlery or relentlessly chugging guitars.

His tone and intonation were never less than perfect and he developed a love for ballad playing, often adding languorous and dreamy introductions, even to fast numbers. He could now employ a soft, breathy tone, using every subtle nuance of his instrument, even using a mute to further soften his sound.

Many of his early trademark licks were ditched, to be replaced with a much larger and more sophisticated bag of tricks, showing that at least to some extent he was not stuck in the 1930s and had adopted many of the new ideas of jazz's development.

Characteristically, his phrases became longer, often starting out with one extended note, followed by a cascade of shorter ones:

Fig 8.16 **Cascading run**

He could turn on the pressure by using triplets:

Fig 8.17 **Triplet run**

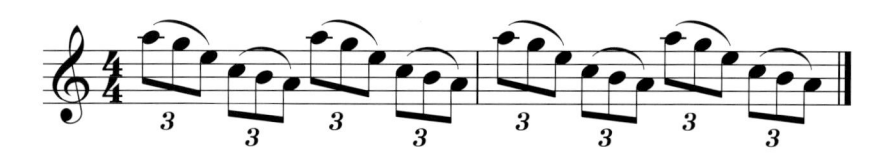

His playing always had a sense of direction, either upwards or downwards. Here's a typical ascending step-pattern:

Fig 8.18 Ascending step-pattern

And here's a favourite descending lick:

Fig 8.19 Descending step-pattern

Chromatic scales are now often in the picture:

Fig 8.20 Descending chromatic run

He could maintain a sense of movement even when 'pedalling' for several bars on a single note – something he was particularly fond of doing on the root note in the key of G. Here, there's just a hint of a ghost note from the D:

Fig 8.21 Pedalling on a single note

In his early recordings there were occasional parallel 5th phrases. In this period they are much more common and more sophisticated. Sometimes just a couple of notes are very effective. If you choose the lower note as the melody, 'inside' note, the upper one will often be something interesting and adventurous. Here on a Gm chord, the lower note is the 5th of the chord, making the upper note a 9th.

Fig 8.22 Parallel 5ths 1

Exploring Jazz Violin

Over a C⁷ this D and A combination gives a big fat 9th and 6th harmony to the chord:

Fig 8.23 Parallel 5ths 2

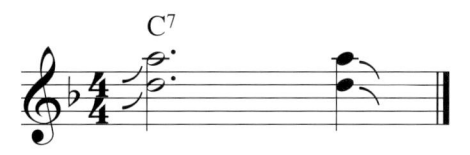

The same notes will work over a chord of G, and would therefore be the 5th and 9th. You may be wondering whether or not you have to work out in your head what relationship these notes are going to have to the chord before you play a parallel 5th lick. Not a bit of it. So long as the lower note is part of a logical melodic sequence – that is to say, it's a note you'd be happy to play on its own – the 5th above will always sound good, whether it's 'in' or not.

Here's one mostly on just the root and 5th, but enlivened by a chopping rhythm:

Fig 8.24 Parallel 5ths 3

Parallel 5ths work well in chromatic runs, always sounding more difficult than they really are (and don't we all want to achieve that!)

Fig 8.25 Parallel 5ths 4

Here, a blues scale is thrown into the mix for good measure:

Fig 8.26 Parallel 5ths 5

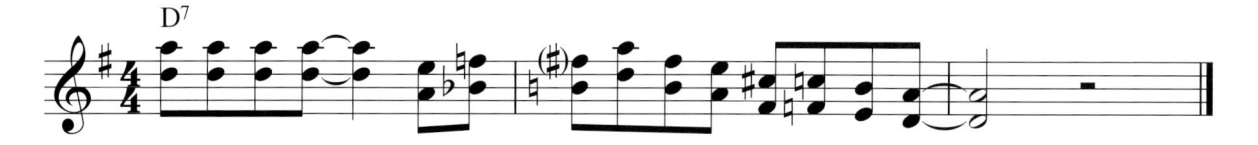

8: Stéphane Grappelli

Grappelli's single slide up to and down from the flattened 3rd is now rarely heard, instead he uses more stylish blues phrases. He makes more use of the flattened 5th note, such as in phrases like this:

Fig 8.27 Flattened 5th phrase

Or he uses both the flattened 5th and flattened 3rd, effectively playing a minor pentatonic over a major chord:

Fig 8.28 Blues scale lick

Here's a strident double stop with a flattened 3rd placed over a 5th:

Fig 8.29 Sliding double stop (flattened 3rd over 5th)

And here's the root placed over a 6th.

Fig 8.30 Root over 6th

Grappelli certainly never became a bebop player, but from the late 40s onwards he began to sprinkle his playing liberally with spicy flattened 9ths, frequently tagging them onto a dominant chord just before returning to the tonic. On a descending run down to the note G, an A♭ always works a treat:

Fig 8.31 Flattened 9th riff

Exploring Jazz Violin

There would often be two flattened 9ths in quick succession:

Fig 8.32 Twin flattened 9th riff

Or even three. This now amounts to an A♭ arpeggio over the chord of G:

Fig 8.33 Triple flattened 9th riff

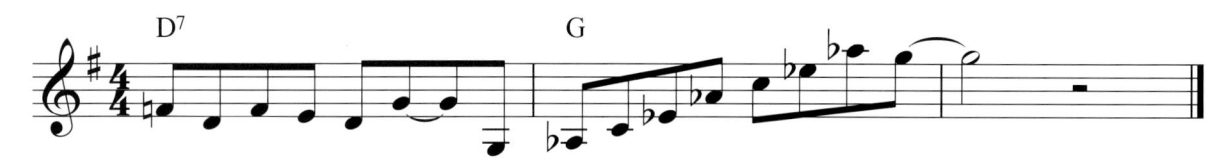

Here a sharpened 9th (notated enharmonically as the flattened 10th) makes a rare appearance along with the flattened 9th :

Fig 8.34 Flattened 9th, sharpened 9th

There's a little 'up and down' scale that would often make an appearance when playing in the keys of B♭ or F. It consists of a tone, semitone, and a tone.

It's function isn't always clear, but here it's emphasising the flattened 7th:

Fig 8.35 Flattened 7th scale

8: Stéphane Grappelli

Here it is extended into a diminished scale, again emphasising the flattened 9th and sharpened 9th (of C7):

Fig 8.36 Diminished scale

Sometimes he would throw caution to the wind with a wide interval lick like this, which defies description or explanation, beyond the fact that it makes a good finger pattern.

Fig 8.37 4-1-0, 4-1-0 lick

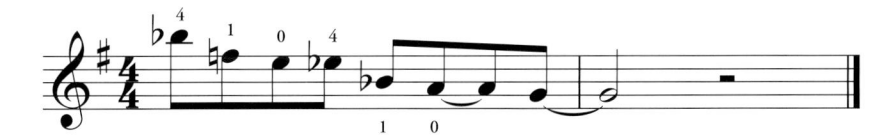

This one ascends in 4ths and is so 'outside', it could have been played over almost any chord. It's literally *Star Trek* territory – cue the theremin!

Fig 8.38 Ascending 4ths

Another area where he went from a small step to a giant leap was harmonics. Where before he was content with a tight little group of three harmonics on one string, in his later years he began to toss them around like Zimbabwe dollars.

Fig 8.39 Repeated harmonics 1

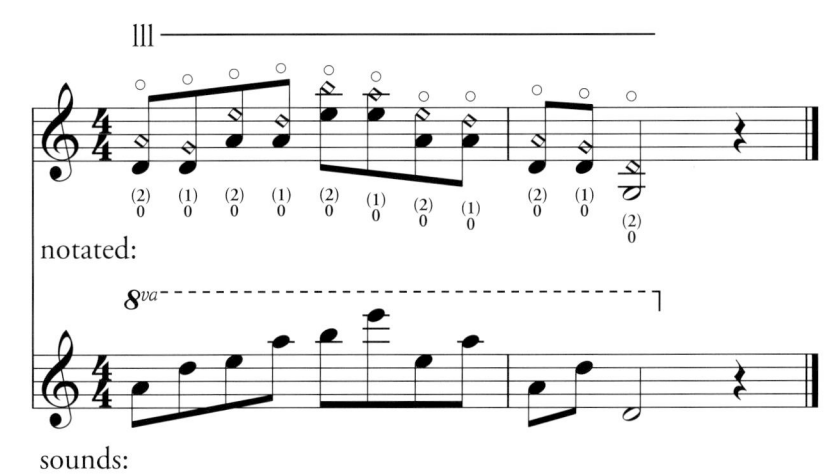

notated:

sounds:

Exploring Jazz Violin

It's all played in 3rd position with the second and first fingers. This three-string pattern would work in the keys of C or G. For the keys of A or D it would be:

Fig 8.40 Repeated harmonics 2

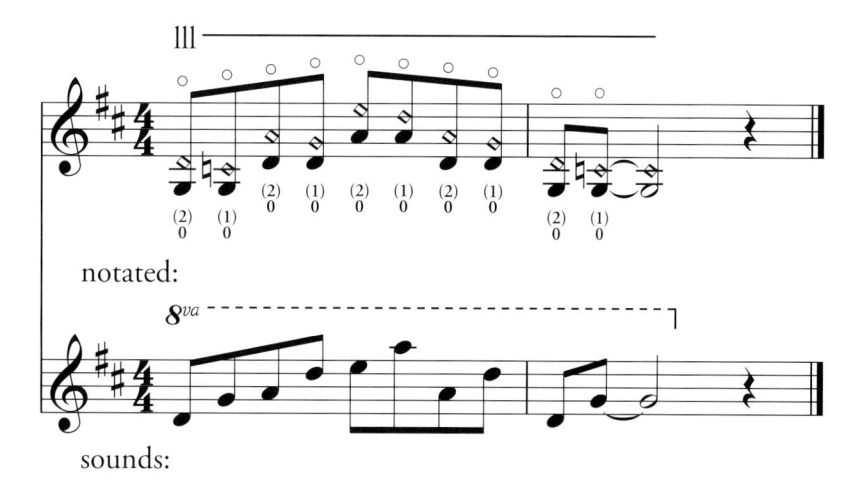

Here's a tune which we can use to try out some Grappelli licks, followed by a solo version.

8: Stéphane Grappelli

Swing Parisienne (head)

Chris Haigh

Medium swing ♩ = 145

Exploring Jazz Violin

Swing Parisienne (solo version)

Chris Haigh

8: Stéphane Grappelli

Bars 1–8

The solo kicks off with the classic slide up to and down from the "little blue note" – the flattened 3rd. Bar 2 runs up to the E string so that you can play the same riff again, an octave higher in bar 3. In bar 4 we go into a slide up to the harmonic in the middle of the E string. A series of rolling phrases descend for two bars, followed by a flurry of ascending triplets in bar 7, topped off with a parallel 5ths chromatic run-down in bar 8.

Bars 9–16

Bar 9 opens with more parallel 5ths, this time with a chop rhythm that develops into a descending blues phrase. The same chops are repeated in bar 11, then a run up to the 0-1-4 finger-pattern lick on the E string in bar 13. The E♭ in bar 14 sees a return of the sliding flattened 3rd (this is the chord of C being anticipated), then a long C and a well-earned rest.

Bars 17–24

The bridge (bar 17), opens with a sliding parallel 5th on the 6th and 9th of C7, then Grappelli's little 'up and down' scale over the F in bar 19. In bars 21–22 there's a fast triplet run over the D7 and then a 'pedalling' phrase on the G7.

Bars 25–32

Bar 25 has a couple of smooth, flowing blues phrases followed in bar 27 by 3rd position harmonics and then flattened 9ths in bar 28 over the Dm7 and G7 chords. The E7 at bar 29 allows you to slip in the 'wide interval' (4-1, 4-1) finger lick. Bar 30 has a full-speed-ahead descending scale of semiquavers (you may have to spend some time on this bar until it runs smoothly off the fingers). A couple of relaxed blues phrases finish the solo on fine style. Vive La France!

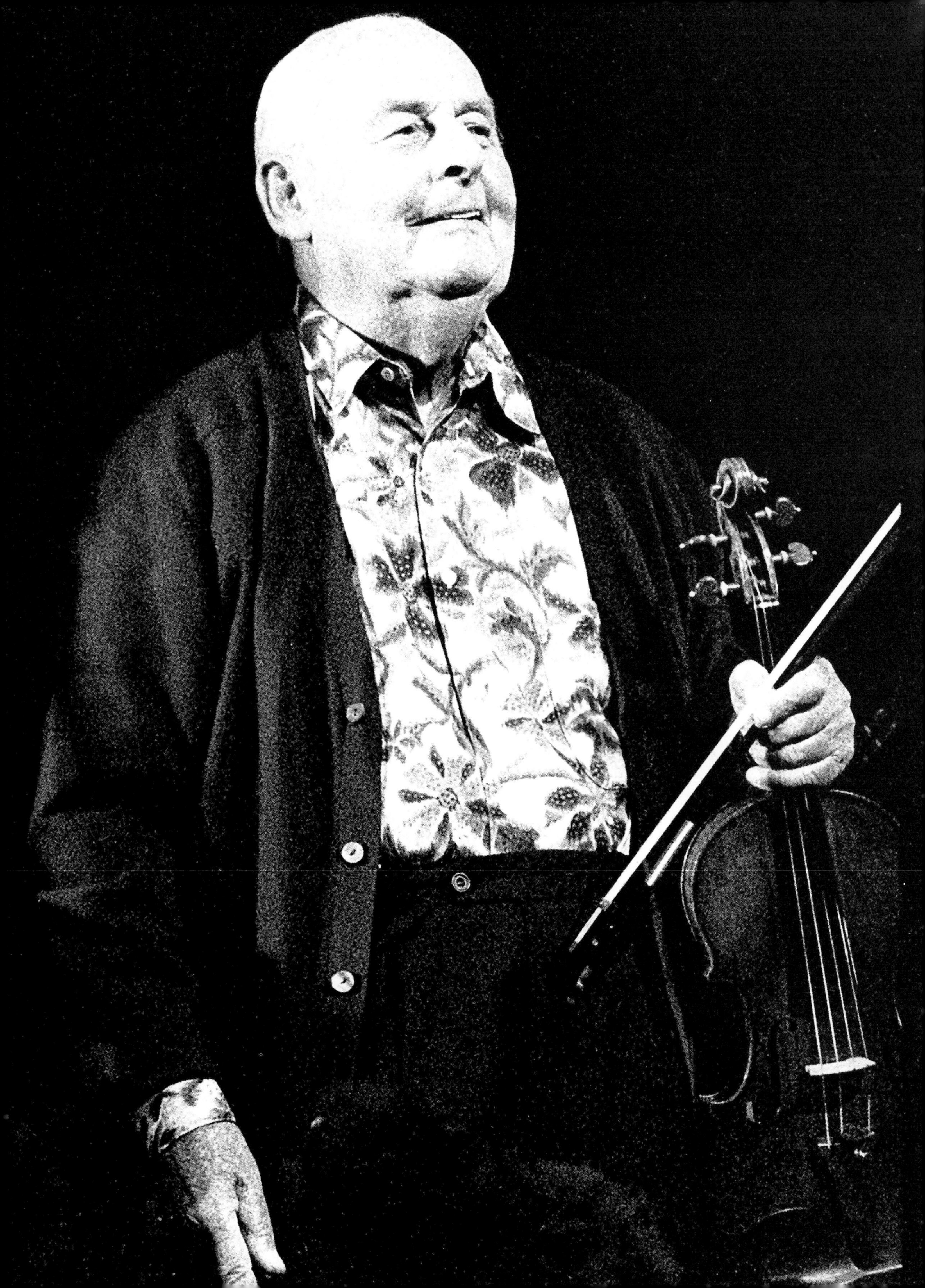

9: Running Wild

So far we have looked at Venuti, Grappelli and Smith – all swing players with a style based in the 1930s and 40s. In this next chapter we will look at the work of more modern players, influenced by bebop, modal and fusion music of the 50s and beyond. Chief among these is **Jean-Luc Ponty**.

Jean-Luc Ponty

The first time I heard **Jean-Luc Ponty** was in the mid 70s on the album *King Kong*, his collaboration with **Frank Zappa**. From the first bar of his entry I knew that this was something special and like nothing I'd heard before.

100% Bebop

He started out as a classical violinist, studying at the Paris Conservatoire, coming out with a technique and qualifications which immediately landed him a job with a major French symphony orchestra. His father had also taught him the clarinet and, with nothing more in mind than the hope of picking up girls, he began playing this in a local college jazz band. He found this an interesting and very different challenge from classical violin playing and, with a new-found interest in the music of **John Coltrane** and **Miles Davis**, he also took up the sax.

This would probably have remained a harmless hobby had he not, one night in 1958, gone to see a jazz gig by the veteran New Orleans clarinettist **Albert Nicholas**. He was so fired up by the performance that towards the end he asked if he could sit in with the band. However, he had neither clarinet nor sax with him, only the violin, since he had just come from an orchestral concert. He launched into playing without having given any thought to how it would sound. The effect was immediate and astounding, and no one was more surprised than him when people stopped dancing in order to listen to him. Ponty was not even aware at this point that there were other people playing jazz on the violin.

To someone raised in the cosy, safe and elegant world of **Stéphane Grappelli**, this was like an axe coming through the front door – alarming, stark and brazen. At this stage Ponty had already undergone a remarkable musical adventure.

He soon discovered **Stuff Smith** and **Stéphane Grappelli**. When he was introduced to Grappelli, the two became friends, but it was the tough and visceral playing of the American **Stuff Smith** that inspired him more. Ponty was much more interested in modern jazz and was encouraged by the fact that, on the violin, he seemed to have that field to himself. When I asked him how he made such a complete transition from classical to jazz player with apparent ease, he told me:

"When I played jazz on sax or clarinet, I was always thinking notes, phrases and rhythm, never thinking about my instrument and I did exactly the same with violin, immersing myself completely in the music without thinking how to hold the bow or which part of it I should use etc., it was totally intuitive. But honestly, I had forgotten how I played when I started until Polygram reissued my first solo album 'Jazz Long Playing' on CD in the late 90s. It surprised me, perhaps as much as you……(laughs) ….that in 1964, four years after I finished my classical studies, I sounded 100% bebop, no hint of classical training and no vibrato at all."

Exploring Jazz Violin

This was an outstanding debut album, a mature and masterful exposition of bebop violin, showing the world once and for all that the violin was as capable as the sax or trumpet of playing modern jazz. He was clearly thinking of lines more as a wind player than a violinist; sweetness and sentimentality were certainly not part of his style. I asked him whether his use of modern jazz harmony – the use of flat 9^{ths}, augmented and diminished scales and so on – was based on a study of jazz theory, or whether he played more by ear:

"By ear. There were no jazz schools in those days, no place to learn jazz theory. But I studied classical harmony for one year as I was preparing to study classical composing, which I gave up as soon as I started playing jazz and it probably helped with improvisation. Also I grew up hearing and playing the music of Debussy, Stravinsky, Messiaen etc. and their complex chords were registered in my brain I guess. But I never prepared improvisations in a scientific way and always improvised by ear in those days. I still do, except when chord progressions are extremely unusual, then I must figure out which notes fit or not until I can improvise without thinking about the chords anymore."

Ponty meets Zappa

In 1966 he was invited to perform at the Violin Summit in Basel, Switzerland, alongside Grappelli, **Stuff Smith** and **Svend Asmussen**. Though a newcomer, he gave an explosive performance and more than held his own; Smith commented: *"Keep an eye on this youngster, he is a killer!"* Several more solo albums followed, including an excellent live recording called *Trio HLP* in 1968 of a performance at the Cameleon Club in Paris, with organ and drums. On these tracks, all cutting-edge bebop, you can hear Ponty's early use of amplification – a contact mic attached to the body of the violin. It's a powerful, round and mellow sound full of low frequencies and ideally suited to his music.

"I was using a DeArmond violin pickup made in the U.S……easy to remember because it was the only decent one available at the time, Stuff Smith also used it…..and even Grappelli who played amplified in those days. Not that great, but it could sound warm depending where it was put on the table of the violin, it also had a volume control on it."

John Lewis (pianist with the **Modern Jazz Quartet**) heard about Ponty playing at the violin summit, and invited him to perform at the Monterey Jazz festival in California in 1967. The performance was a big success and Ponty was signed to the World Pacific record label. He began playing with the young pianist **George Duke**, with whom he struck up a great musical rapport. The two were introduced to the archetypal Californian psychedelic hippy rock star **Frank Zappa**, who was looking for musicians of high technical competence to play the challenging new material he was writing.

Ponty played on one track on the *Hot Rats* album (which also featured some outstanding playing from fellow violinist **Sugarcane Harris**) and Zappa was so excited by Ponty's playing that he asked him to collaborate with him on his next album, *King Kong*. This was a rambling and experimental mix of **Stravinsky**, jazz, funk and rock, which gave Ponty free rein to stretch out on some long solos, mostly over single chord modal grooves. To someone who had disciplined himself to play over the complex changes of bebop, this must have been like being let out of school early to run wild in the playground. His tenure with Zappa was brief but valuable, bringing his name to a wider public than could ever have happened in jazz circles.

A second Zappa album, *Electric Connection*, followed and some touring with the **Mothers of Invention**, but this was not a marriage made in heaven. Zappa's fans didn't want to see long, difficult, avant-garde instrumentals, they wanted the wacky and satirical songs for which he was famous, so Ponty hardly got any chance to solo.

He left Zappa, but was soon playing with **John McLaughlin**'s **Mahavishnu Orchestra**, with whom he recorded two albums: *Apocalypse* (1974) and *Visions of the Emerald Beyond* (also 1974).

Cosmic Messenger

He began using electronic effects on his instrument, particularly phasers and delays, giving a warm, fat and distinctive sound that was well suited to the genre. I asked him how he got hold of these effects, many of which were new to the market, and he told me:

"People like Tom Oberheim would bring their prototypes (of effects pedals) to famous musicians like Frank. These were the first sound effects small enough to be used on stage…..and the whole band tried them. This is how I got the first Maestro phase shifter. It continued while I was with Mahavishnu and even after I started my band in 1975."

He was by now using a Barcus Berry electric violin; the baritone and later 5-string models allowed him to play in a low register so that he could play in unison with sax or guitar lines. He dropped many of his bebop inflections – the flattened and sharpened 9ths, and dissonant double stops for example, opting for a more melodic and relaxed style. He also picked up a liking for deep, spiritual and meaningful song and album titles.

This was all instrumental music and much more suited to Ponty. By this time he was adapting to the new jazz / rock / fusion environment.

From 1975 onwards he produced a long series of albums under his own name, with titles such as *Enigmatic Ocean* and *Cosmic Messenger*. Many of these were superb flights of fantasy and were tight, funky and imaginative. One of his finest and most popular tunes was 'New Country' from his 1975 *Imaginary Voyage* album; a snappy country-tinged number featuring some super-fast staccato bowing.

Since the 90s he has taken a change of direction, moving from moody, dense electronic textures towards a cleaner, more acoustic sound, and, since the 1991 *Tchokola* album, incorporating African rhythms into his sound. Five decades of recording have given us a huge wealth of Ponty material to listen to and compare. Certain features of his playing have altered markedly over the years as he moved from bebop to jazz fusion. However, other elements have remained constant and there are many melodic, harmonic and rhythmic approaches as well as individual motifs which are instantly recognizable.

One such idea is the descending pattern, typically built on a three-note motif:

Fig 9.1 Descending lick 1

The golden age for this particular lick was the *King Kong* and *Electric Connection* period. The individual three-note motif is tightly rhythmic, but the timing of the overall phrase is usually very free; the length may vary from two to six repetitions of the three-note motif. In the above example the notes outline an arpeggio, but it is often more of a scale:

Exploring Jazz Violin

Fig 9.2 Descending lick 2 (scale version)

It can take different shapes:

Fig 9.3 Descending lick 3 (scale with alternative pattern)

It can be more slurred:

Fig 9.4 Descending lick 4 (slurred)

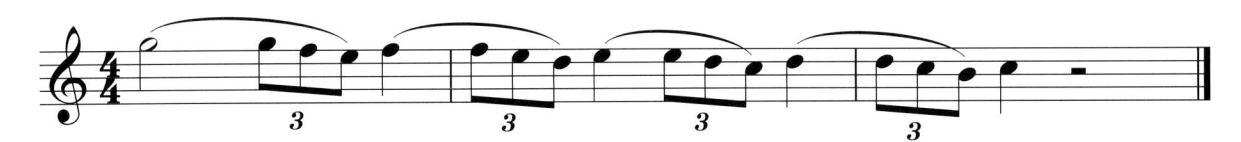

Or less slurred:

Fig 9.5 Descending lick 5 (no slurs)

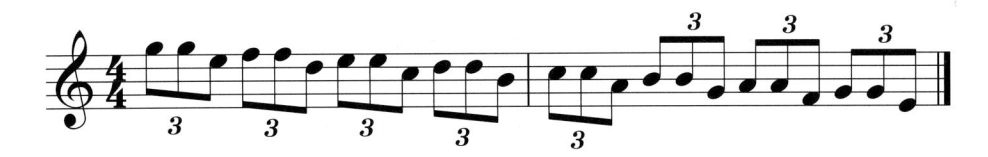

Sometimes the three notes within the motif are connected by slides, up and down, giving an almost Indian effect:

Fig 9.6 Descending lick 6 (slides)

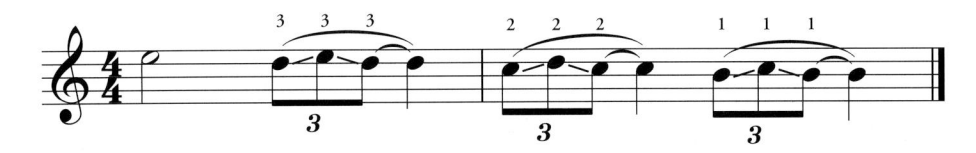

This kind of scale is particularly effective in modal tunes, where a single chord may last for eight bars, or even eight minutes.

But Ponty also makes use of them over changes of chord where the scale will change partway through:

Fig 9.7 Descending lick 7 (over chord changes)

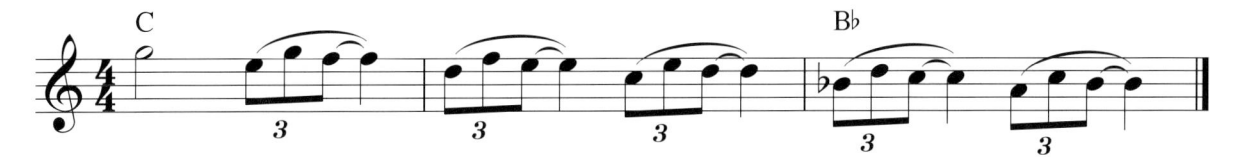

Ponty also creates an element of surprise by changing it suddenly to a whole-tone scale:

Fig 9.8 Descending lick 8 (changing to whole-tone scale)

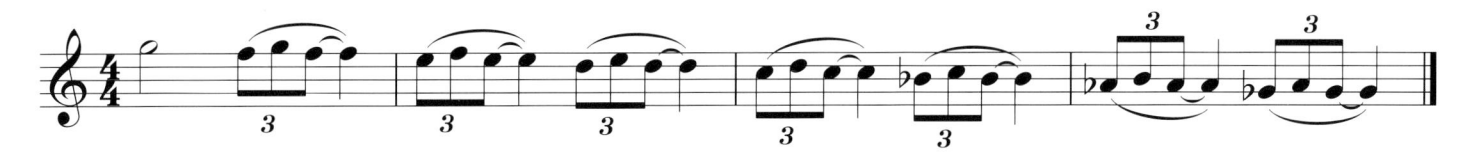

Whole-tone scales are a common feature of Ponty's improvisations. They will usually start with part of a conventional scale which has two whole tones anyway. So an E^7 chord could lead into:

Fig 9.9 Whole-tone scale

This is following the rule we established earlier about playing 'outside'. Start 'inside' to set up a firm harmonic anchor for the phrase, then move outside with some confidence that you're going to sound as if you know what you're doing. With Ponty, you're never in any doubt.

Here's a couple more three-note descending patterns using a whole tone scale. (Notice that I've indicated some of the accidentals as flats, and some as sharps. I'm not just being sloppy – it makes it clearer which fingering is more appropriate.)

Fig 9.10 Whole-tone scale 2

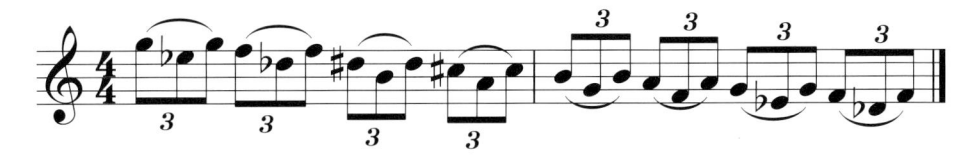

Fig 9.11 Whole-tone scale 3

Exploring Jazz Violin

The augmented descending arpeggio also makes an appearance, starting with the 3rd of the chord, then the tonic, augmented 5th and the 3rd (here the pitches are enharmonically written to illustrate the major 3rd intervals that form the augmented sound):

Fig 9.12 Augmented descending arpeggio

Here's a lick that demonstrates a very strange property – two separate whole-tone scales descending like twisted staircases in an **Escher** painting.

Fig 9.13 Twin whole-tone descending scales

Enough of whole-tone scales. Ponty often goes in for very fast triplet runs:

Fig 9.14 Triplet runs

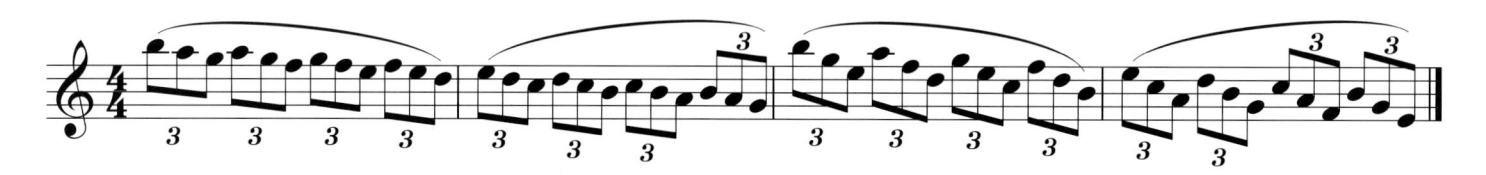

In case you were getting a certain sinking feeling, here's a couple of ascending runs for a change. The second of these is based on a pentatonic scale:

Fig 9.15 Ascending riffs

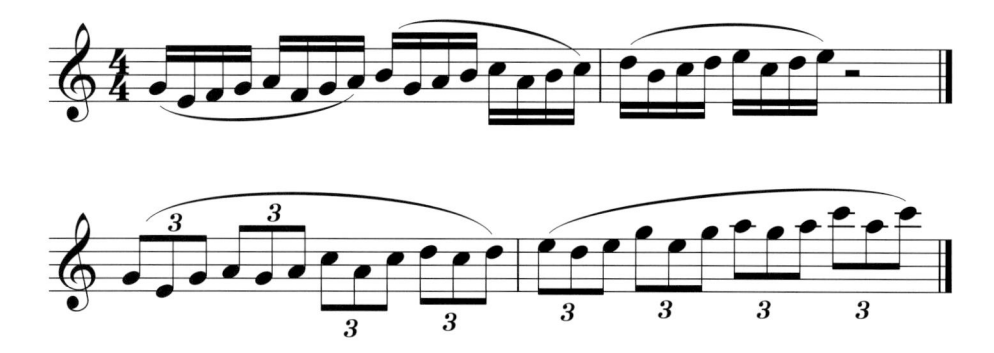

Repeated three-note riffs are a common device:

Fig 9.16 Repeated three-note riff 1

Sometimes the upper notes will alternate:

Fig 9.17 Repeated three-note riff 2 (alternating)

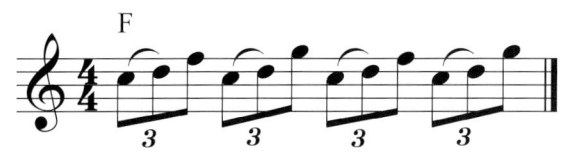

Sometimes it's very bluesy:

Fig 9.18 Repeated three-note riff 3 (bluesy)

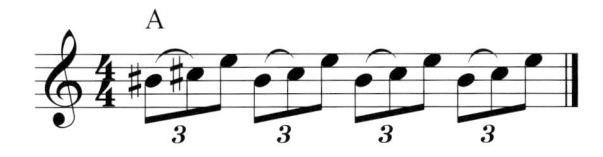

Sometimes the pattern is elaborated:

Fig 9.19 Repeated three-note riff 4 (elaborated)

This three-note pattern is often the launching pad for some outside playing. If there are no open strings involved, it's an easy matter to shift the whole thing up a semitone and then down again:

Fig 9.20 Three-note riff (leading to outside)

This inside-outside-inside idea also crops up with four-note arpeggio phrases with a major 7th shape. This pattern moves from 1st to 2nd position and back:

Fig 9.21 Major 7th arpeggio riff (leading to outside)

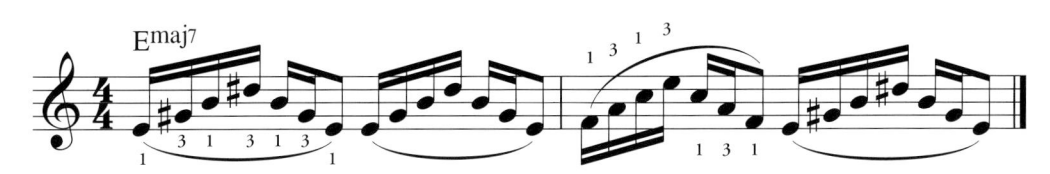

Exploring Jazz Violin

Or with a minor 7th arpeggio:

Fig 9.22 Minor 7th arpeggio riff (leading to outside)

Fast, semiquaver, ostinati-type figures often make an appearance. Play this one in 3rd position:

Fig 9.23 Semiquaver ostinato 1

A more accented variation would be:

Fig 9.24 Semiquaver ostinato 2 (accented)

Here the ostinato takes the predictable upward step:

Fig 9.25 Semiquaver ostinato 3 (shifted upwards)

A couple of points to bear in mind when approaching these kind of phrases. Firstly, make sure your initial lick doesn't have any open strings. If it does it'll be a lot harder to shift it. Secondly, you don't need to work out what the notes will be when it shifts up, or how they will relate to the chord – some will be inside, others outside. Throw caution to the wind!

Instead of coming safely back to land, the lick will sometimes take off, like an out-of-control skyrocket, ascending not necessarily in neat semitones but in a crazy upward trajectory. At this point the idea of writing the phrase down becomes somewhat arbitrary…

Fig 9.26 **Upward trajectory**

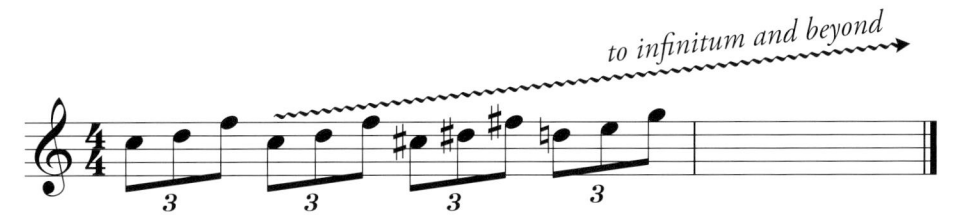

These explosive take-offs are one of the most exciting features of Ponty's playing – possibly inspired by **Stuff Smith**, certainly not by the always-in-control **Stéphane Grappelli**.

Many of Ponty's techniques seem to be a deliberate attempt to move away from the thin, clean sound that the violin is normally associated with to the fatter, dirtier sound of the sax or electric guitar.

One such technique is the doubling of a note using an open string.

At its simplest, this is an open string played with the same note stopped (played normally). Play the stopped note with the second finger in 3rd position. In the example below, if the stopped E is played perfectly in tune, little would be gained. But if you slide up to the stopped E, a dissonance is created:

Fig 9.27 **Double E riff – upward slide**

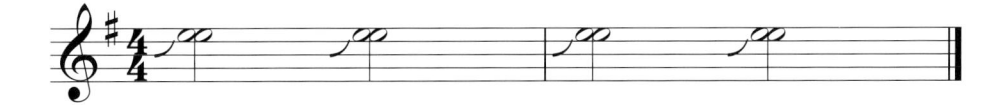

These sustained double notes work particularly well if they are the 6th or 9th of the chord they are being played over; the 'double E riff' would therefore be ideal for over a chord of G or D major. The stopped note can also be slid down, creating a plaintive wail:

Fig 9.28 **Double E riff – downward slide**

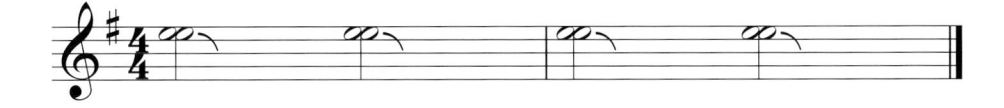

You can introduce other notes, particularly those harmonically close to the drone:

Fig 9.29 **Drone riff**

Exploring Jazz Violin

These phrases are often powerful rhythmic chops:

Fig 9.30 Drone with chops

It can also provide a launch-pad for another crazy take-off – the note on the lower string (the stopped note) can slide up while the drone of the open string stays the same, the bow meanwhile hammering away like an AK47. Go easy on licks like this if you're playing at a dinner dance!

Fig 9.31 Chromatic ascending chops with drone

Ponty also makes widespread use of double stops to create ear-grabbing intervals. They come in a variety of shapes and sizes. A third finger over a first finger gives an interval of a flattened 7th:

Fig 9.32 Flattened 7th double stop

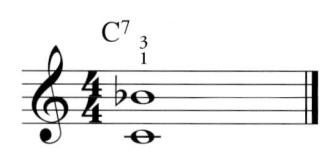

This is played over a C^7 chord, but it would also work in different contexts; over an E♭m chord for example, the lower note would be a raised 6th, the upper note a 5th.

A second finger over a third finger, or a third finger over fourth finger produces an interval of a 4th:

Fig 9.33 Double stopped 4th

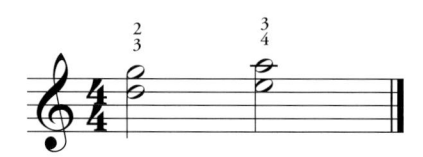

Perhaps the most strident of these double stops is the interval of a 2nd, with the first over a fourth finger shape. The first finger is on the tonic and the fourth finger provides the ear-shredding (inverted) 7th.

Fig 9.34 Inverted-7th double stop

Sometimes several different tricky double stops occur together. The Ponty composition 'Summit Soul', which he premiered at the Violin Summit, is full of patterns like this:

Fig 9.35 Multiple double stops

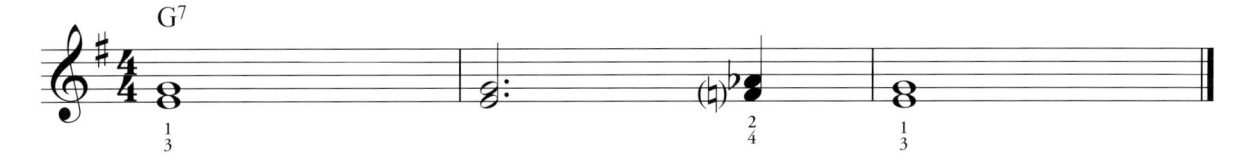

It will come as no surprise that after any of these double stops has been clearly stated, they can be followed by the same shape a semitone up, or sent into orbit on a one way trip.

Another favourite double stop is the octave. This is the hardest to play in tune, particularly when a whole lick is made up of octaves. The all-pervading descending sequence is shown here in octaves:

Fig 9.36 Descending octave riff

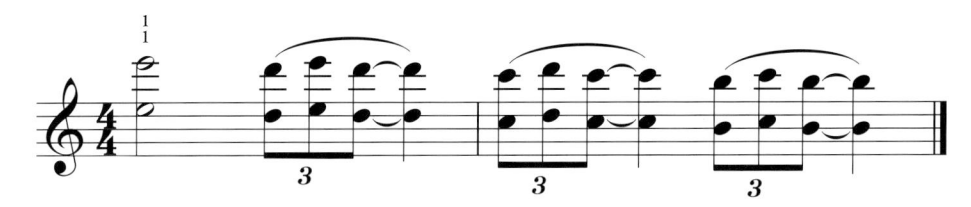

In a lick like the above, the triplets have to be slurred, which means sliding the hand up and down for each consecutive note change. No one said this was going to be easy! Octaves can also be used for rhythmic chop patterns, sometimes so aggressive they sound like frenzied knife attacks.

Finally, note alterations such as the flattened or sharpened 9th were part of Ponty's stock-in-trade during his bebop period. Here you get them together twice in the same lick:

Fig 9.37 Altered notes

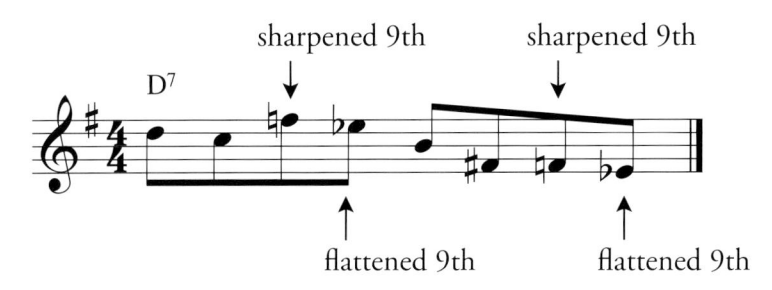

Here's a tune and short solo in mid-70s vintage **Jean-Luc Ponty** style:

Exploring Jazz Violin

Cosmic Voyager

Chris Haigh

The Head

The melody is a simple 4-bar phrase which is repeated three times over a 12-bar blues.

Bars 13–24

We launch into the solo at bar 13 with a double D riff, played in 3rd position. Slide up the second finger each time until it matches the open D string. This off-the-beat phrase alternates with a flourish that uses flattened 3rds and 7ths in bars 14 and 16.

At bar 17 we get an three-note ostinato figure repeated three times, which is then taken up a semitone (and therefore outside the chord). At bar 19 our opening rhythm is repeated, but this time with octave As. Bar 21 begins the 'twisted' whole-tone scale pattern, while bars 23 and 24 have a minor pentatonic pattern ascending over two octaves to a high D.

Bars 25–36

The next chorus starts on the same note and proceeds down in a classic Ponty-style, three-note-motif sequence. The first three motifs (in bars 25 and 26) have a slide up and down – use just one finger for this. The pattern continues but the rhythm changes in bars 27 and 28, and in bars 29 and 30 it becomes a whole-tone scale.

In bar 31 we return to the same figure as bar 13, we then switch to 3rd position for a high octave Ds. In bar 33, give it all the speed you've got until you reach escape velocity and slide all the way up to the high A.

Assignment

You may have found the solo example hard to read – Ponty-style rhythms are often complex and writing them down robs them of their fluidity and spontaneity. A more fruitful approach might be to take each of the licks described in the previous section, change the key where necessary and play them repeatedly over the backing for 'Cosmic Voyager', allowing the rhythm and timing to become flexible.

Any of the licks will bear repetition and most will work when shifted up a semitone. You may also find it difficult to place these kind of licks in their proper context without hearing Ponty's playing. Listen to a selection of his recordings, particularly from the late 60s to mid 70s and it will all start to make sense.

Didier Lockwood

On the planet Kobaïa, far into the future, settlers from the doomed Earth have taken refuge from the ecological and sociological mayhem of the home planet. Such is the legend told by **Magma**, the French prog-rock band formed in 1969 by the demented visionary **Christian Vander**. His 40-year Wagnerian space opera, still very much alive to this day, is all the more remarkable for being sung entirely in the umlaut-infested and totally impregnable alien language of Kobaïan. Such was the unlikely springboard for one of Europe's finest jazz violinists, **Stoht Malawelekaahm**, or to give him his Earth name, **Didier Lockwood.**

Lockwood was born in 1956 and studied violin and composition at the Calais Conservatoire. He developed a fine technique, but found the discipline of classical music too stifling. At the age of 14 he broke his arm and was unable to play for six months. During this time he listened to a lot of rock and blues artists such as **John Mayall** and **Jimi Hendrix**, and decided he wanted to take a different direction with his music. This six-month period was the opportunity he needed to break the link between reading and playing – a transition which many classical players find so difficult. In 1972 he quit his studies; by now he had heard **Jean-Luc Ponty**'s *King Kong* album and knew that jazz-fusion was his new raison d'être.

It was soon after this that he joined **Magma**, a big name in France in the early 70s, he stayed with them for three years; his work in this period can be best heard on the 1975 album *Magma Live*. This was also the year that Lockwood appeared for the first time at the Montreux Jazz Festival; here he met **Stéphane Grappelli**, who was now riding high on his revived career. Grappelli was struck by the young man's talent and invited him to come on tour with him, joining him for the last few numbers of each concert. Grappelli considered him almost as his adopted Grandson and gave him a great deal of encouragement.

In 1977 Lockwood joined the **Magma** off-shoot **Zao**, another experimental jazz-fusion band in the **Weather Report** mould. He then formed **Surya**, a jazz-rock band much influenced by early 70s Ponty.

Didier's Style

In terms of his range of expression, **Didier Lockwood** is virtually unique in the jazz violin world. He is at home anywhere in the spectrum of rock, jazz-rock and jazz-fusion, and has mastered the use of electronic effects including phaser, delay, wah and distortion. He can play faultless bebop to a level only ever matched by the earliest Ponty recordings; 'Don't Drive So Fast' on the 1995 *New York Rendezvous* album will take your breath away.

He ventures successfully into avant-garde and almost free music, such as on the spine-tingling 'Spirits of

1979 was a good year: he released his first solo album *New World* and had a series of tour de force performances. These ranged from hard-bop to jazz-rock, including a breakneck version of **John Coltrane**'s notoriously difficult workout 'Giant Steps', **Sonny Rollins**'s 'Pent Up House' (which he had frequently played with Grappelli) and 'Zbiggy', a tune he wrote in memory of the recently departed Polish cutting-edge violinist **Zbigniew Seifert**.

In the same year Lockwood was also presented with the Warlop violin. This was an instrument **Michel Warlop** had originally given to Grappelli in 1937 when he realized that his friend and former employee was the better jazz violinist. Grappelli in turn handed it on to **Jean-Luc Ponty** – a tradition had evolved with the violin being presented to the most promising new French jazz violinist.

A series of further albums followed under his own name – all melodic, bouncy and accessible material, mostly with keyboard, electric guitar, bass and drums. In 1999 he produced a beautiful acoustic gypsy jazz album *A Tribute to Stéphane Grappelli*, who had died two years previously. Particularly spectacular on this album are the slow ballads, 'Nuages' and 'Misty'. In 2001 he established his own jazz school, the CMDL (Centre Musique Didier Lockwood), where he takes a personal interest in the teaching.

the Forest' on his 1996 album *Storyboard*. He can play delicate, elegant and very French music, as he showed on the 2006 *Waltz Club* album with accordionist **Marcel Azzola**. Perhaps the area where he shines most brightly is on acoustic ballads where he displays a sensual, breathy tone and uses every kind of harmonics known to man. The 32-bar solo on 'Nuages' from his tribute to Grappelli would bring tears to the eyes of a Marseille dockworker.

Unlike certain other French jazz violinists I could name, **Didier Lockwood**'s playing is virtually free from clichés and it is difficult to find phrases which characterize his playing. One consistent and enviable aspect of Lockwood's playing is his use, where appropriate, of an extremely soft, breathy tone with a rich palette of harmonics.

Can you remember back to those first few painful weeks (months?, decades?) when you were trying to make your instrument sound like a violin rather than a drowning cat? There were two problems with the bow. If you pressed too hard or moved too slowly it would squawk like a chicken. Too little pressure, or too much movement, and you would get a whistle instead of a clean note. There can be great beauty in imperfection, and this is the sound we're looking for.

Play a single long A note on the G string. Look at your right hand and feel the downward pressure that your first finger is applying to the bow. Control of this pressure is what Lockwood refers to as his 'secret weapon' and gives him his unique sound. Keep playing that note, but reduce the pressure. You'll start to hear less pure note and more bow 'noise'.

But mixed in with this noise you will hear an array of harmonics and overtones – notes higher than the one you're fingering – which are constantly changing as your pressure alters. Now, keeping that low pressure to maintain the ghostly whispers, try playing the following. (If you have difficulty maintaining the tone, move your bow closer to the bridge.)

Whispers

Demo 59

Chris Haigh

© 2010 Schott Music Ltd, London

Now comes the difficult bit. You might think this style of playing is going to be all vague, new age and wishy-washy. Not a bit of it. Lockwood combines these soft notes with a very hard-edged, precise articulation, controlled again from that first finger of the right hand.

Play 'Whispers' again, but this time make every bow an up bow, and do *all* of the bow movement with your wrist and fingers. Your upper arm should be no more than twitching. If you can remember all the way back to chapter 1, we tried the 'endless bowing', where the bow acts like a spring, jumping back into position after every note, so that your arm doesn't have to move, no matter how many up bows you play. You probably tried it for a few minutes, decided it didn't quite work and then moved on. Slapped wrist! This is a *very* valuable skill and will amply repay the many hours that I'm sure you now intend to spend on practising it. Listen carefully to **Didier Lockwood**'s recording of 'Minor Swing' on his *A Tribute to Stéphane Grappelli* album.

Another closely related aspect of Lockwood's playing is his use of slides, which he probably uses more than any of the other leading brands of jazz violinist, some are subtle, some exaggerated. Another feature of his playing is the way he will often close a ballad, with a soft ascending scale, going up several octaves to the very top of the E string.

Michal Urbaniak

In a similar league and jazz-fusion ball game to Lockwood and Ponty is the Polish-American violinist **Michal Urbaniak**. Born in Warsaw in 1943, he learned classical violin and jazz saxophone at school. From 1962 to 69 he worked with various bands as a sax player on successful tours in Scandinavia and the U.S. He then returned temporarily to Poland and, perhaps inspired by the early success of Ponty, transferred his attention back to the violin. He formed the **Michal Urbaniak Group**, playing electric jazz-fusion and in 1971, at the Montreux Festival, was awarded the 'Grand Prix' for the best soloist, he was also offered a scholarship to Berklee College in Boston.

In 1973 he emigrated to the U.S., but chose not to take up his place at Berklee, as he was too busy with the continued success of his career. As well as performing with his own groups, Urbaniak has also worked with many of the big names in American jazz, among them **Weather Report**, **Herbie Hancock**, **Freddie Hubbard** and **Chick Corea**.

His biggest inspiration in jazz has always been **Miles Davis** and he can hardly have been more delighted when Miles, seeing Urbaniak on TV one night, is reported to have demanded *"Give me this Polish fiddler, he's got that sound!"* The two met up and Urbaniak performed on the song 'Don't Lose Your Mind' on Miles's 1984 *Tutu* album. In 2009 he released *Miles of Blue*, a tribute to Miles, incorporating aspects of urban, hip hop and rap which had been increasingly influential on Urbaniak in recent decades. He plays various electric violins – including a 5-string violectra, and he sometimes uses the 'talking violin' – a kind of synthesizer which enables him to shape the sound of his instrument with a microphone near his lips. You can hear the effect on 'Fall' on the *Miles of Blue* album.

L. Shankar

Finally, we have to mention **Lakshminarayanan Shankar**, also known as the more easily pronounced **L. Shankar**, for whom four strings are not nearly enough and of whose style, all analysis or imitation is futile. Born into a family of musicians in Southern India, he mastered the Carnatic tradition of classical improvisation.

When he moved to the USA in 1969 he soon found himself working with guitarist **John McLaughlin** in a groundbreaking east-west fusion band called **Shakti**. What followed was a dazzling career including Grammies, film scores and collaborations with a host of rock stars. His technique is nothing less than mind-blowing and his separation from mere mortals of the violin world was emphasized in 1980 when he unleashed his ten-string, double-necked electric violin, with a range going all the way down to the double bass. If he ever sits in on your jam session, I suggest you beat a hasty retreat!

10: Other Styles, Other Players

We have spent most of this book looking at the core of the mainstream jazz technique and theory. In this section we take a brief look at some of the many sub-genres that make jazz so fascinating; from gypsy jazz to bebop and from modal and Latin to free jazz.

Gypsy Jazz

In many branches of jazz, the violin is seen as something of a pretender, struggling to 'elbow' its way in among the saxes, trumpets and pianos. Not so with gypsy jazz!

But we've spent a whole chapter on **Stéphane Grappelli**. Doesn't that cover gypsy jazz in more than necessary detail? Today the term 'Hot Club' jazz (the music of the **Quintette du Hot Club de France**, of which Grappelli was co-leader with **Django Reinhardt**) is synonymous with the term 'gypsy jazz'. Since Django's death in 1953, gypsy jazz has grown and developed – there are now hundreds of bands worldwide playing this music, many of them Rom (gypsy) and many more still who get their Rom only on CD. In this section we'll look at the gypsy and the east European influence on the music, and see its development in the last half-century.

Gypsies arrived in eastern Europe some time in the middle ages, where they plied their numerous trades, the most prestigious of which was music. Unlike the part-time peasant musicians with whom they came into contact, gypsy musicians did not work the land and were able to play professionally, passing on their skills down the generations. As a result, they have always been valued for the mastery of their instruments. They quickly picked up the local tunes and elaborated them in ways which had never been heard before. They were highly prized by the nobility, not least for the fact that unlike trained, classical players, they did not use notated music but performed directly to the listener. In Hungary in particular, gypsies came to dominate the musical profession.

When the nationalistic fervour of the struggle for liberty from the Hapsburg Empire in the 18th and 19th centuries took hold of Hungarians rich and poor, it was the gypsies who were performing the freedom songs and manning the bands which enticed young men into the army. Soon every czardas (village inn), city restaurant and chandeliered ballroom had its own gypsy band. These groups often comprised of: accordion, cymbalom (a kind of hammered dulcimer), guitar, clarinet, bass or cello and, particularly in Russia, a singer, but generally speaking it was the violinist who ran the band, got all the glory and most of the money.

Among the stylistic embellishments used by the gypsy fiddlers were harmonics, slides, trills and 'bird calls' high up on the E string (as in the Romanian showpiece 'The Lark'), left-hand pizzicato, extended rubato improvisations, dramatic changes of tempo, and chromaticism. A master musician could make his fiddle sing, laugh, and weep.

By the 20th century, there were many gypsies in western Europe; the Sinti in Germany, and the Manouche in France. Typically, the gypsy musicians of France during Grappelli's childhood were playing whatever was popular at the time: Musette music (French waltzes), light classical music, popular chansons and, increasingly, the new swing music which was starting to come over from America.

When **Django Reinhardt** began playing jazz, he brought to it a distinctive style which was partly personal, but also owed a lot to his gypsy heritage.

Exploring Jazz Violin

The rhythm-guitar style is a driving, highly percussive series of on-the beat chops, negating any need for drums, whilst his solo lines were dazzling and explosive, full of rising arpeggios, diminished scales and startling chromatic runs. With a rhythm section entirely made up of strings, the violin was a natural front-line instrument. With less volume than a drums-and-horns band, the violin, in the days before satisfactory amplification, had a much better chance of being heard and also there was no pressure to play in the cursed flat keys.

For the violinist, gypsy jazz lies towards the conservative end of the trad / modern spectrum, though that doesn't stop players like **Didier Lockwood** or **Daniel John Martin** (a great English fiddler living in Paris) from putting some very exciting modern harmony into their playing. With Grappelli as the brand leader, the tone has to be rich and romantic; the vibrato-free style of bebop and fusion would sound distinctly odd in this setting.

Repertoire

Django and Stéphane composed many tunes, which still form the core repertoire of Hot Club / gypsy jazz music today. Perhaps the most famous of these is 'Minor Swing', a very simple but powerful tune in A minor with a dark, gypsy feel. It was featured in the film *Chocolat*, played (yes, he really can play!) on guitar by **Johnny Depp**.

Other must-have medium and fast-tempo compositions of the genre include 'Belleville', 'Daphne' and 'HCQ Strut' (both of which have melodies built on harmonics), 'Djangology', 'Swing 39', 'Swing 42', 'Stomping at Decca', 'Douce Ambiance' and 'Dinette'.

Among the slow ballads the best known are: 'Nuages', along with 'Manoir de mes Reves', 'Melody au Crepescule' and 'Tears'.

There is some crossover with the east European and Jewish repertoires. The Russian tear jerker 'Dark Eyes' was recorded by Django and works equally well as a ballad or a tear-away number. Monti's 'Czardas' is a great crowd pleaser, as are tunes such as 'Bei Mir Bist du Sheyn' or anything from *Fiddler on the Roof*.

Gypsy jazz has also taken on many jazz standards, such as:

'After You've Gone'
'All of Me'
'Cheek to Cheek'
'Crazy Rhythm'
'Don't get Around Much Anymore'
'Honeysuckle Rose'
'I Can't Give you Anything but Love'
'I Got Rhythm'
'I'll See you in my Dreams'
'In a Sentimental Mood'
'It Don't Mean a Thing (if it Ain't got that Swing)'
'It had to be You'
'Just one of those Things'
'Lady be Good'
'La Mer'
'Limehouse Blues'
'Love for Sale'
'Pennies from Heaven'
'September Song'
'The Sheik of Araby'
'Smoke gets in your Eyes'
'Sweet Georgia Brown'
'Sweet Sue'
'Tea for Two'
'Them there Eyes'
'Tiger Rag'
'Undecided'

I refer to these as jazz standards, but they are by no means mainstream; the majority of jazz players outside the Hot Club scene would consider this a strange repertoire, being mostly from the 20s and 30s, and including little in the way of 'modern' jazz.

Some of the tunes common to both the Hot Club and mainstream repertoire would include:

'Ain't Misbehavin'
'Autumn Leaves'
'Blue Skies'
'Body and Soul'
'Caravan'
'A Foggy Day'
'Georgia on My Mind'
'Here's that Rainy Day'
'How High the Moon'
'In a Sentimental Mood'
'It Had to be You'
'Night and Day'
'A Nightingale Sang in Berkley Square'
'On the Sunny Side of the Street'
'Out of Nowhere'
'Pent-up House'
'Satin Doll'
'What is this Thing called Love'

The gypsy-jazz style can, perhaps tongue in cheek, be applied to almost any tune. I recently heard the theme from *Star Trek* given the gypsy-jazz treatment!

Gypsy-jazz players

Two of the finest contemporary gypsy-jazz violinists are east Europeans. **Florin Niculescu**, from a family of musicians in Bucharest, Romania had a full classical training before moving to Paris, where he began playing with the **Férre Brothers**. They were two of the leading Manouche guitarists and determined modernisers of gypsy jazz, along with **Biréli Lagrène**. Florin can also be heard in great form with the **New Quintette du Hot Club de France**, fronted by guitarist **Babik Reinhardt**, Django's son. His playing is marvellously clean and accurate – effortlessly adjusting from gypsy to concert violinist and from traditional style of Hot Club to bebop.

Equally eclectic, is the playing of Budapest gypsy and moustachioed maestro **Roby Lakatos**. Descended from the famous **János Bihari**, he was playing in a band at the age of nine and studied at the Budapest Béla Bartók conservatory. At his concerts he moves with consummate ease between classical, traditional and modern jazz, Latin and 19th century Hungarian traditional material. A unique feature of his playing is the occasional use of two- or three-finger rolling pizzicato, reaching an almost balalaika-like speed. It would be fair to say that he is more of his own man than Niculescu and less integrated into the gypsy jazz scene, but for flair, style, versatility and beauty of tone, I could not choose between them.

The blind, Belgian violinist **Tcha Limberger**, grew up playing gypsy jazz and performs with the **Lollo Meier Quartet**. However, he combined this with a deep love of Hungarian traditional music; he studied for three years in Budapest and now lives in Transylvania. On his recording of 'What is this Thing Called Love' he plays a whimsical solo full of Romanian / Hungarian inflections and trills.

Frenchman **Pierre Blanchard** is a player with great respect for the Grappelli tradition, as you can hear on his 2004 album *Rendez-vous* with **Dorado Schmitt**, who although best known as a guitarist, also plays the violin. In 1984 Pierre was awarded the Warlop violin.

Another Grappelli disciple is the Dutch violinist **Tim Kliphuis**, who has played with many of the leading gypsy-jazz guitarists including **Fapy Lafertin**, **Angelo Debarre**, **Boulou Ferre**, **Samson Schmitt** and **Stochelo Rosenberg**. He is the author of the fine book *Stéphane Grappelli, Gypsy Jazz Violin*. Other gypsy jazz violinists to look out for are the Belgian **Watti Rosenberg** and the German **Titi Winterstein**.

Exploring Jazz Violin

With so many groups playing in this style, there is plenty of opportunity to see this music live. There is an annual pilgrimage of Django devotees every June to Samois sur Seine, near Paris, where a festival in his memory has been held since 1968. More recently a series of 'Djangofests' have been held at different locations in California, and in London there is Le Quecumbar, a venue dedicated entirely to "Live Parisien Swing". As well as hosting most of the great names in gypsy jazz, it is also an excellent place to go for the weekly jam sessions.

Bebop

Jazz in the 1920s and 30s was all about swing, and it was primarily dance music. It could be either big band music, highly arranged and densely textured with the solos carefully arranged, or small band music, with more emphasis on less restrictive soloing. Either way it was commercial, with mass appeal and was generally easy on the ear. Bebop on the other hand, which began in the early 40s, was definitely not dance music and made no concession towards the casual listener.

Musicians like saxophonist **Charlie Parker** (often referred to as Bird), trumpeter **Dizzy Gillespie** and pianists **Bud Powell** and **Thelonious Monk** developed a small-band style of jazz which emphasized technical prowess at improvisation, above all else. Tempos became much faster, solos became longer and chord sequences more elaborate. Whereas before the melody had been of great importance, it was now almost an afterthought. Tunes such as **George Gershwin**'s 1930 hit 'I Got Rhythm' were used almost as templates; a new Head based on the (chord) changes would be composed, or almost improvised on the spot and the chords extended and elaborated. You can impress your friends by slipping the word 'contrafact' into your next conversation. It refers to a new tune written to replace an old one, whilst maintaining the original chord sequence.

Some bebop standards worth learning include:

'Anthropology' (based on 'I Got Rhythm')
'Au Privave' (based on the 12-bar blues)
'Billie's Bounce' (based on the 12-bar blues)
'Crazeology' (based on 'I Got Rhythm')
'Donna Lee' (based on 'Indiana')
'Hot House' (based on 'What is this Thing Called Love')
'Ornithology' (based on 'How High the Moon')
'Salt Peanuts' (based on 'I Got Rhythm')
'Scrapple from the Apple' (based on 'Honeysuckle Rose')
'Serpent's Tooth' (based on 'I Got Rhythm')
'Straight No Chaser' (based on the 12-bar blues)

Rhythms, both on the head and on solos, became jumpy and unpredictable. Although still swinging powerfully, phrases were often of odd lengths, starting and ending in unexpected places. The name 'bebop' itself is thought to derive from the scat singing of phrases where the accent falls on the off-beat 'bop', instead of the on-beat 'Be'.

Here's a typical bebop line:

Fig 10.1 **Typical bebop line**

Notice how the first phrase starts on the off-beat and ends, in bar 2 – also on the off-beat. The first two notes of bar 2 could in fact be sung as "be-bop". The difficult syncopation of bars 2 and 3 is typical, as is the use of triplets in bars 1 and 4, and the rests in the middle of bar 2 and at the end of bar 4.

When it comes to soloing, lines are usually a series of swung quavers (8th notes), ending with an accent on the last note – often an off-beat. If the tempo is slow to medium, the soloist will often double up the tempo of his lines to semiquavers (16th notes). Depending on the tempo, the semiquavers may be swung or, if it's too fast, straight.

Fig 10.2 Doubling up the tempo

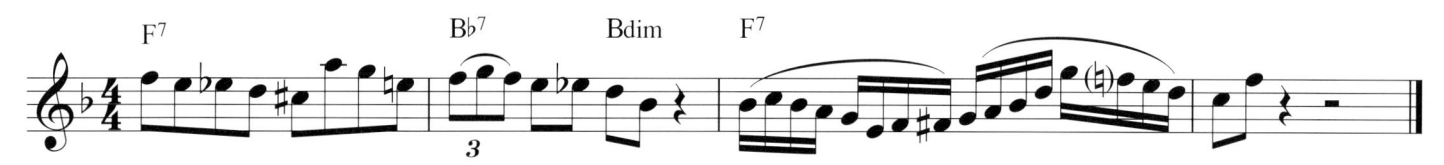

Perhaps the most important feature of bebop soloing is the close attention that you must pay to the chords. Each chord must be adhered to and addressed carefully. Whereas in swing the solo line can drift over the top, in bebop, you've got to be right in there with every chord change. It should be possible to hear the chord changes even if the accompanist stops playing. If you were soloing with just a single blues or pentatonic scale, this would leave no clues as to what the underlying chords were.

Let's look at two techniques that will help you, both of which we have touched on earlier:

1. Arpeggiate the chords by playing the roots, 3rds, 5ths and 7ths.

Fig 10.3 Arpeggiated chords

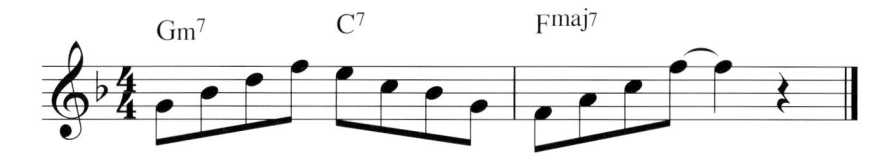

Often the upper extensions of arpeggios will be used. Shift the whole thing up a 3rd and you will get:

Fig 10.4 Arpeggiated chords – upper extensions

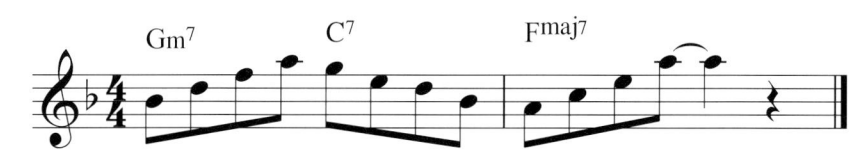

Exploring Jazz Violin

2. Play bebop scales – eight-note scales with an added chromatic note, allowing you to place the chord tones on the beat.

Fig 10.5 Bebop scales

Better still, combine both techniques, ascending on the arpeggio and descending on the scale. At the same time, avoid starting or ending on the root notes:

Fig 10.6 Ascending arpeggio, descending scale

Even with these elaborations, a solo can still sound like a mathematically generated set of scales and arpeggios, so bebop lines also deviate from the predictable by using 'enclosure'. This involves preceding a chord tone with two neighbour notes, one step above and below. The note below will be chromatic (one semitone below) whilst the note above may be either chromatic or the next note in the scale.

Here, the note E (on the chord of C^7) is preceded by an F and a D♯, whilst the note A (on the F chord) is preceded by a B♭ and a G♯:

Fig 10.7 Enclosure

Finally, you'll find many altered notes in bebop. One of the simplest ways to achieve this is by substituting a diminished scale in place of a dominant one. If you start ascending diminished scale over a IIm^7 chord, the first four notes will be 'in', then you get a 'boptastic' flattened 9th (D♭) and sharpened 9th (E♭/D♯) over chord V^7 (C^7). This particular lick also has an enclosure for the final note F:

Fig 10.8 Altered notes

178

If you have a longer chord over the dominant, you can start the diminished scale, descending this time, on the root note of the chord. Again, the scale starts off 'in' for four notes, then unveils a sharpened 11th, sharpened 9th and a flattened 9th, before landing neatly on the 5th of chord I. (It's worth noting, that a diminished scale can start with an interval of either a tone or a semitone, so long as the pattern is preserved – T, S, T, S, T, S, T, S.)

Fig 10.9 **Descending diminished scale**

The standard line-up for a bebop band, which has changed little since the 1940s, is: piano, bass, drums, sax and / or trumpet. With a few notable exceptions, violin didn't get a look-in. So why do you even need to know anything about bebop? Whether you like it or not, the techniques developed by the bebop players have become part of the fabric of the jazz vocabulary and if you want to be taken seriously by other jazz musicians, you'll have to be able to blow over bebop tunes like 'Anthropology' or 'Scrapple from the Apple' without breaking into a cold sweat.

Bebop players

Some fiddle players have demonstrated that their instrument is as good as any for playing bebop. **Stuff Smith** certainly led the way, as you can hear on his version of 'I Got Rhythm'. He spent a good deal of time playing with people like **Charlie Parker** and **Coleman Hawkins**, and **Dizzy Gillespie** considered him a major influence. His punchy, adventurous and exploratory approach was certainly well suited to the style, Smith never considered himself a bebop player as such; he once referred to bop as "*The illegitimate child of swing*".

Two players who have undoubtedly done most for bebop violin are **Jean-Luc Ponty** and **Didier Lockwood**. Ponty's early albums *Sunday Walk*, *Jazz Long Playing* and *Trio HLP* are superb examples of the genre – there can be few fans of bebop violin who do not rue the day he was enticed away into jazz fusion. **Didier Lockwood**, though always eclectic in his stylistic choices, has also produced some excellent bebop throughout his career, notably on his albums *New York Rendezvous*, *New World* and *Storyboard*. **John Coltrane**'s 'Giant Steps' is often regarded as one of the most challenging bebop numbers to play, with its constantly changing keys. Lockwood tackles it on his album *New World* and you can hear a version from young, British fiddle player **Billy Thompson** on **Barbara Thompson**'s 1997 *Never Say Goodbye* album.

There are many other fiddlers who have had a brave stab at bebop. The fount of all knowledge in this field is **Anthony Barnett** who runs the AB Fable publishing house; his website, books and rare-recording albums chronicle in the minutest detail the works of many jazz violinists. His album *I like Be I like Bop* brings together countless pre-bop, proto-bop, true-bop and post-bop violinists, several of whom are a mere full stop to an appendix to a footnote in jazz history. Many of them were jazz musicians for whom the violin was their second or third instrument. **Ray Perry**, for example, was also an alto sax player, notable for being the first fiddler to hum in unison with his solos. **Dick Wetmore**, described by some as the first bop violinist, was also a trumpeter, as was **Gene Orloff**.

Players like these, because of their experience on horns, were able to play fine and convincing bebop lines. That they never became well known, must be largely down to the fact that audiences have a certain expectation about the sound of a violin, whether they are thinking about **Stéphane Grappelli** or **Jascha Heifetz**, namely that it should sound sweet, rich and powerful. Any weakness in bowing, intonation or tone is immediately obvious and for players of the violin as a second instrument, this is often a challenge too far.

Violinists who did pull it off convincingly include the Scandinavians **Odd Wentzel Larsen** and **Soren Christiensen**, both of whom had excellent technique and tone. The Budapest-born **Elek Bacsik** is often cited as one of the finest bebop violinists, though most of his career was spent in America as a guitarist. **Johnny Frigo**, from Chicago and the black, female bandleader **Ginger Smock**, were also excellent bebop players, but both found it to be an unrewarding genre and moved on to pastures new.

It seems to be the case that at the time when bebop was all the rage, many violinists had a go, with varying degrees of success, and then moved on.

As we must ourselves.

Modal Jazz

In 1959 jazz did a handbrake turn. For the previous half century it had been evolving in one direction, from simple melodies with only a few chords, towards ever-more complex heads and chord sequences. This movement culminated in bebop in the late 40s and 50s, where highly technical and cerebral 'cutting sessions' pitted musicians against one another to see who could play with the greatest speed, fluidity and creativity over lightening-fast chord changes.

When **Miles Davis** released *Kind of Blue* everything changed. The album introduced the idea of modal jazz, in which long sequences of dense and complex chords were replaced by a few, simple modal scales. The idea was to give freedom and space to the improviser instead of an obstacle course, allowing a much more melodic approach to soloing. In conventional jazz there was a key and a tonal centre, and all the chords within the song related to that key according to the rules of music theory. The II-V-I progression and its associated licks were the backbone of jazz. In modal jazz, there are extended periods of just a single chord, over which the soloist can explore a single scale or mode. "*There will be fewer chords*" explained Miles, "*but infinite possibilities as to what to do with them*". It sounds kind of academic and you're probably thinking that even if you understood what I was talking about, it doesn't seem such a big deal. The fact is that *Kind of Blue* triumphed, persuading jazz musicians, critics and the public alike that this was indeed the future of jazz. It is frequently cited as the best-selling jazz album of all time and the ideas that it bravely introduced have been central to jazz theory and practice ever since.

So, the first thing you want to know is, what is a mode? The concept and the names which we use today go back to the ancient Greeks and were used in early European church music. The idea of modes is actually pretty straightforward. If you play just the white notes on a piano, starting on C, you have the following C major scale:

Fig 10.10 **C major scale (C Ionian mode)**

This scale, from C to C, is also called the C Ionian mode and the chord which would fit it best is C^{maj7}. Because this scale is so prevalent in Western music, it is not usually considered as a mode, even though strictly speaking it is. If we stick to the white keys, but start and end on a D, we get this:

Fig 10.11 D Dorian mode

This scale, D to D, is called the D **Dorian** mode. By starting in a different place, the intervals are different from the previous mode. Even though the key signature (no sharps or flats) is the same, any melody built around this, with D as the tonal centre, will sound quite different. It is clearly a minor-type scale (Dm^7 would be the appropriate chord). And so we proceed with E to E; this is the E **Phrygian** mode (Em^7).

Fig 10.12 E Phrygian mode

F to F is the F **Lydian** mode ($F^{maj7add\,\sharp11}$)($\sharp4$).

Fig 10.13 F Lydian mode

G to G is the G **Mixolydian** mode (G^7).

Fig 10.14 G Mixolydian mode

A to A is the A **Aeolian** mode (Am^7).

Fig 10.15 A Aeolian mode

And finally B to B is the B **Locrian** mode ($B^{\emptyset}$).

Fig 10.16 B Locrian mode

Exploring Jazz Violin

Here are the essential elements of the modes of the major scale:

Mode	Degree based on	Tonality	Main features	Chord type
Ionian	1st	Major	Major scale	maj7
Dorian	2nd	Minor	♭3rd, ♭7th	m7
Phrygian	3rd	Minor	♭2nd, ♭3rd, ♭6th, ♭7th	m7
Lydian	4th	Major	♯4th	7 add ♯11(♯4)
Mixolydian	5th	Major	♭7th	7
Aeolian	6th	Minor	Natural minor scale	m7
Locrian	7th	Minor/diminished	♭2nd, ♭5th, ♭7th	half dim

In practice, some of these modes sound so strange that they are rarely used. The Dorian and Mixolydian are probably the most useful. In addition to those described above, there are many other possible modes. **Ric Sanders**, violinist with British-jazz rock band **Soft Machine** of the 70s, told me:

"I got a John McLaughlin book with lots of the Mahavishnu repertoire written out, and in the introduction John wrote out a lot of 'synthetic' modes, Enigmatic, Hungarian Minor, Symmetrical etc., with the advice that he'd included them because you could find so much hidden within them, particularly in the extraction of their scale-tone chords."

To get the feel of modal music you need to listen to some. 'So What' and 'All Blues' from the *Kind of Blue* album would be the obvious place to start. The tenor sax on this album was played by **John Coltrane**, who went on to become possibly the leading exponent of modal jazz. Listen to his 'Impressions' or 'A Love Supreme', **McCoy Tyner**'s 'Naima' and pianist **Freddie Hubbard**'s 'Maiden Voyage'.

If you want to hear violinists playing modal jazz, listen to **Didier Lockwood** playing 'Impressions' on *The Kid* album, or **Jean-Luc Ponty**'s version of **Herbie Hancock**'s 'Cantaloupe Island'. Coltrane also used 'Scarborough Fair' as a modal vehicle; Ponty covered this on the *Electric Connection* album and much of his early 70s work was modal in character. For an uncompromisingly modern interpretation of **Miles Davis**'s 'All Blues', listen to **Michal Urbaniak**'s version on his *Miles of Blue* album.

The chords used by pianists in modal music are often sus chords – harmonically ambiguous because they avoid the 3rd. The overall feel is cool, drifting, searching and meditative. When it comes to soloing, you may be forgiven for thinking that, compared to blowing over a complex chord sequence, it would be very easy. In a sense it is, but with no chord changes to give structure to the piece, it's very easy to quickly run out of ideas and end up with something amorphous and vague. For this reason, soloists of the genre create their own micro-structures. Pentatonic scales are ideal and in the free-for all melee, that is modal jazz, you usually have a choice of several. Over D Dorian, for example, the eight available notes encompass the pentatonics of F major, C major and G major, and their relative minors.

Using these scales gives a temporary stability to the music and sets up an expectation which can then be upset by sidestepping – repeating a phrase up or down a semitone. The kind of chords and bass lines used in modal music make sidestepping appear a much less risky business than in mainstream jazz. Whole-tone scales also fit well into modal music – either temporarily in solo lines, or in the melody (as in **Wayne Shorter**'s 'Juju').

10: Other Styles, Other Players

Here's a tune typical of those written during the 'great chord shortage' of 1959.

Some modal tunes you will find written without a key signature, others with. In this piece I have written in the key signatures to show the link between the keys and the modes. The piece uses the Dorian mode, in two different keys, so the first mode is D Dorian (the scale that starts on the 2nd degree of C major), followed in the B section with E Dorian (the scale that starts on the 2nd degree of D major). The structure is AABA.

Dorian Grey (head)

Demo 60

Chris Haigh

© 2010 Schott Music Ltd, London

On the following page you'll find a solo of 'Dorian Grey' which examines some of the distinctive approaches to modal playing.

Exploring Jazz Violin

Dorian Grey (solo version)

Bars 1–16

The solo kicks off with a short, punctuated phrase, immediately followed by a 'yawning' gap. Think of modal jazz as the 'Final Frontier'; it requires space. The three strong notes on the first line are all outside the Dm triad; G is a 4th, B a 6th and E a 9th. This sets the mood for a solo with an unsettled and searching character, which continues through line 2. Bars 9 and 10 finally outline the Dm^7 chord, whilst bars 11 and 12 extend it to the 9th and 11th. Bars 13 to 15 are similar to a Coltrane phrase from 'So What' – also remarkably similar to the lick which was **Jean-Luc Ponty**'s staple diet in the early 70s. Could this have been the source?

At bar 16 we're approaching the modulation. In a tune with so few changes, it's important to make the most of them when they occur. One tactic would be to anticipate the change by half a bar or so; another would be to hold a note which is common to both modes over the modulation. A third would be to start a scalar phrase over the Dm chord, modifying it to take into account the change in mode. A fourth approach, which we've taken here, is to play a pentatonic phrase in Dm and then repeat it up a tone as the key changes.

Bars 17–24

At bar 17 we finally arrive at the new mode of E Dorian. Bars 20 to 24 all make use of wide intervals – lots of 4ths, emphasizing the melodic openness of the solo.

Bars 25–32

The return to Dm (D Dorian) comes at bar 25, this echoes the phrase from the previous bar. Neat, because the mode is shifting back down, but the solo line completely disguises the fact. At bar 27 we've had enough of wandering lonely as a cloud. We change gear, moving into a bar of semiquaver notes. We also change to a G major / E minor pentatonic scale. In bar 28 we set up a 'three-over-four' phrase in Em. After playing it twice, we do a side-step, taking it up a semitone. This is a very typical strategy for modal tunes where harmonic tension is otherwise hard to come by. In bar 30 we use another Coltrane-type lick – a descending whole-tone scale pattern – again, a way of escaping the potentially monotonous expanse of Dm. Notice that in this solo we've taken most of our reference points not from violinists, but from horn players. If you want to play a lot of modal music, this is the way you need to start thinking.

Free Jazz

We have **Ornette Coleman** to thank for 'free jazz' – music in which rhythm, harmony, melody and structure are largely abandoned in favour of free expression. He started his career in the early 50s playing sax in various R&B groups and soon graduating to bebop. This he found restrictive and was soon developing his own voice, throwing out all the rules and making himself very unpopular with other musicians, many of whom would leave the stage when he started to play.

His 1960 album *Free Jazz – A Collective Improvisation* proved both highly divisive and influential. Many hated it and everything it stood for, but it opened up new avenues for a whole host of modern, free-thinking jazz musicians. In the 1960s Coleman began playing the violin – he was left-handed and self-taught. The fact that he had no technique to speak of made little difference within the style of music he was playing. "*I think he should stick to his alto sax*" was the comment of veteran swing fiddler **Stuff Smith**.

Among the violinists to follow Coleman's lead into free jazz are a trio of black-American players and a plucky Brit...

Free-jazz players

Leroy Jenkins (1932–2007) was a classically trained violinist who trod an uncompromising and highly individual path within modern jazz. His music, either free or composed, was harmonically challenging to say the least. He often performed solo, but was best known for his work with the **Revolutionary Ensemble**. If you're looking for hummable melodies, foot-tapping rhythms and sweet harmonies, keep looking.

Although rougher in tone and weaker in intonation than Jenkins, nevertheless **Billy Bang** (who names Jenkins as his chief inspiration) has a much more approachable style. Along with some free and experimental sounds Bang has a strong dose of swing and blues in his playing and in 1992, with **Sun Ra** (with whom he worked for 10 years), he recorded a tribute to **Stuff Smith**. He has over 14 albums under his own name, as well as a number with the **String Trio of New York**.

Michael White, based in San Francisco, was another pioneer of free-jazz on the violin and despite having made little impact on the jazz world as a whole, has worked with a number of leading artists including **Sun Ra**, **Pharoah Sanders**, **Stevie Wonder**, **McCoy Tyner** and **John Coltrane**. He manages to mix total cacophony with some quite accessible material.

A fierce and uncompromising contemporary British exponent of free-jazz violin is **Graham Clark**. You can hear him on the album *Improvisations Series One* with pianist **Stephen Grew** – recorded with "*no prior preparation and no subsequent manipulation*". He is also well known for his work with the reformed jazz / rock / fusion band **Gong**.

Unlike many of the styles of jazz violin covered in this book, I have no scales, licks or exercises to help you if you're keen on exploring free jazz. Be bold, shed your inhibitions, and hang on to your day job.

Latin

Latin music is based around a series of complex rhythms originating from South and Central America. From the 1930s onwards, they have had a consistent influence on jazz, finding their way into swing, big band, bebop and jazz-fusion. It is very common for almost any jazz band, which for most of the night might be playing straight-ahead swing rhythms in 4/4 time, to throw in one or two Latin numbers for some variety.

In the context of jazz, there are two main branches of Latin music: Afro-Cuban and Brazilian.

Cuban effect on Latin music

Cuba was colonised by the Spanish in 1511 and they soon began populating the island with African slaves. Along with the remnants of the indigenous population, plus a large number of French and Creole refugees from Haiti (in 1791) and Louisiana (in 1812), this created a fertile mix of musical cultures. The formal, French 'Contradanse' was transformed into the 'Danza'. By 1898, when Cuba gained its independence, the dance had evolved into the 'Danzone' and was being seen as a symbol of national identity.

It was performed by the 'Orquesta Tipica' (a band that plays popular music), consisting of two violins along with clarinets, horns, timpani and a guiro – a serrated gourd. By the 20th century the flute and piano had been added, followed by more percussion and the clarinets were dropped. Through the early 20th century the 'Son' became increasingly important – a song-form consisting of two parts: the first with a distinct length and structure, the second an open-ended vamp or 'montuno' section, where both lyrics and music could be improvised.

An important development came in the 1940s when a new band was formed, the **Orquesta Melodias Del 40**. It featured a sensational violinist **Miguel Barbon** nicknamed **El Niño Prodigo** (the child prodigy) or **Brindis** (after the famed Cuban classical virtuoso **Brindis Di Sala**). He is seen as the role model for all future improvising violinists in Cuba, his solos a showcase of techniques. His playing is diametrically opposite to someone like Grappelli. There is no swing in Latin music; all the quavers are played straight. Instead of long, sinuous, flowing lines, Barbon produced short, simple and highly rhythmic phrases repeated many times. Instead of lots of slurs, he used almost all separate bows.

When not soloing, the role of the violinist in Afro-Cuban music is as part of the rhythm section, playing endlessly repeated 2-bar phrases or 'montunos' which lock in with the complex rhythms of the rest of the band. The soloing style takes this very much into account. With very simple chord sequences and a powerhouse rhythm section, the soloist can afford to leave space, developing and repeating ideas at leisure. Many different rhythms are used, particularly 'lazy' crotchet-triplets. Octaves, interesting double-stops and chromatic sections all add spice to the solos of **El Prodigo**. He developed a favourite, and much imitated, ending – an ascending-octave-tremolando glissando.

The violin has remained a key feature of Cuban music and many other fine musicians have continued to follow the example El Prodigo set. **Jose 'Chambo' Silva**, who was also a sax player, brought a good knowledge of jazz to his playing and, after moving to New York in 1957, was influential in disseminating Cuban violin to the outside world. **Alfredo De La Fé** was an extremely talented young violinist, gaining scholarships to Warsaw at the age of 10 and then Juilliard in New York. He learned Cuban music by transcribing Barbon's solos, practicing them in every key and mixing up the phrases to create his own solos. He brings a modern outlook to the music, with the electric violin, the use of effects pedals, a knowledge of rock music and some pyrotechnic technique.

The Clave

Cuban rhythms, when you hear them played by a full band, sound extremely complex. The pattern may be only two bars, endlessly repeated, but every instrument is playing a different part of the groove.

The key to understanding what's going on is the 'clave' (pronounced clah-vay). This does **not** refer to the wooden block percussion instrument (which, confusingly, may or may not be involved). The word clave in Spanish means key or code, it can be thought of as the keystone or centre of the complex rhythmic pattern. The clave is two-bars long and is asymmetrical, being either a '3:2' or a '2:3' pattern – one bar has three strokes or hits, the other has two.

If you want to delve further in Cuban music, I would suggest that your first stop has to be **Sam Bardfeld**'s book *Latin Violin – how to play Salsa, Charanga and Latin Jazz Violin*. It includes an album with extracts of solos from many of the great violinists, along with transcriptions and a detailed analysis of the solo style. Sam explained to me:

"*The clave pattern frequently exists as a 'virtual thing' – whether it's played or not, everyone in the band has usually internalized it – it determines the direction of the montunos, the way the melodies are written, the way solos are played, etc.*

Clave is a two-bar pattern, with a 'strong' measure and a 'weak' measure – or in more practical terms, a measure that stresses the downbeat and a measure that stresses syncopation."

Let's see what a clave looks like when it's notated:

Exploring Jazz Violin

Fig 10.17 **3:2 clave**

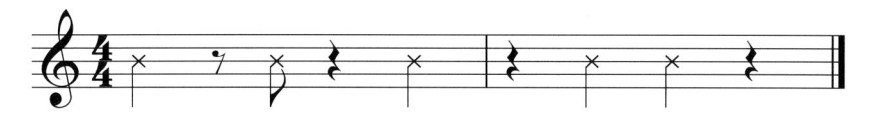

[Musical notation: 3:2 clave pattern in 4/4 time]

And here it is reversed, as the 2:3 clave:

Fig 10.18 **2:3 clave**

[Musical notation: 2:3 clave pattern in 4/4 time]

This is the template on which all the other rhythm parts are based; they will all have the same 3:2 or 2:3 pattern. An experienced player will recognize the clave immediately and can deduce it from all the other parts, even if the clave itself is not actually being played.

Deep study into Afro-Cuban improvisation is beyond the scope of this book, but here are a couple of montunos – the repeated, rhythmic figures that the violin might play behind the son and on which you might build an improvisation.

Fig 10.19 **Montuno (2:3 clave)**

[Musical notation with chords D, G, A7, G]

Fig 10.20 **Montuno (3:2 clave)**

[Musical notation with chords Em, B7, Em]

A couple of things to notice about these montunos. They do not duplicate the clave; instead they interlock with it. You can usually recognize the '2' part of the montuno because this will start on the beat, whilst the '3' part will be a syncopation, or begin on an off-beat.

The second example (fig. 10.20) is four-bars long, not two. This is dictated by the chord sequence. Melodically it is four bars, but rhythmically, it is still a 2-bar, repeating pattern.

Brazilian effect on Latin music

Whilst Cuban music began to enter American jazz in the 30s and 40s, with the Rumba and Mambo dance crazes, and the creation of what was at first called 'Cubop', the Brazilian influence came later, in the 50s and 60s. The Cuban influx had been hot and fiery, whilst that from Brazil was cool and languorous. Most important was the Bossa Nova.

10: Other Styles, Other Players

This grew out of the Samba, a lively and highly percussive dance with strong roots in African drumming and close associations with carnivals. The Bossa Nova (often referred to just as Bossa), was created in the late 1950s by **Antônio Carlos Jobim** and **João Gilberto**. Unlike the Samba, Bossa was very cool and controlled, frequently played just on an acoustic guitar, it often had complex jazz-chord sequences. Like the music of Cuba, it can be described in terms of a clave: one interpretation of the rhythm is an asymmetric two-bar phrase. This is often played on the snare drum rim and can be a '3:2' or '2:3' version. It's similar to the regular clave, but the last beat of the '2' bar is slightly earlier:

Fig 10.21 **Bosa Nova clave (3:2)**

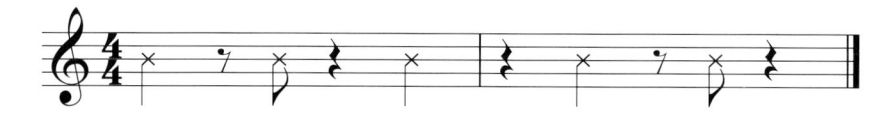

Fig 10.22 **Bosa Nova clave (2:3)**

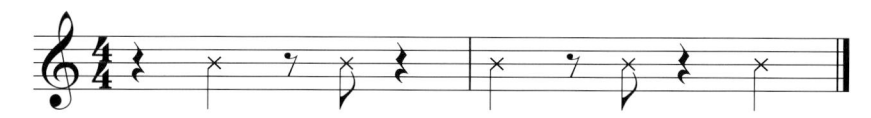

The first, and still most famous hit song in the Bossa Nova style is 'The Girl From Ipanema'. It was written by Jobim in 1962 and recorded by the cool saxophonist **Stan Getz** and singer **Astrud Gilberto**. Jobim was responsible for many Bossa standards including 'Wave', 'How Insensitive' and 'Quiet Nights'. Other classics include 'Morning of the Carnival' (from the 1959 film *Black Orpheus*), 'Blue Bossa' and 'Desafinado'. Many slow- to medium-tempo tunes that might ordinarily be played with a swing feel can be readily adapted to Latin rhythms; a good example would be 'Here's that Rainy Day' – often given a Bossa treatment.

An extreme, and highly entertaining example of this is *Django Latin* – an album of Django tunes by American fiddler and multi-instrumentalist **Joe Craven**, where every number is given a different, but very authentic, Latin rhythm.

When it comes to playing a Bossa, from the viewpoint of the violinist, you don't really need to know the intricacies of the underlying rhythms. Whether it's a Bossa, a Samba, a Rumba or a Mambo, you can let the rhythm section worry about whether what they're doing is authentic. In fact, many jazz players will simply refer to a number as being 'Latin' and leave it at that.

Having said that, it's important that you listen to the rhythm section and play appropriately. A Bossa, with its easy and lazy feel will allow you to play 'behind' the beat, whilst for something Cuban you have to think much more rhythmically and sit right 'on' the beat. From your point-of-view, the most important thing to recognize is that your quavers (eighth notes) have to be straight, not swung. And if you're playing a Bossa, you had better take a look at the chords first. They won't be easy!

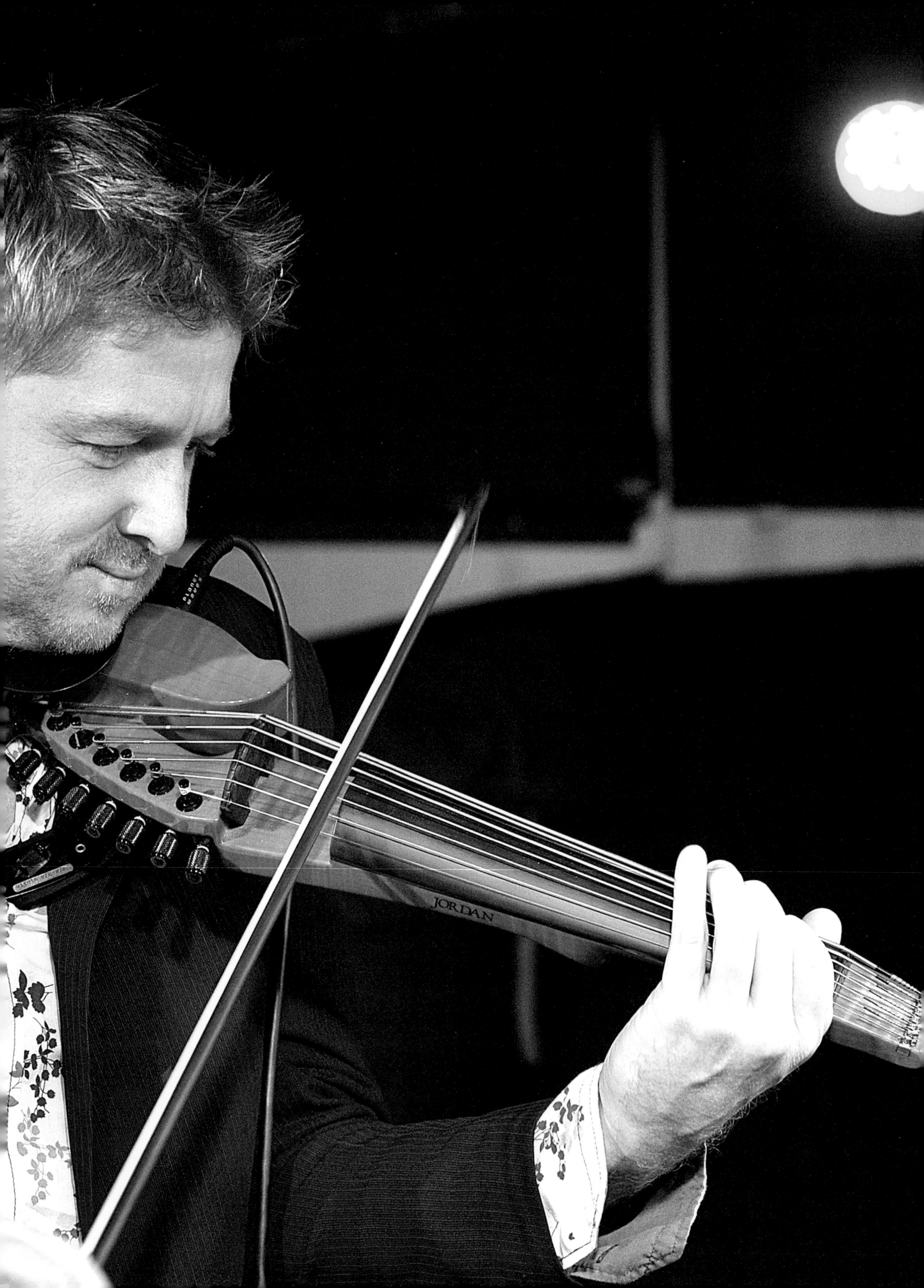
JORDAN

11: The Big Night

OK, here's the scenario. You've read this book cover to cover, broken the bank buying jazz violin cds and you spend every waking hour practising. The only trouble is you've yet to do your first gig. Your mum, ever helpful, says she knows a few people and will try to sort something out. A week later she comes up with the goods. She was being modest when she said she knows some people. She has in fact fixed you up with a gig at the Albert Hall. It's a guest spot and you only have to play one number – but there'll be 3,000 people in the audience including royalty, visiting heads of state, celebs and music and press moguls aplenty. So, no pressure!

If you've never done a jazz gig in your life you should read this final chapter with care. It's a final run through of everything you need to know about learning a new tune, finding your way around it, deciding how you're going to play the melody, how you're going to interact with the band and pull off the solo of your life. There are a few things you might want to think about…

Can I Use Sheet Music?

If you're from a classical background, your first question when faced with a gig, might well be – can I use sheet music? There's no clear cut answer to this one. It's not unusual to see jazz musicians using a music stand. This might happen if the band is playing arrangements – fixed parts where harmonies, counter melodies, backing riffs and so on are written out for the band. It might also happen if there are original compositions being performed and the musicians are new to the material. If it's an informal jam session, or if it's a long-standing band where everyone knows all the numbers well, you're unlikely to see any music.

I used to consider it extremely un-cool to be seen bringing music to a jazz gig, since it marked me out as a beginner who, unlike the rest of the guys, didn't know hundreds of standards. If it came to a number I didn't know, I would just bluff. I now take a more relaxed approach. Particularly if it's a 'wallpaper gig' (where you're hired to play jazz at a party but no one is actually listening), it's actually great to bring along a pad. It allows the band to play new, interesting and unusual numbers which not all the musicians are familiar with. In the context of your Albert Hall gig (certainly not a wallpaper gig!), you're definitely going to play your one number without music.

The Key

So, take a good look at the sheet music. This being jazz, even here not everything is as it seems. Let's say you've been given the title of the number you're going to be playing, but no more than that. It might be easy enough to get hold of some sheet music – from a music shop, online or from a friend, but if you take it too literally you could come a cropper. To begin with, you need to think about the key. It could be that your sheet music is in a difficult flat key; you sweat over learning the head and the changes with all the difficult fingerings involved and then on the night the bandleader asks 'what key would you like to do it in? G?' Worse still, it may be that you learn it in an easy key only to be informed on the night 'five sharps, OK?' Most experienced jazz accompanists will be able to transpose at the drop of a hat, so in your situation it's well worth finding out in advance what the key will be, or what your options are.

Versions and phrasing

The written melody on your sheet music can also be taken with a pinch of salt. If it's an old standard, the sheet music may have the melody of the original sung version of the tune; half a century of usage by jazz musicians may well have modified the tune considerably.

A good source of reliable sheet music is the *Real Books* – written by, and for, jazz musicians. Not only are they usually based on recordings by famous jazz performers, but the books themselves are a common 'currency' among musicians.

Playing the head

Don't underestimate the importance of playing the head. Even before you get to the solo, your audience will have made up their minds whether they're going to give you a standing ovation or 'nul points'. It's not just a question of playing it nicely and in tune, you have to stamp your musical identity firmly all over the melody.

Even supposing you know the right key and have some reliable music, that's still not the end of the story. When playing the head, you have a lot of leeway to rephrase parts of the melody. What works great on a sax or guitar may not be so good on the fiddle. Whilst some violinists would go to any extreme to play just like **Charlie Parker**, others would say, 'this is a violin, not a sax; this is how I'm going to play it'. I would suggest that you listen to as many different versions of the tune as you can. Once upon a time this would have meant a huge amount of research followed by a costly trip to the record shop, but nowadays it's very easy and inexpensive to do online. Look out for fiddle versions of the song, but also versions from other instrumentalists or singers. Listen out for the tempo, the arrangement, the rhythm, the phrasing, the way the soloist deals with the chords – you may get a very different impression of the number than you originally got from the sheet music. So, listen to different versions, work out a part that suits you, practise it and memorize it.

So far, so good. Here's an assignment for the piece with which you're going to rock the Albert Hall – 'The Big Night' – a snappy, bebop blues.

Assignment

Play through the tune. The most challenging aspect of this number is the rhythm and syncopation, as is often the case with bebop. I've put in my suggestions for bowing, I'd play it all down at the heel of the bow, where you get the best control. Most of the jazz music you'll be playing from now on won't be from violin arrangements, so if something feels uncomfortable with the fingering, bowing or phrasing, you have to decide:

1. Is this simply difficult, but will be OK if I practise it enough? Or:

2. Should I modify it in some way to suit my instrument, my style and my playing ability. Unless you're playing the head in unison with someone else, it won't matter.

If there's a couple of notes in a phrase which you are going to struggle with every time you play them, then substitute them for something more appropriate. It may be the Albert Hall, but this is not the 'Beethoven Violin Concerto'. People want to hear your interpretation of the tune, not a perfect reproduction of the original.

The Big Night (head)

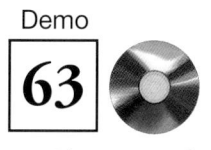

Demo 63

Chris Haigh

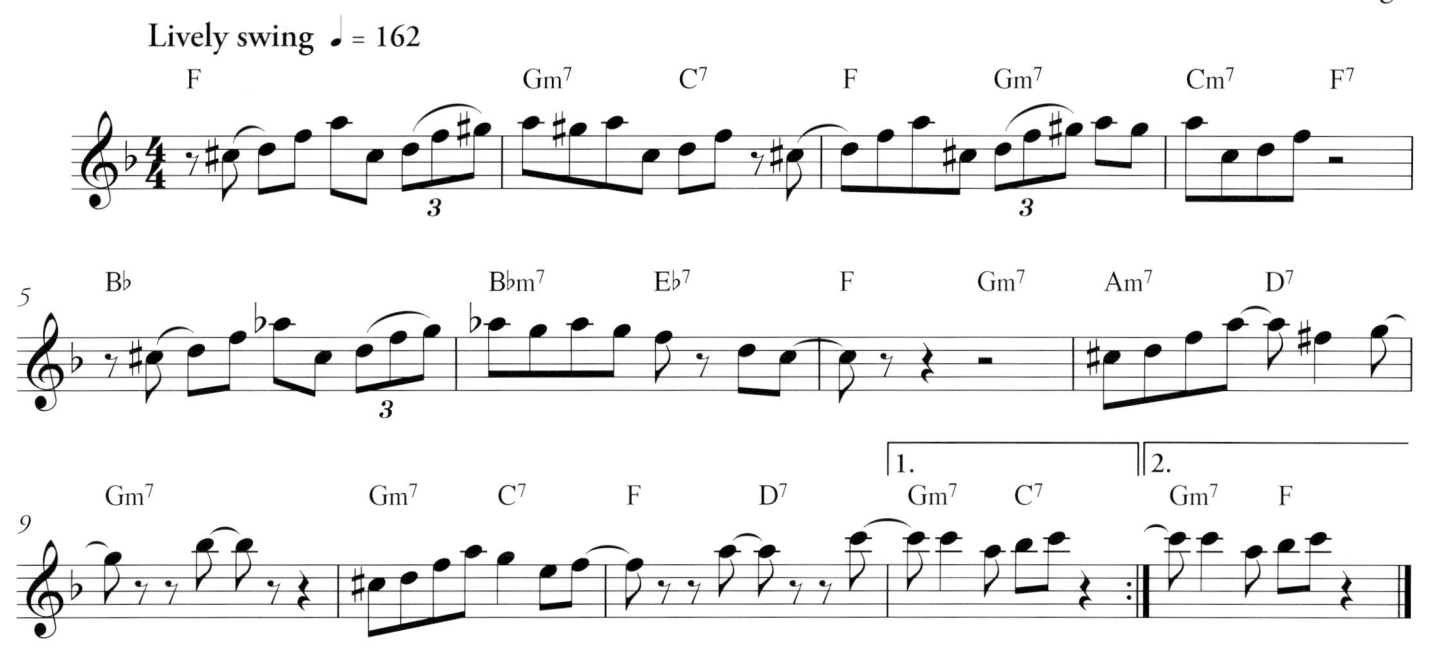

Lively swing ♩ = 162

© 2010 Schott Music Ltd, London

Is there an arrangement?

Jazz standards are often played in an ad-hoc way, with no discussion about the arrangement. For example, the pianist or guitarist might give a few chords in (as an 'intro' or introduction), and one of the instrumentalists goes straight into the head. A few solos, back to the head and then off to the bar! Some numbers, however, might have an arrangement. This may include a written 'intro' and 'outro' (ending), a special arrangement of the melody, or possibly some changes in rhythm or key at a certain point. **Stéphane Grappelli**, particularly in later years, always liked to have neat intros and outros.

The tune 'Honeysuckle Rose', a mainstay of the gypsy jazz repertoire, is often played 'with all the trimmings' – with a particular guitar / fiddle intro and outro, and a set way of playing the head which relates to the original Hot club recording, but not to the original song. 'I Got Rhythm' has a 'tag' (a 4-bar section usually played on the head but not during the solos) and it is often played in half time on the final head.

These are the kind of things you pick up with experience, by playing the same number with different people, or by listening to different recordings of the same song. So don't turn up to your big gig and start playing without asking the crucial question – is there an arrangement? Whereas in a 32-bar tune, the head will usually only be played once before the solos. With a short, fast tune like this one, it will often go round twice at the beginning and end.

Exploring Jazz Violin

Learning the chords

It is possible to play a solo by ear, or to sight-read the chords, but at this stage you may not be ready to take that chance. You need to study the chord sequence carefully, work out how you're going to deal with it and then memorize at least the 'skeleton' of the changes.

We've already looked at the idea of listening to different recordings of the piece. It's also very valuable to have a 'minus one' version to practise with. You have several options: If you play guitar or piano, or can persuade a friend to help, you can make your own recording to work on. If you're very lucky, you may find a commercially recorded backing track such as those produced by **Jamey Abersold**. The third and to my mind best option is to use 'Band in a Box' or something similar. This is a piece of software into which you can quickly input a chord sequence. It can then play it back in any key, any tempo, almost any style and with a large selection of instrumental line-ups. It will even, with a little persuasion, generate a sample solo in the style of a heavenly host of top jazz names.

Practising a solo without backing of some sort is of fairly limited use. The best that you can do is to arpeggiate the chord sequence. This will at least give you a good feel for the chords and can suggest phrases which you might use over the trickier changes.

Let's look at the first four bars of 'The Big Night'. The simplest way to play the arpeggios would be:

Fig 11.1 Bars 1–4 simple arpeggios

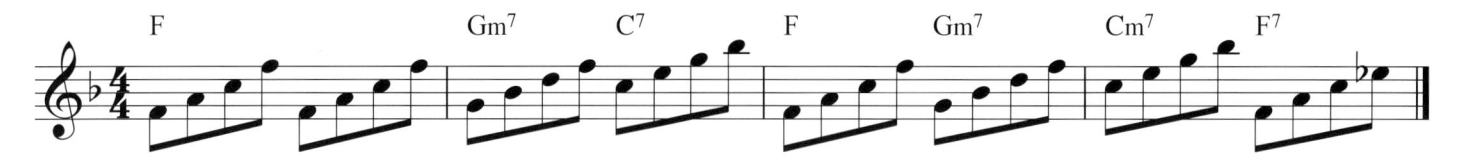

This will give you a useful outline of the chords, but is far from musical. As we saw in the bebop section, it's possible to make arpeggios more flowing and musical. Initially, instead of starting on the root notes and ascending every time, alternate between ascending and descending, starting each arpeggio with whichever chord note lies closest to the last one that you've played.

Fig 11.2 Bars 1–4 ascending / descending arpeggios

From here it's only a couple of steps further to making an actual musical line. Add a few longer or shorter notes to break up the rhythm, sprinkle in a rest or two and a few chromatic or scalar notes and you have a fairly creditable solo line. Here's bars 5–8 treated in this way:

Fig 11.3 Bars 5–8 embellished arpeggios

Assignment

Try arpeggiating the whole sequence. As above, start off with just the basic skeleton of the chords, then gradually add more ideas to make it run more smoothly and sound more interesting. This is a very valuable exercise and worth repeating on every new tune you learn.

Analyzing the chord sequence

We saw in earlier chapters how the tonal centre can change though a tune, with a number of temporary key changes. As a blues, this piece can be played very simply, with a single tonal centre. However, the chords have been deliberately embellished to include a series of II-V-Is. Here's the whole sequence mapped out:

Fig 11.4 **The Big Night with II-V-Is highlighted**

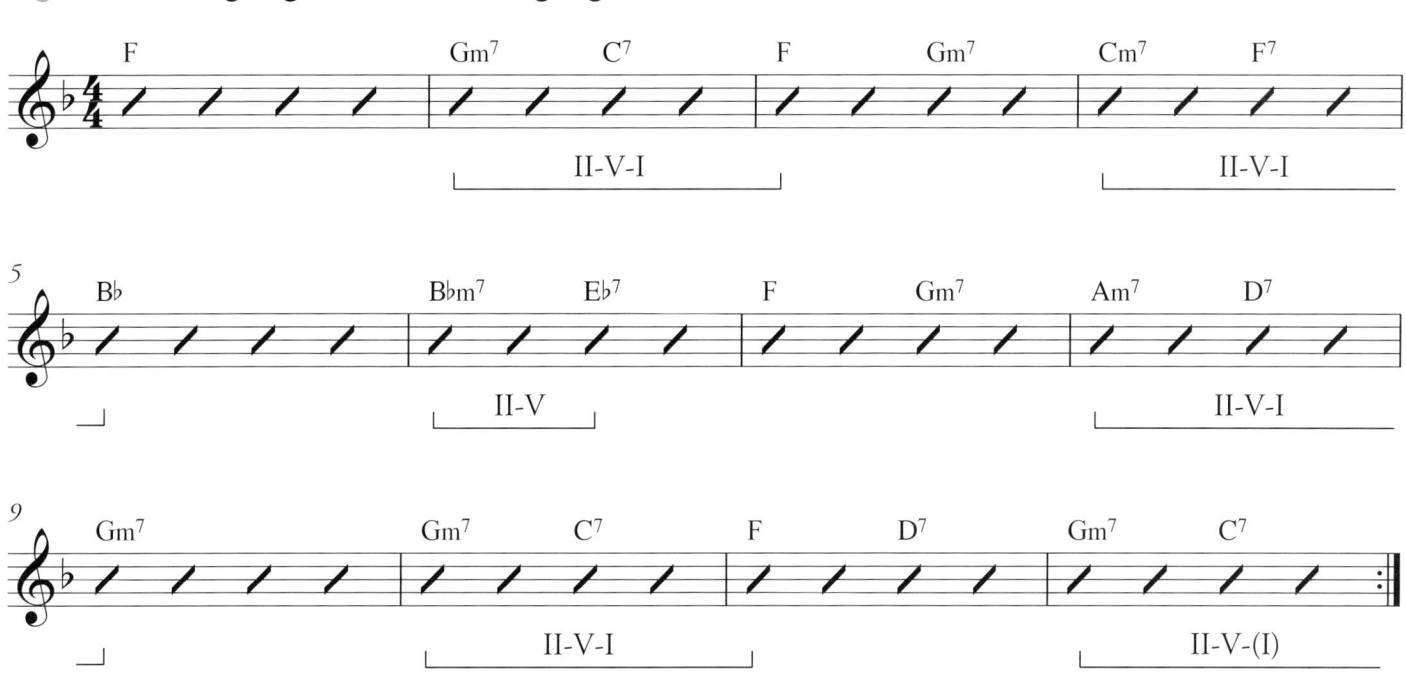

It begins with the chord of F – chord I. Bars 2–3 are a II-V-I in F. This leads, via Gm^7, to a II-V-I in B♭. Bar 6 is a II-V but it leads not to the expected I (A♭), but back to F. Bars 8–9 are a II-V-I in Gm. Bars 10–11 are a II-V-I in F, as are bars 12–1 (when you repeat back to the beginning). So, instead of thinking about each individual chord, you can now just concentrate on memorizing 'chord areas'.

The Big Solo – When Do I Start?

At a jazz gig, to someone in the audience, the order of solos may be a complete mystery. Is it all organized in advance or is it a free-for-all? If there are five members in the band, on any particular number there may be just one soloist, or all five may have a go. Since this is your first gig, it may be a complete mystery to you too. If the band has a leader (some do, some don't), you may get some clues from him or her. When I'm in charge of a band, I will usually turn around and look straight at the person I want to take the next solo. No words are spoken but the message is pretty clear. When I've

Exploring Jazz Violin

been in a band but not the leader, I've had everything from, 'let's hear that fiddle, boy!' to a miniscule relaxation of the guitarist's posture. Sometimes the bass player and drummer may expect to solo as well as the 'front line' (melody) instruments.

Once, when leading a band of musicians that I wasn't familiar with, I made the mistake of forgetting to invite the bass player to solo. After the fourth number he packed up and left (and no, I'm really not kidding!).

So, at the end of the head, don't be daydreaming or fiddling with your tuning. Pay close attention to what's happening. If there's been no prior arrangement it may be up to you to come tearing in after the head or the previous solo and hope that no one gets in your way.

Your opening gambit

How to start your solo? If you're the first soloist coming straight after the head, you may want to base the opening of your solo on the melody, even if this only means referring to one or two key phrases. You may decide to come in at full tilt with something strong and flashy, or to start off really gently. If you're following another soloist, it's often a good idea to go for contrast – so follow the previous soloist's rip-roaring climax with something quiet and sensitive. Don't feel that because all eyes are on you, you have to immediately lay out your credentials. One of the best openings to a solo I've come across is by **Florin Niculescu** on **Bireli Legrene**'s *Gypsy Project* album. On his first solo on the album's opening track, 'Djangology', he plays a single note, then stops for two whole bars before continuing. Now there's a man with absolute self-confidence!

Phrasing

Take a look at this section of solo. It follows the chords nicely, runs smoothly and has no wrong notes. Unfortunately it stinks. In the event of a medical emergency during your concert, if someone were to call out 'is there an anaesthetist in the house?', some wag would be sure to call out 'Yes, he's on the stage!'.

Fig 11.5 Solo line

Beginner-jazz soloists tend to follow the same pattern. They're terrified of stopping, so they ramble on without a pause or a gap anywhere. There are no clean lines, no riffs, no melody, no repetition or development of ideas, no contrasts and no surprises. Here's a few simple suggestions to consider. You don't have to follow all of them all of the time, but ignore them at your peril!

1. Leave some space!

A good speaker doesn't talk continuously without a pause. The spoken word uses phrases and sentences, punctuated by short pauses. Your solo lines should do the same. Don't be frightened to leave space.

There's a band behind you who will keep playing no matter how long you stop for. Listen to them, trust them and use them.

2. Vary your note lengths

The unfortunate solo above offers a choice of crotchets or quavers, hardly an alluring menu. A good solo will have notes of any and every length; a slow tune can have passages of very fast notes, or a fast tune like this can have long, slow notes.

Syncopation, repeated three-over-four phrases, triplets and unexpected gaps will all help to keep the audience on the edge of, rather than slumping comatose into, their seats. The next example has a good selection.

Fig 11.6 **Variation of Rhythm**

3. Vary the width of your intervals

It's all too easy, when you've learned to improvise using scales and arpeggios, to limit yourself even without realizing, to intervals of a semitone, a tone, or a 3rd. Put in some larger intervals.

It will create more harmonic interest and generate more unusual and striking phrases. Here we see a mixture of different intervals, both large and small:

Fig 11.7 **Variation of intervals**

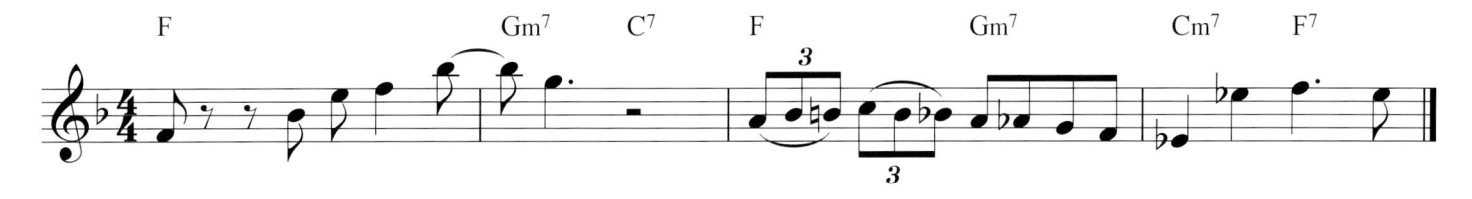

4. Use the full range of the fiddle

Don't restrict yourself to the easy and 'safe' notes in 1st position. You've got four octaves to play with – make the most of them! By using the pentatonic and blues patterns we looked at earlier, you can easily play right up the neck without having to worry about what notes you're actually playing.

5. Use repetition

At first you may find yourself with the problem that every phrase you play is a slight disappointment, but you live in constant hope that the next one will be better. So you're constantly noodling from one bar to the next, with no sign that you have confidence in anything you're playing. As soon as you find a half-way decent phrase – repeat it! And again! This shows confidence and decisiveness, and gives the listener something to hang on to.

Fig 11.8 **Repetition**

6. Predictability and surprise

The whole essence of music, whether it be jazz or anything else, is getting the right balance between predictability and surprise. In each of the above examples we tried to extend the range of expression, allowing more chance of surprise. With too much repetition and too little variation in your range – your solo quickly becomes boring. Go the other way and your audience will feel that you've lost the plot.

When talking about 'playing outside' we looked at the idea of setting up an expectation, then breaking it. Without one, you can't have the other.

7. The element of risk

You could think of soloing in the same way as you might some sports, such as skiing, quad biking, canoeing or caving. They all have an element of danger. The chance of breaking a limb, drowning or being horribly mangled is admittedly slim, in a jazz club, but improvisation shares the unpredictability, risk and the potential of an adrenaline rush when you pull off a good move.

Find out what your limits are in terms of technique and your understanding of jazz theory. You don't want to cross these limits too often and end up out of tune, out of time or out on your ear. But nor do you want to be playing safe all the time. The real buzz of soloing comes from trying new things and surprising yourself, as well as the audience.

8. The special effects department

People in the audience are shuffling their feet, glancing at their watches, muttering under their breath – things could get ugly. Time to reach for the special effects department.

Playing a '**quote**' is a common way to provide interest or humour in a solo. **Stuff Smith** was very partial to including a line from some little ditty like 'The Sailor's Hornpipe', 'The William Tell Overture' or 'Comin Through the Rye'. The 'Marseilleise' (French national Anthem) often gets a walk-on part in gypsy jazz and Jean-Luc Ponty slipped it neatly into 'Rhum 'n' Zouk' on his Tchokola album. I recently heard the 'I love you baby' line from 'Can't Take My Eyes Off of You' played over 'Djangology'. Such quotes are great when you first hear them, but 'The Flintstones' or 'The Muppet Show' over 'I Got Rhythm' are very passé.

Quotes from within the actual jazz violin genre are rather a different matter. In this book I've loaded you up with an armoury of licks in the style of various players. It's up to you to decide how you balance, on the one hand, being original and creative and on the other hand, producing a carbon copy of someone else's style. Even **Tim Kliphuis**, whose career largely revolves around the recreation of Grappelli's style, told me he would never copy a whole solo verbatim. By all means transcribe, analyse and learn other people's solos, but to trot them out at a gig goes against the whole ethos of jazz.

There are plenty of other tricks available to enliven your solo. Venuti of course was famous for his '**four-string**' technique, his **double shuffle** and the elaborate use of **harmonics**. **Pizzicato** solos can be very effective as a novelty, particularly if you're able to get the band to lay low for a while. **Mike Piggott** has a fine example on 'The Gift' on his *Take a Walk* album. **Singing** or **humming** in unison with your solo line is another good trick, possibly first tried on the fiddle by the bebop player **Ray Perry**. Besides it being a crowd pleaser, it's intrinsically a good technique because it forces you to play more simply and melodically than you might otherwise do and throws up non-violinistic lines.

'**Trading fours**' can be a lot of fun and shows that you're actively interacting with the rest of the band.

The band leader or soloist will give a signal and then several musicians will take it in turn to play a 4-bar solo – often including the bassist and drummer.

The Punch Line

How long to make your solo? In terms of a normal gig, the best guide is to listen to what the other soloists are doing. For a medium-tempo, swing number the average is probably two choruses (twice round the sequence). For a fast number it could be three or four choruses and for a ballad, it's more likely to be one. If you're the bandleader, of course you have plenty of scope, but as one of the rank-and-file you don't want to be seen to be taking much longer solos than everyone else. It also depends partly on what type of jazz you're playing. Swing generally is pretty disciplined in terms of solo length, whilst with fusion or modal jazz, you can often stretch out (maybe even on a single chord) for as long as your imagination will allow. One thing's for sure, as soon as you find yourself running out of ideas, it's time to stop!

And how to finish your solo? One thing to bear in mind is that unusual creature, the 'jazz applause'. Jazz audiences have the habit of applauding some, most, or all solos, rather than waiting till the end of the number. To many musicians this is more of an annoyance than an encouragement, as it often breaks up the flow of the performance. Most hazardous is the audience which will applaud some, but not all solos. The temptation for the soloist is then to 'top off' the solo with something flashy and spectacular, possibly at the expense of good taste and artistry. We've seen how the Cuban **El Nino Prodigo** violinist used the ascending-tremelando-glissando to drive his audiences into a frenzy. **Didier Lockwood** ends many of his solos, particularly on ballads, with an ascending scale which goes all the way to the top of the neck and then a bit further, getting softer all the time. To me that's a real 'killer' ending.

Particularly if it's a two-way interaction, you have a chance to feed off one another, listening carefully then repeating and developing one another's lines.

Whatever ending you choose, make sure it sounds natural, logical and thought out in terms of the whole solo, rather than just noodling on until the end of the 32 bars and then stopping abruptly.

So, here's a sample solo:

Exploring Jazz Violin

The Big Night (solo version)

Chris Haigh

Chorus 1 (bars 1–12)

The solo opens with a Niculescu gambit – a punchy double-A note (notice it's the 3rd, not the root of the opening chord), followed by a long pause as you look around to make sure all eyes are on you. Bar 3 quotes the original tune, while bar 4, a pair of descending arpeggios, shows that you're driving with due care and attention and not bluffing the II-V-Is.

We follow with a few bluesy flattened 3rds, adding some downward slides à la **Stuff Smith**. Bars 7 and 8 follow the ascending line of the chord sequence. Bar 9 has some aggressive double stops followed by a Venuti-style descending 'yodel'. The last two bars are a reminder that this is a bebop tune, dropping in the 'enclosure' lick from the previous chapter.

Chorus 2 (bars 13–24)

You've made it through the first chorus without a hitch and no one is trying to jump in, so round we go again. It's a surprise straight out of the SWAT armoury, a switch to pizzicato. The drummer, surprised and impressed, eases off on the decibels to give you some space. It's a cool, 4-bar, jazz-funk lick you just pulled out of nowhere. It repeats easily when the chords change in bar 17 and 18, with just a flattening of the A over the E♭ chord. You could carry this lick on endlessly, but the audience is getting restive. You change tactics and switch to the D minor pentatonic descending lick in bars 21–22. After hearing it played 48 times by **Michal Urbaniak**, you know you're onto a winner and a sea of Polish flags are waving as you double the tempo in bar 23.

Chorus 3 (bars 25–36)

The bandleader is looking anxiously at his watch, so better settle for another 12 bars then quit while we're ahead. We start the third chorus in circa 1973 with the old Ponty double-A riff. Remember all those hours, or was it months, you spent practising the closed-position pentatonic scale? Here's your payoff, in bars 26–27 you effortlessly sweep up two octaves of triplets. Bars 29–30 are a diminished substitution – again, it's 'one you prepared earlier' and rolls right off the fingers. When was the last time you took a breath? If this were a sax solo you'd be turning blue by now, so bar 31 gives a strategic pause, followed by a surprise raised 6th (the F♯) over the Am7 chord in bar 32. Whatever its merits, this solo is not going to score highly on stylistic purity, so why not throw in another Venuti yodel. Spontaneous applause bursts out from the Italian Americans in the audience, followed by a roar of approval from the Gallic contingent as you climax with a reckless quote from the Marseillaise.

A stunned silence follows and then the Albert Hall erupts. A thousand cigarette lighters are held aloft. A thousand cameras flash. The servers at YouTube.com crash as a thousand out-of-focus files are uploaded simultaneously. The ghost of Grappelli is nodding in approval. A beaming Simon Cowell is rushing towards the stage, trying to overtake the MD of Warner Bros., who is frantically waving a recording contract at you. In the Royal box H.R.H. is having a word with an assistant about a late addition to the new year's honours list. You've made musical history. You've ushered in a new golden age. You've made your mum break out the tissues and the writer of a certain best-selling jazz fiddle book is looking exceedingly proud. Well, you can dream!

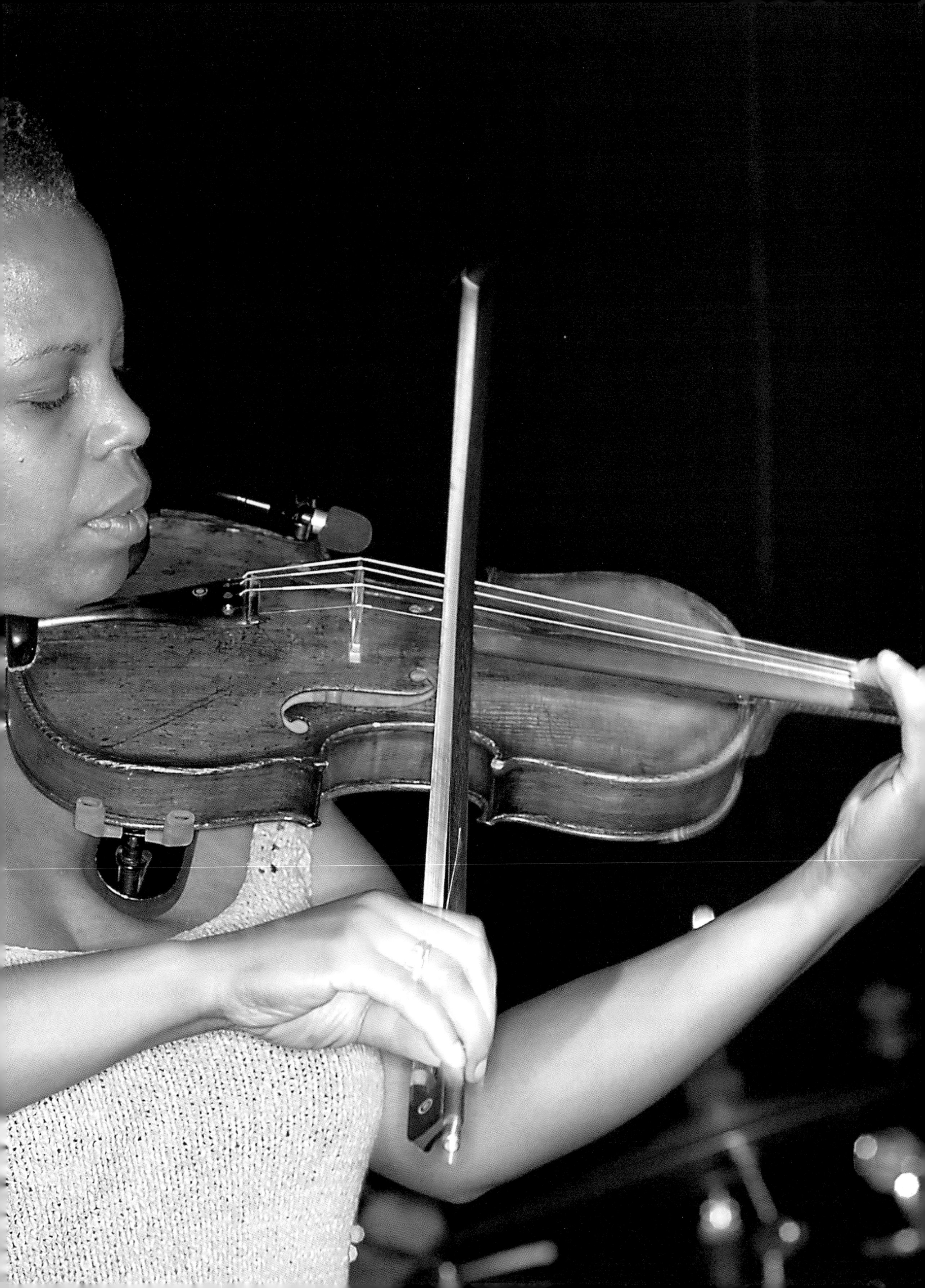

12: Final thoughts

Gear

As a gigging jazz violinist, even if you're playing gypsy jazz (which doesn't include the drums), you're going to need some form of amplification. There are various options available, which can be summarised as:

1. Standard mic
2. Close-up mic
3. Pickup on the violin
4. Electric violin
5. Amp

Standard mic

With the standard mic you don't have to do anything to your violin and many venues will make available a mic and a PA (an amplifier with speakers). This is a good choice in a concert situation providing you have a good PA, good soundman and not too much noise on stage; this is the kind of set-up Grappelli relied on for most of his later career. However, unless you are Grappelli, which seems unlikely, I wouldn't rely on it! It doesn't give you any control over your sound and leaves you at the mercy of someone who would possibly prefer to be mixing **Metallica**, rather than a jazz violinist.

Close-up mic

A close-up mic (clip mic) is a tiny microphone designed to be attached to the violin in some way. The brand leader is the **DPA** supercardioid condenser mic. You don't need to know what it means, just that its reassuringly expensive price tag guarantees a really natural, high quality sound. **Tim Kliphuis** and **Tscha Limberger** both use them – they are ideal for the relatively low volumes of a gypsy-jazz gig.

Pickup on the violin

The most common and best all-round solution to amplification for the violin is a 'pickup' or 'bug' – it attaches to the violin, either temporarily or permanently, directly transforming the vibrations of the instrument into an electrical signal rather than the vibrations from the air. **Barcus Berry** and **Fishman** are well-established makers, but for me the **Baggs** pickup is top of the tree. Built into the bridge, it gives a clean, powerful sound, requiring little or no EQ (equalization or tone adjustment) or preamp (a device to enhance tone quality before amplification). **Billy Thompson**, **Ric Sanders** and **Chris Garrick** all use the Baggs pickup. I use one in conjunction with the DPA mic – the Baggs provides stability and solidity, whilst the DPA supplies sensitivity.

Electric violin

The electric violin is a solution best used in a jazz-rock or jazz-fusion setting. Its solid body eliminates the danger of feedback and is ideal if you're into using effects or midi. If you're looking for a natural violin sound, something like a **Skyinbow**, sometimes used by **Graham Clark**, comes very close. **Chris Garrick**, **Ric Sanders**, **Billy Thompson** and **Jean-Luc Ponty** use the **Zeta**. The low action allows you to play very lightly, with much less digging-in from the bow, but electric violins in general suffer from lack of sensitivity.

Amps

You will also need an amp. Something between 60 and 100 watts will be fine for small to medium gigs. For a larger gig that has a PA system, having your own amp on stage is still preferable to going direct to the PA, as it gives you some independence and control over your sound. The choice is an easy one. Over the last decade, the **AER** amp has swept the board. Light to carry, powerful and clean, they are ideal. **Chris Garrick** described it to me as "Like a little PA in a box; portable and with plenty of welly!"

Software

Finally a plug for Band-in-a-Box. Whether you're learning jazz as a beginner, or learning and practising new material as a professional, it's essential to have some chordal and rhythmic backing to work with. This piece of software allows you to easily and quickly create your own endlessly repeating, infinitely adaptable, cheap, tireless, uncomplaining, punctual, sober and professional backing band. Now where else are you going to find one of those!

Suggested Listening

Pierre Blanchard and Dorado Schmitt
Rendez-Vous, Le Chante du Monde 2004
Delicate and sensitive playing, a true connoisseur of the Grappelli style.

Graham Clark (and Stephen Grew)
(http://www.grahamviolin.com)
Improvisations Series One, GCImprovi 2008
Free improvisations with pianist **Stephen Grew**. Impressive technique, impeccable tone and intonation from Graham.

Miles Davis
Kind of Blue, Columbia / Legacy 1959
Not a violin to be seen, but this is an essential album for anyone interested in modern jazz.

Chris Garrick
Four Spirits, Flying Blue Whale 2001
Superbly fearless modern playing.

Stéphane Grappelli
Live at the Cambridge Folk Festival 1999
Most of the tracks are from a 1983 appearance with the **Martin Taylor Trio**. Only four tracks are from the 1973 gig with the **Diz Disley Trio** with exuberant playing and ecstatic reception.
Duke Ellington Jazz Violin Session, Wounded Bird Records 1963
Features **Stéphane Grappelli**, **Ray Nance** and **Svend Asmussen** (viola). An interesting and historic session, marred by poor recording quality.

Stéphane Grappelli and Stuff Smith
Violins No End, Pablo 1957
Smith plays like a streetfighter, whipping up both band and audience with the sheer forcefulness of his playing while Grappelli sounds polite and diffident.

Stéphane Grappelli and Joe Venuti
Venupelli Blues, CD Charly 1969
The Frenchman plays up a storm but Venuti sounds tired and sloppy in places. Nevertheless, to quote Trevor Salter's pithy liner notes 'It presents two grand old men of music swinging their respective asses off'.

Tim Kliphuis (www.timkliphuis.com)
The Grappelli Tribute, RWP 2005
As perfect a reproduction of the Grappelli style as you're likely to hear.

Birelli Lagrene
Gypsy Project & Friends, Dreyfus 2002
Including **Florin Niculescu** – modern, gypsy jazz.

Eddie Lang and Joe Venuti
New York Sessions, JSP records 1926–1935
Box set with detailed notes and track listings. Many tracks do not include Venuti, but is still good value.

Didier Lockwood
The Kid, MPS 1983
Fun, high energy jazz-rock with some very memorable tunes. Excellent 'outside' playing and interesting use of effects.
Tribute to Stéphane Grappelli, Dreyfus 2000
Birelli Lagrene (guitar) and Orsted Pederson (bass), a beautiful album – 'Nuages' is breathtaking.
Storyboard, Dreyfus 1996
Bebop to fusion.
New York Rendez-vous, JMS 1995

Modern and exciting, some superb 'outside' playing.
Magma Live, SNAP 1975
Didier Lockwood's finest moment with the crazy Kobaians. Surprisingly accessible.

Lollo Meier Quartet (featuring **Tcha Limberger**)
Rosas, 2006
Includes an extraordinary Transylvanian-style fiddle solo on 'What is this thing called Love'.

Mike Piggott
Take a Walk, 2006
Stylistic nods towards Venuti, Smith and Grappelli, with an excellent piano trio backing.

Jean-Luc Ponty (http://www.ponty.com)
Visions of the Emerald Beyond, Columbia 1974
A menagerie of effects pedals. A jazz-rock-fusion masterpiece.

Trio HLP, Dreyfus 1968
Live bebop performance on standards including 'Summertime', 'Round Midnight' and 'So What'.
Electric Connection / King King Gottdiscs
Transitions between his bebop and modal phases. Superb playing and great big-band arrangements.
Cantaloupe Island, BGO 1969
Live recording with a trio featuring pianist **George Duke**. Electric violin with no effects. Exuberant playing, mostly modal material.
King Kong, BGO
Re-released on the same CD as the above. Material written by Zappa.
Tchokola, Epic 1991
An unexpected but successful departure with some rich and seductive west-African grooves.

Django Reinhardt
Djangology, Membran
10-CD box set with lots of early QHC recordings.

Stuff Smith
Cat on a Hot Fiddle, Verve 1959
Clean, punchy and often explosive playing on a fine set of standards.
Time and Again, Proper
A double CD set with over 50 tracks covering 1936–1945. Excellent detailed sleeve notes.

Eddie South
The Dark Angel of the Fiddle, Soundies 1944,
From classical to gypsy, swing to bebop, showing what an underrated player South was.

Barbara Thompson's Paraphernalia
Never say Goodbye, 2005
Features the violin of **Billy Thompson** (no relation!), with a particularly fine solo on 'Are You Real'.

Michal Urbaniak
Ask me now, Steeplechase Productions 1999
Free-wheeling, bebop standards including 'Ornithology', 'Yardbird Suite', 'My Little Suede Shoes' and 'Moose the Mooche'. Played on a 5-string violin.
Live in the Holy City
Jazz-fusion band / symphony orchestra / rap, top of the range playing by Urbaniak on 5-string electric.
Fusion, Columbia / Legacy 1973
Asymmetric rhythms and fairly extreme electric violin sounds, surprisingly accessible and melodic.
Miles of Blue, Sony 2009
A tribute to **Miles Davis**'s *Kind of Blue* album. Uncompromisingly modern and urban, with strong elements of rap.

Various Artists
I Like Be I Like Bop: Odds & Svends of Early Bebop Violin & Contemporary Violin Curiosities,
Able Fable 2005
A labour of love by **Anthony Barnett** to create this collection of rare bebop violin recordings. Includes a 90 page booklet packed with detailed research.

Joe Venuti and Tony Romano
Never Before, Never Again, Nucool 1954
Recorded with guitarist Tony Romano. Early Venuti suffered from a thin tone, here his sound is pure gold and technique effortless.

Bibliography / Suggested Reading

Sam Bardfeld
Latin Violin: how to play Salsa, Charango and Latin Jazz Violin, Gerard and Sarzin 2001
An excellent and detailed look at the violin in Latin music – includes a CD. With solo extracts from past masters and many sample montunos.

Bill Crow
Jazz Anecdotes, Oxford University Press, 1990
Packed with jazz jokes and stories from the lives of jazz players, not least the notorious **Joe Venuti**.

Matt Glaser and Stéphane Grappelli
Jazz Violin, Oak 1981
Long and detailed transcriptions of Grappelli and other jazz violinists. Not as useful as you would think, unless you're a great reader, or have all the original recordings.

Tim Kliphuis
Stéphane Grappelli Gypsy Jazz Violin, Mel Bay 2008
Detailed and authoritative introduction to Grappelli's playing style.

Frank Zappa
Hot Rats, Rykodisk 1969
Legendary album featuring blinding solos from **Don Sugarcane Harris** on 'Willie the Pimp' and 'Gumbo Variations'. A low-key debut for **Jean-Luc Ponty** on 'It Must Be a Camel'.

Mark Levine
The Jazz Theory Book, Sher Music 1995
This is the Holy Bible of jazz theory. Other faiths also available.

The Real Book, Hal Leonard 2005
The Real Book has been around in various illegal versions for many years. Finally here's a legal version; a big fat book stuffed with hundreds of jazz standards – the common currency of all jazz musicians.

Geoffrey Smith
Stéphane Grappelli: A Biography, Pavilion 1987
A detailed and engaging biography.

Track Listing

1. Fig 1.4 G major scale – swing quavers
2. Swingin' the Scale (head)
3. Swingin' the Scale (backing)
4. Swingin' the Scale (slurred pairs)
5. Head First (head)
6. Head First (backing)
7. Head First (with slides)
8. Fig 1.20 Bars 17–18 with downward slides
9. Head First (rephrased)
10. Come Home (head)
11. Come Home (backing)
12. Come Home (scale fragments)
13. Fig 2.31 Chord change (C to C7)
14. Fig 2.32 Chord changes (C to Dm7 to D7)
15. Fig 2.33 Chord changes (C to E7 to Am7)
16. Snakes and Ladders (head)
17. Snakes and Ladders (backing)
18. Snakes and Ladders (solo version)
19. Mind the Gap (head)
20. Mind the Gap (backing)
21. Vamp in G major
22. Vamp in E minor
23. Mind the Gap (solo version)
24. The Glass Slippers (head)
25. The Glass Slippers (backing)
26. The Glass Slippers (solo version)
27. Fig 4.1 Basic blues in G – arpeggios
28. Fig 4.2 Blues boogie
29. Fig 4.3 Basic blues with double stops
30. Fig 4.4 Blues melody – minimal changes
31. Fig 4.12 Blues with repeating riff
32. Fig 4.13 Blues with transposing riff
33. Head First (Blues Pentatonic version)
34. Fig 4.31 Blues scale melody over major chords
35. Fig 4.34 E minor blues melody
36. Fig 4.38 Jazz blues
37. Fig 4.39 Bebop blues
38. Gmaj7 (backing)
39. Am7 (backing)
40. D7 (backing)
41. II-V-I in G major (backing)
42. II-V-I in E minor (backing)
43. Cycle Ride (head)
44. Cycle Ride (backing)
45. Cycle Ride (solo version)
46. Fig 6.5 II-V-I phrase in every key
47. G diminished (backing)
48. G7 augmented (backing)
49. Fig 6.36 Blues with substitutions
50. Jumpin' with Joe (head)
51. Jumpin' with Joe (backing)
52. Rhythm Changes (solo)
53. Rhythm Changes (backing)
54. Swing Parisienne (head)
55. Swing Parisienne (backing)
56. Swing Parisienne (solo version)
57. Cosmic Voyager (solo)
58. Cosmic Voyager (backing)
59. Whispers (head)
60. Dorian Grey (head)
61. Dorian Grey (solo version)
62. Dorian Grey (backing)
63. The Big Night (head)
64. The Big Night (solo version)
65. The Big Night (backing)

Recording Acknowledgements

Chris Haigh Violin

Tracks 1–20, 23–42, 47–49, 54–56, 59:
Jez Cook Guitar
Stuart Blagden Guitar
Raph Mizraki Double Bass

Tracks 43–46, 50–53, 57–58, 60–65:
Geoff Castle Piano
Dudley Phillips Double bass
Roy Dodds Drums
Recorded and mixed by **Roy Dodds**, August 2010 at Kitchen Floor Studios